# THE OPTIC OF THE STATE

D1547421

ILLUMINATIONS:
CULTURAL FORMATIONS OF THE AMERICAS
John Beverley and Sara Castro-Klarén, Editors

# The Optic of the State

VISUALITY AND POWER
IN ARGENTINA AND BRAZIL

Jens Andermann

University of Pittsburgh Press

Published by the University of Pittsburgh Press, Pittsburgh, Pa., 15260
Copyright © 2007, University of Pittsburgh Press
All rights reserved
Manufactured in the United States of America
Printed on acid-free paper
10 9 8 7 6 5 4 3 2 1

Library of Congress Cataloging-in-Publication Data
Andermann, Jens.
    The optic of the state : visuality and power in Argentina and Brazil / Jens Andermann.
        p.    cm.— (Illuminations)
    Includes bibliographical references and index.
    ISBN-13: 978-0-8229-4337-2 (cloth : alk. paper)
    ISBN-13: 978-0-8229-5972-4 (pbk. : alk. paper)
    ISBN-10: 0-8229-4337-9 (cloth : alk. paper)
    ISBN-10: 0-8229-5972-0 (pbk. : alk. paper)
    1. National characteristics, Brazilian. 2. National characteristics, Argentine. 3. Museums—Influence. 4.
National state. I. Title.
    F2510.A73 2007
    306.20981--dc22                                    2007018695

*For Ana and Maja*

# CONTENTS

# ILLUSTRATIONS

# ACKNOWLEDGMENTS

The idea for this book originated in a research project on Latin American national iconographies that William Rowe, Patience A. Schell, and I started working on in 1999. The British Arts and Humanities Research Council (AHRC) funded initial trips to Buenos Aires, São Paulo, Rio de Janeiro, and Berlin that allowed me to gather the material analyzed on these pages; subsequently, the School of Languages, Linguistics, and Culture at Birkbeck College, University of London, and the AHRC provided financial support for further research trips and a sabbatical leave that made it possible to finish the manuscript. To William and Patience, as well as to our research assistant Jennifer Fraser, I am grateful for continuous critical support and inspiration. I thank Beatriz González-Stephan, Sylvia Molloy, Andrea Noble, Mary Louise Pratt, and Adriana Rodríguez Pérsico for agreeing to act as referees for subsequent grant applications and helping to convince skeptical boards of the hidden merits of this project. This book is only one of its outcomes—the full collection of visual sources on which its argument is based is available online in a virtual exhibition hosted by Birkbeck College (http://www.bbk.ac.uk/ibamuseum). Readers are very much encouraged to consult this resource in order to add to the necessarily reduced selection of images illustrating this book.

In every project of this kind, the patience and goodwill of staff at museums, libraries, and archives is critical to its success or failure. For letting me use their resources, despite the bulky photographic equipment I brought into spaces intended for peaceful reading and note taking, I am tremendously grateful to the librarians and curators of the *Museu Nacional* (UFRJ), *Museu Histórico Nacional, Museu Nacional de Belas Artes, Museu da República, Biblioteca Nacional Brasileira,* and *Casa de Rui Barbosa*, all in Rio de Janeiro; and in São Paulo, *Museu Paulista* and *Pinacoteca do Estado*. In Buenos Aires, the staff at the *Archivo General de la Nación,*

*Museo Argentino de Ciencias Naturales, Academia Nacional de la Historia, Museo Nacional de Bellas Artes, Museo Histórico Nacional, Museo Mitre, Sociedad Científica Argentina,* and *Museo de La Plata* provided invaluable help. With calm efficiency, the friendly staff of the *Ibero-Amerikanisches Institut*, Berlin, provided me with many materials I could not get hold of elsewhere. In particular, I would like to thank all institutions that have generously granted me permission to reprint images held in their collections.

Working on this project has allowed me to make new friends in a variety of disciplines, from art history to anthropology and geography. I lack the space to account for the ways each and every one of them has widened my horizons and inspired my thoughts to advance in more exciting directions. Nonetheless, I would like to express my gratitude for their advice and orientation to, in Brazil, Antonio Carlos Souza Lima, Claudia Oliveira, Myrian Santos, Fernando Rabossi, Nicolau Sevcenko, Carlos Roberto Maciel Levy, Sergio Nunes, Maria Inez Turazzi, and the late Afonso Carlos Marques dos Santos, to whose memory I would like to dedicate the chapter on the Planalto Expedition. In Argentina, special thanks go to Florencia Garramuño, Paola Cortés Rocca, Javier Trímboli, Andrea Giunta, Axel Lazzari, Alejandro Kaufman, Juan Manuel Obarrio, Fermín Rodríguez, Claudia Torre, Emilio Bernini, Gonzalo Aguilar, Irina Podgorny, Horacio González, Roy Hora, Pedro Navarro Floria, and the Centro de Estudios Patagónicos, Neuquén.

I was fortunate to be able to discuss a first draft of the manuscript with the participants of the Spanish and Latin American postgraduate research seminar at Duke University in the spring term of 2006. To all of them, my gratitude for their enthusiasm and critical acumen in discussing ideas, arguments, and images. Special thanks go to Teresa Vilarós and Alberto Moreiras for their generous hospitality, and for discussing theoretical positions and references with me during the final stages of revising the manuscript. I am indebted to John Beverley and Sara Castro-Klarén, the series editors, and to Devin Fromm and Sara Lickey at the University of Pittsburgh Press for their patience and the gentle insistence with which they made me go back to work on the clumsier parts of my argument, as well as for bringing the editing process to a smooth conclusion.

A special thanks, finally, goes to my colleagues at Birkbeck, Luciana Martins, Carmen Fracchia, Mari Paz Balibrea, María Elena Placencia, Eleanor Wake, David Hanlon, Jessamy Harvey, and especially to John Kraniauskas and Philip Derbyshire, for their inspiring comments and suggestions. For many years now, Alvaro Fernández Bravo has been a persistent critic and friend, whose academic interests have evolved so closely to my own that he can claim ownership to many of the insights and concepts he generously allowed me to pillage. Above all, I have to thank Ana Alvarez for the encouragement and critical intelligence with which she has accompanied this project. I cannot express in words my gratitude for her endurance of my doubts and despairs. I dedicate the book to her and to Maja, our daughter, to whom belongs the future.

# Introduction

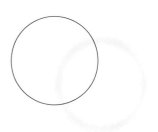

Child! You will never see another land like this!
Look, what a sky, what a sea, what a forest!
—Olavo Bilac

Over the final decades of the nineteenth century, Brazil and Argentina saw the emergence of new forms of power that expressed a substantial shift in the relation between society and the state. At the core of this shift was the consolidation of the state as a distinctive agent, set apart from the field of social relations. Paralleling this process was a dramatic expansion of capitalist forms of production and exchange into areas formerly regulated according to traditional patterns of patriarchal authority. This mutually constitutive enhancement of state power and of capitalism depended on new forms of knowledge that registered, classified, and distributed human and natural resources in time and space. As a means of observation, ordering, and storage of natural and social forms the state could be figured as set apart from social practices—as a way of seeing that yielded an impersonal, "objective" type of knowledge. This knowledge of society as object could, in turn, be exhibited, exemplified, and illustrated: made plain to see. This new way of seeing—the optic of the state—and the subjects and objects of the gaze it posited are the topics of this book.

Contrary to most conventional histories of the state in Latin America, I attempt to show that, rather than the necessary outcome of social or economic processes, the kind of modern state that emerged in Argentina and Brazil in the closing decades of the nineteenth century was but one option among others.[1] Its "necessity" was, then, an effect of the images of nature and of history generated by a new way of seeing, which posited these as announcements of the modern state. Hence the state, we might say, is just as much a cultural form as it is a particular organization of the political. It is a specific correlation between politics and aesthetics, or rules of perception, in which the latter sustains the former as its own cause and end. Timothy Mitchell has suggested that, rather than merely expose and reject the metaphysics of the modern notion of the state, we need to ask how and why its "ghostlike effect" of historical necessity and its similarly transcendental association with the nation-form became "the distinctive political arrangement of the modern age." The state, he concludes, should be examined "not as an actual structure, but as the powerful, metaphysical effect of practices that make such structures appear to exist. [...] What we call the state, and think of as an intrinsic object existing apart from society, is the sum of [...] structural effects."[2]

This book proposes to take the state as a visual form: as a way of looking and as the objects that command observation. A visual form is neither in the eye of the beholder nor in the artifact that claims her or his gaze (for everything that "claims a gaze" is already set up as an image, and thus involves artifice, visual composition). Rather, it is the relation that binds a certain gaze to a particular artifact. We could call this relation a "perspective," following Erwin Panofsky's classic analysis of Renaissance optics: a way of setting subjects and objects up for one another and of making calculable the terms of their mutual engagement. Perspectival seeing turned the beholder into a sovereign viewing subject commanding an external object world, at the same time as subjecting her to its impersonal laws. "The claim of the object," in Panofsky's words, "confronts the ambition of the subject."[3] Here, then, a relation between visuality, subjectivity, and the law takes shape that harks back to the very origins of Western modernity. However, in order to capture its concrete manifestations in certain places at a particular moment in time, one needs to read it against a history of optical devices and contemporary notions of representation and the observer. To make the notion of visual form analytically productive, it has to be put to work in the specific interplay between imaging technologies, compositional forms, and the objects they capture in a given time and place.

Juan Gutiérrez's photograph of the inauguration ceremony for General Osório's equestrian monument on Rio de Janeiro's Paço Imperial square, which you see on the cover, appears to me to convey better than any other image this relation between the rituals of showing and of spectatorship in which the optic of the state takes shape. Taken in 1894, five years after the overthrow of the Imperial monarchy, the image depicts a defiant ritual of whose triumphalist rhetoric the camera was in many ways the main addressee. Only the previous year, Gutiérrez had published an album depicting the defeat of a monarchist naval uprising in Guanabara Bay. The photograph of the statue's unveiling was part of Gutiérrez's subsequent project, an album entitled "Memories of National Feasts," published on the fifth anniversary of the Brazilian Republic's proclamation, in which he collected pictures of official celebrations staged by the victorious army. The album was aimed at fellow Republicans: an object of political devotion that each member of the crowd could purchase and take home to restage the public ritual of state worship within the privacy of domestic space.

Pedro Karp Vasquez has exhaustively analyzed the various forms of stagecraft involved in Gutiérrez's subsequent shot of the unveiled Osório (fig. 1).[4] Here the bronze general is shown at the focal center of a *contre-plongée* shot, taken from below, making his head appear above the roofline of the Imperial palace in the background, next to the window from which, in 1822, Emperor D. Pedro I had declared Brazil's independence from the Portuguese motherland. The photograph thus enhances the political message implied in the monument's

FIGURE 1. Juan Gutiérrez, General Osório's statue during its inauguration (Rio de Janeiro, 1894). Albumin print, 20.5 x 26.9 cm (1894). Instituto Moreira Salles, Rio de Janeiro.

FIGURE 2. Anonymous, Inauguration of the statue of D. Pedro I on Largo do Rocio (Rio de Janeiro, 1862). Albumin print, 32 x 40 cm (1862). Coleção Américo Jacobina Lacombe, Acervo Institucional da Casa de Rui Barbosa, Rio de Janeiro.

erection, a kind of symbolic revenge against the installation, in 1862, of the first emperor's own equestrian statue on nearby Largo do Rocio square—the very spot where the Republican hero Tiradentes had been executed by the Portuguese authorities in 1792 (fig. 2). If Republicans had always regarded this monumental inscription of the monarchical state as a calculated provocation, Osório's equestrian monument repossessed urban—and national—space in the name of the victorious Republic. The Brazilian commander in chief during the Paraguayan War of 1865–70, Osório was a plausible candidate to become military nationalism's founding hero, through whose glorification history could be rewritten as a tradition of victorious military struggle, always striving towards the Republic. Osório's sculptural and photographic immortalizations were the visual components of a complex rite of repossessing an urban space that had been the ceremonial center of the Imperial state. Its ritual process also involved the burial of the general's remains in a small crypt beneath the monument, and the rebaptism of the square as Praça 15 de Novembro, in remembrance of the Republican revolution.[5]

Yet if the almost exact repetition of monuments, rituals, and their photographic representations from the image of 1862 to the one of 1894 also speaks to the continuity between the monarchical and the republican state form in Brazil, dismissing the "revolutionary" claims of the latter, it is Gutiérrez's first image of the still-veiled Osório that stands out. Screened off from our gaze, and that of the crowd on the square, behind an enigmatic catafalque of black canvasses, Osório (or whatever is behind the screen) paradoxically attracts the eye in a much more powerful way than his unveiled sequel. Seen from our early twenty-first-century vantage point, it is impossible not to catch in this black box a visual echo of the famous black monolith from Stanley Kubrick's *2001: A Space Odyssey*. As in Kubrick's film, a monolithic invisibility is at the center of Gutiérrez's photograph, at the point of convergence of the gazes of the crowd with our own, external gaze. And it seems to be this shared invisibility, too, attracting and rejecting the eye of internal and external viewers alike, that produces the sublime, even sacral, status of this object of invisibility within the photograph's visual space.

The analogy with Kubrick's film is less capricious than it may seem: both images can be taken as meditations on visuality and truth, as processed through their respective apparatuses of capture (photography and the cinema). Both images take hold, within their visual space, of a figuration of the invisible in which, quite literally, their own visibility is rooted. This figure, in both images, is the black box, solid darkness that marks out, within visual space, a space of not-seeing, of absolute blindness. It is thus a figuration of the lightless space, the darkroom, through which photography and film must pass (or, in the case of Kubrick, a figuration of the darkness that fills the nonspace between one frame and the next, thus setting them in motion). However, the paradoxical incarnation of this space of blindness in a visual object is also a scandal of visuality, since it violates the invisibility of the invisible as the main premise of representation itself. Truth, the truth of representation, crucially depends on the clear-cut separation between the visible and the invisible, the non-objectness of the latter. Truth is the effect of what we could call the catachretic nature of visuality, the way in which the world of visual objects can point to the invisible domain of pure being only by obsessively pointing to itself. Therefore, the fashioning of the invisible as an object to be seen is a violation of the fundamental pact of representation that brings the beholder into the troublesome presence of an impure sacred. This is the ritual function of the black box on Gutiérrez's photograph, and also the reason why it must immediately be removed to release yet another bronze equestrian, reconstituting the order of repetition it had momentarily interrupted. In the monumental rite of unveiling, the visible allegory of the state is magically invested with the sacred power of the invisible, which it both invokes and helps to keep at bay. This is what the optic of the state is all about.

In some ways, this ritual of visions in which the truth of power is posited as a transcendental unseen recalls the political image world of the baroque, elements of which were still present in the visual culture of Brazil's early nineteenth-century monarchical state. Walter Benjamin, in *The Origin of German Tragic Drama*, refers to the setting—the princely court as *Schauplatz* or, literally, show-place—as an allegorical representation of the world at large. In a "veritable dialectic of the setting," baroque theater constructed the "stage of history" as the image of a "nature fallen from grace," just as it turned nature into a reservoir of emblematic images of history. Nature, in becoming allegorical, became afflicted with the arbitrariness and transience of meaning proper to human language: the things of the world, in baroque culture, could turn into signs because things and signs were similarly godless and insubstantial. Borrowing the term "panoramatic" from Herbert Cysarz, Benjamin applied it to this spatial image of historical time—this "movement from history to nature which is the basis of all allegory"—and returned to this notion in much of the work related to his unfinished *Arcades Project*.[6] Indeed, as Susan Buck-Morss has shown, Benjamin wielded the visual forms of the baroque to a strategy of "dialectical seeing," a "critical allegoresis" of nineteenth-century modernity in its proliferation of mass-cultural forms offered to the gaze of a consumer. The "dialectical image," which re-actualized the baroque visual genre of the emblem through the modern cinematographic technique of montage, was to serve as a critical interruption of the nineteenth century's equally panoramatic way of seeing, which had once again conflated history with nature. In the "panorama of evolution," progress was introduced as the "natural time" of human history, a time that (in exhibitions, museums, and fairs) could be represented as space.[7]

In nineteenth-century visual culture, the baroque spectacle of tragic (or rather, in Benjamin's terms, sorrowful or melancholic) mutual allegorization of nature and history was being recast in the vein of comedy, to quote Hayden White's distinction between historical genres.[8] Evolutionary nature was the template and foundation for humanity's progress that culminated in the Western liberal state. This transformation in the system of representation itself can be observed, for instance, in the differences separating the modern museum from its seventeenth- and eighteenth-century forerunners, the *studioli* and cabinets of curiosities. Unlike museum exhibits focussing on the structural relations between species descending from a common ancestral root, these earlier displays had foregrounded their diversity and variety, as an image of the wealth and vastness—but also the irredeemable dispersion—of God's creation. Thus, even though it radically changed the status and internal logic of the image, the nineteenth century reintroduced the baroque predilection for visual ostentation, specularising social and political hierarchies out of a similar concern with appealing to the affections of an emergent mass audience.[9] As Gutiérrez's photographs of General Osório's unveiling make it clear, the ritual performances of showing and seeing in the public arena were not merely illustrations of a fully written-out historical script. On the contrary, they were the stage productions of national history's myths of origin, pointing us to the state's theatrical dimensions as "display, regard, and drama," which, as Clifford Geertz has argued, have become overshadowed in modern political theory by the state's exclusive identification with governance and dominion.[10] As José Murilo de Carvalho and Lilia Moritz Schwarcz have eloquently shown, nineteenth-century politics in Brazil, at least from the Portuguese Court's arrival at Rio de Janeiro in 1808, evolved in a "theater of shadows," in which a complex system of public processions, ephemeral monuments, stage decorations, and Imperial regalia, as well as painterly and theatrical productions, served to invisibilize the more embarrassing aspects of a slaveholding plantation society.[11] A similar predilection for public ceremony on behalf of Argentina's de facto ruler for most of the early decades after independence, Juan Manuel de Rosas, was already noted in the writings of his political opponents, notably Domingo F. Sarmiento.

Towards the end of the century, however, rather than serving as emblems of the sovereign himself, visual representations of nature and of history turned into figurations of the nation and thus attained a hegemonic function. As I shall argue in this book, the kind of visual ostentation proper to what Michel Foucault calls a "sovereign power" gradually gave way to a concern with the disciplinary education of the gaze, which had to be trained to see the nation-form in its spatiotemporal emanations.[12] "Peoples are in need of relics and sanctuaries to preserve their tradition," as Argentina's president Miguel Juárez Celman put it in a speech before congress in 1887: "Patriotic feeling also requires a temple, and the images of the Fatherland's great men, just as the monuments that tell us of their victories, are useful objects of worship and education for the generations to come, shaping the national character without which Greatness, Power, even Independence and Freedom, are but ephemeral conquests."[13]

In this book I will study the visual forms used to express this limited and contradictory attempt to hegemonize society: not merely monuments and temples, as in Juárez Celman's proposal to construct a memorial in honor of the heroes of independence, but also less explicit (and thus often more persuasive) forms such as museum displays, photographic travelogues, landscape and historical paintings, maps, and atlases. In the new representations of space as nature and of time as history manufactured in the final decades of the nineteenth century, the state became the transcendental condition of the real itself. This new political metaphysics was very much the consequence of a visual logic of presence and absence, of the internal organization of the image and the way in which it invited the gaze of a spectator.

In setting up this book as a comparative study between state formations in two very different societies with distinct colonial histories and experiences of internal struggle following emancipation from the Iberian metropolis, I have sought to avoid the illusion of historical inevitability so often found in analyses of a single national context. In comparing how, in both countries, visual forms expressed, and produced, the capture of social exchange in the political form of the state and in the economy of capital, I hope to show the contingency of effects and outcomes of these processes in local situations, as well as their shared structural elements. Brazilians and Argentines, in fact, already practiced this comparative approach in the period under study here, watching one another anxiously and measuring their own progress or backwardness in the light of the achievements or shortcomings of the other. More intensely than with any other neighboring countries, Argentina and Brazil cultivated a relation with one another as "noble rivals," in the words of the writer and diplomat Estanislao S. Zeballos, vying for each other's approval but also for the preference of European culture and capital (fig. 3).[14]

I have divided the book into two large sections, the first dedicated to the museum and the second to the map as figures of visual order. I use "museum" and "map" both in a figural and a historical sense. Drawing the boundaries of national space and its internal relations, and collecting and exhibiting its contents as a natural, historical, and artistic heritage were the fundamental symbolic practices of making sovereignty visible. In a sense, collecting and mapping represent but different approaches to the question of the state's production as a visual form: to collect also implies to postulate a space or territory; to map is also to fashion a synthetic image of a collection of data. Throughout my argument I will move from nature to history, tracing the way in which the latter, in late nineteenth-century discourses on the national, gradually took precedence over the former. I start with a comparison of the transformations in Argentine and Brazilian museums of natural history over the second half of the century. I then focus on a particular event, Brazil's Anthropological Exhibition of 1882, to examine the ways in which a national modernity was construed in the encounter of a gaze and its object, an indigenous past both native and alien to the view-

FIGURE 3. Pereira Neto, *December 8th, 1889*. "After a long period of mistrust, the Argentine Republic and the United States of Brazil seal a pact of frank and unshakeable friendship." *Revista Illustrada*, December 14, 1889. Biblioteca Nacional Brasileira, Rio de Janeiro. This image, in which the Brazilian Republic is welcomed by its Argentine sister into the concord of modern nation-states, is striking in its complete omission of cultural or ethnic markers of the national. Both countries are impersonated by classicist Mariannes, imported straight from French revolutionary iconography, their hands touching (in an imitation of the Argentine national coat of arms) to carry a Phrygian cap on a pole. Brazil and Argentina not only contemplate themselves in each other's image, but also in that of a European model that watches, as it were, from the mirror that is their very point of contact.

ing subject. Next, I compare the first attempts at defining a national heritage of historical memorabilia, seeking the ways in which the competing logics of the archive and the antiques collection shaped a dispute about the place and status of the past in the present.

In section two, I compare the Brazilian Republic's symbolic reappropriations of the backlands of the interior (the *sertão*) as a providential center of the nation with Argentina's violent expansion into Patagonia and the Chaco. The frontier, in both of these processes, was captured simultaneously as cartographic space and as landscape. Whereas internal others were largely absent from these representations of space as nature, I argue that it is in a different visual register—photography—that the foundational violence of this purging operation came to the fore of the image. I end with some concluding remarks on the crisis of the nineteenth-century image world in the emergent age of the cinema and the way in which it can help us understand the crisis of the image in our own day, as well as the crisis of the modern political formations to which this image had once been attached.

# MUSEUMS

The German word "museal" has unpleasant overtones. It describes objects to which the observer no longer has a vital relationship and which are in the process of dying.
—Theodor W. Adorno, "Valéry Proust Museum"

When one enters an exhibition worthy of that name for the first time, one's first impulse is to get out.
—Junio, "Pelas exposições," *Revista Illustrada*, 1881

## Still Lives

In a series of writings containing the first sketches of ideas and formulations that would later become the core of the "Artwork" essay and the "Theses on the Concept of History," Walter Benjamin characterizes the collector as an archetypal figure located at the emergence of the modern capitalist order.[1] Alongside the flâneur, the gambler, the virtuoso, or the prostitute, the collector incarnates a romantic rebellion against capital, even as he exposes the extent to which it has taken hold of all things. For, in his attempt to reencounter an ontological source of value in the objects that pass into his possession, he tries to ward off the alienation of a material universe subsumed under the commodity's regime of abstract universal equivalence. Like the alchemist, the cabbalist, and other cultivators of secret knowledges who are his predecessors, the collector attempts to find gold at the heart of things, refusing to acknowledge its abstraction into a mere sign of equivalence. What the collector opposes in its deepest sense is representation, even if to do so he has to craft an encyclopedic image of the universe, a limited form of totality that has to be unmade and remade whenever a new piece of material enters his object system. Immersed in a hopeless struggle against dispersion, the collector's concern is with an order of things capable of restoring the ontological bond between materiality and language, that is, of restoring nearness in a mode of possession that defies the bourgeois logic of accumulation.

As critics of the modern "system of objects" have pointed out, this salvage of the material world is irredeemably bound to fail. It can only preserve the aura of things at the price of mythicizing the real process of their acquisition. Collecting thus becomes an originary act, a "labor of consumption," in which production and experience are erased in favor of the order of classification.[2] Like the naturalist's distribution of dead specimens across the tabular space of the *systema naturae*, the collector's relation with his possessions can only take place in the realm of a spectral afterlife. The collector can oppose commodity fetishism only in an aesthetic of melancholy, of mourning, which testifies to the incontestability of its historical triumph. Collecting is a way of simultaneously acknowledging and denying the catastrophic demise of the subject as a creative or constituent instance under the regime of capital and of alienated labor.

Benjamin, however, in a subtle twist of his argument, distinguishes between a "museal" and a "pioneering" mode of collecting. Whereas the former, he argues, is concerned with completeness in the sense of a finite canon of masterpieces (and the notion of the "master," the signature, is to be understood here as the site of commodification, where art is turned over to the market), the pioneering collector is restlessly on the lookout for new sources, revalidating and bringing to our attention the anonymous artifacts of mass culture. Thus, the pioneering collector challenges reified bourgeois notions of art and culture. For Benjamin, the passionate collector, the *ramasseur*, is potentially a cultural revolutionary. His compiling activity is a practical response to the aporias of theory—here, of dialectical materialism's difficulty in conceptualizing the aesthetic beyond conventional notions of singularity and within a context of mechanical reproduction. Pioneer collecting provides the material base for a kind of thinking that had not been possible in terms of the museal canon. Collecting comes, in this sense, before words; as the action of a pioneer it permits the development of a critical discourse on (or against) reified culture as it has been assembled at the museum. A collection that has entered the museum is one that has lost its critical edge and has become an instance of reification.

This journey of collections and collectors towards the museum—and thus also towards the state—is largely the itinerary that the next three chapters will take in following different kinds of objects through space and time. Of course, all collecting is always to a certain extent both conservative and constituent. It simultaneously defies and anticipates the museum that is both its horizon and its point of departure. The museum, in modernity, is the historical condition under which every new act of collecting operates, an instance of capture that is always already implied even in the most defiant, anticanonical gesture of countercollecting. Yet every project of extending the museum's grasp into areas of the material world formerly beyond its reach must invariably contain aspects of pioneer collecting that question the validity of the extant order of classification and the social order expressed in it.[3] The museum, as Didier Maleuvre reminds us, came into being in modernity as a revolutionary rather than restorative device, a monumental representation of the dispossession of the aristocracy. Nevertheless, it immediately forsook this revolutionary energy in associating the sovereignty of the new collective subject it thus projected with a notion of ownership, of property and propriety.[4]

Historians of collecting and museums have shown how, in the transition from the late Renaissance to the modern bourgeois era, a new space of order emerged. Within this new space, visuality and materiality became linked to a politics of truth and a concept of sovereignty permanently and ubiquitously embodied in spatiotemporal performances of seeing and being seen. Renaissance collecting and connoisseurship had been concerned foremost with the reimposition of order on a world that had become vertiginously contradictory and multiperspectival in the aftermath of the voyages of discovery and the wars of religion. As Paula Findlen explains, in the princely and scholarly *Kunstkammern, gabinetti,* and *studioli* of the sixteenth and seventeenth centuries, the sovereignty of ownership and the validity of knowledge sheltered in the space of the collection remained a function of the *hermetic* character of this space. The cabinet of curiosities was neither private nor public, in the modern sense, but rather was a realm of selective exposure in which truth and sovereignty were bound up with secrecy, enclosure, and the control of access.[5]

Upon the advent of print culture, this mode of knowing and of displaying was radically modified, and the collection turned, as it passed into the museum, into an open secret: a space of disciplinarity rather than of sovereignty. Together with the development of a new architectural frame typically associated with Graeco-Roman models, which inscribed the museum's authority into the heart of urban space, a new internal organization of collections emerged. This new order of things was based on principles of chronology and locality as well as on typological distinctions between families, classes, and species, in the domain of nature, or between genres and schools, in the domain of art. The museum's external and internal forms of organization predetermined the visitor's engagement with the objects on display. Walking past the spoils of history, the forms of nature, or the creations of art, all of them arranged in a sequence of gradual becoming that invariably pointed to the present as its moment of fulfillment, visitors would at once see and embody the making of a modern subject. They were thus simultaneously addressing, and addressed by, the state as the invisible custodian of this space of (self-)knowledge. The museum, Carol Duncan and Alan Wallach suggest, "is the site of a symbolic transaction between the visitor and the state. In exchange for the state's spiritual wealth, the individual intensifies his attachment to the state. Hence the museum's hegemonic function, the crucial role it can play in the experience of citizenship."[6]

This movement from cabinet to museum is paralleled, on an individual level, by the museumization of the bourgeois interior, which reconstructs a dream of sovereignty by holding fast to an already redundant form of collecting. Bourgeois house building is always at heart the construction of a mausoleum. It monumentalizes the historical demise of a form of sovereign subjectivity, which the collector of precious objects tries in vain to call back to the scene. Whereas at the museum the state literally makes itself at home, taking hold of a space formerly attached to the residence of the sovereign, the domestic interior internalizes its inhabitants' subjection by becoming museal space, confiding selfness to questions of selection, classification, and display. Museums, in fact, invariably have to draw on the private space that is presumably their opposite in order to renovate and thus ensure the validity of their collections. Most, if not all, state museums contain objects that had previously dwelled in private collections: if bourgeois domesticity has incorporated the museum, the museum itself is, in fact, continuously occupied in making the home public.

Two pictures may help to illustrate what I am trying to say here. The first one, a photograph taken towards the end of the nineteenth century, shows Andrés Lamas, the Uruguayan politician, antiquarian, and archivist, in his Buenos Aires home, surrounded by items of his collection (fig. 4). The second, a postcard distributed by the Museum of La Plata in 1910, is entitled "Anthropological Section" and depicts the museum's collection of indigenous human remains, complete with the portraits and death masks of Amerindians who had lived at the museum after the conquest and occupation of their lands (fig. 5). The scene is presided over by a museum scientist, possibly (though it is hard to tell from the image) Robert Lehmann-Nitsche, a German anthropologist and the section's curator at the time. The absence of proper names from the second photograph's caption, the anonymity of the subject of collecting, is of course far from irrelevant. Rather, it indicates the passage from subjectivity, privacy, and belonging to disciplinarity and publicness. Despite their almost identical formal composition, the two pictures—the collector at home, and the state custodian of objects colonized, quite literally, by their arrangement on the museum's shelves—are located

FIGURE 4. Anonymous, Andrés Lamas in his study. Albumin print (ca. 1890). Museo Mitre, Buenos Aires.

FIGURE 5. Anonymous, Museo de La Plata, anthropological section. Postcard (1910). Archivo General de la Nación, Buenos Aires.

at opposite ends of a particular figure of state power. The antiquarian collects the memorabilia of national history—the busts of Mitre and Sarmiento that frame the scene, alongside genre paintings and precious furniture—in order to forge an interior space of sensibility and nobility. This patrician domesticity ennobles the liberal state by juxtaposing its monuments with an array of precious objects, simultaneously exposing and disavowing the nexus between state formation and capital accumulation. The "anthropological" display of indigenous corpses and body parts, in contrast, forges a gruesome allegory of state conquest by exposing, in the museum interior, the radical exteriority of an otherness that the rationality of liberalism can only conceive as—and thus turns into—a space of death. I want to leave aside for the moment the histories and politics of collecting and display that these two scenes call forth. Instead, I want to concentrate on the analysis of formal relations, the critical mode of inquiry that Panofsky called the level of formal identification and description of "motives" and "compositions," a task which must precede any iconographic discussion of the image in terms of themes and concepts.[7]

The most striking parallel between the two images is the way in which both collectors are installed, by the arrangement of the objects themselves, at the focal point of the scene. The men are thus placed, quite literally, at the crossroads of the dead gazes of things: the busts and portraits, in the first picture; the skulls, death masks, portraits, and the mummy in her glass cage in the second one. We see the objects of the collection looking towards their custodian as if confirming the sovereignty he has exercised by putting them in their place, as if awaiting his gaze that might redeem them from their purgatory but which, instead, he concedes exclusively to the camera lens that stands in for the gaze of the spectator. Not merely the statues and human remains look towards the collector-curator, we should add, but all the materials as well as the space they open up and delineate. The arrangement of furniture and carpet in the photograph of Lamas's collection; the diagonals of the showcases, cupboards, doorways, and columns in the museum photograph—all converge on the human subject in their midst. Or rather, the upper half of a human subject, for what we have in both pictures is really half a human body, a bust. The lower half remains hidden behind the institutional and symbolic embodiment of his knowledge, the place from which the entire arrangement has supposedly originated: the desk (even in the photograph of the museum, the showcase at which the curator is seated figures as a desk, in the absence of a real one). This reduction of the body—which, in the Lamas picture, is echoed by the busts of the two statesmen invigilating, as it were, the entrance to the scene—is no minor detail, since what it suppresses is precisely the part where the body is at its most bodily. This substitution of the body's generating power by a material duplication of the head, a brainy piece of furniture, we might say, constitutes the first, original substitution from which all the others derive. The place of the collector is defined in both pictures as the site of an originary, fetishistic disavowal that projects, along the vanishing lines of perspectival space, a metonymic chain of objects that always return their gaze to the initial site of lack. Collecting, Jean Baudrillard observes, is an activity most frequently observed in male subjects prior to the awakening, or towards the apogee, of genital sexuality. There is, he suggests, "a manifest connection between collecting and sexuality," the former being a tendency that "clearly runs counter to active genital sexuality, although it is not simply a substitute for it. Rather, as compared with genitality, it constitutes a regression to the anal stage, which is characterized by accumulation, orderliness, aggressive retention, and so on."[8]

And indeed, something more than merely phallic substitution seems to go on in our two pictures: something we might describe as a mental engendering of rigidity. In the ensemble of human torso and desk, the production of order is represented as a mental act taking the place, quite literally, of genital activity. Instead, or in the place of, the reproduction of life the collector is seen here as immersed in a metonymic accumulation of death. The collection does not merely substitute genital desire but actively wards off any kind of fluidity or fleshiness; in this sense the collected object is quite the opposite of the fetish as a thing that is invested with life. Modern collecting is, on the contrary, a systematic investment of things with death: to become object is to be stripped of the fluidity of living things (hence, also, the importance of taxidermy to the origins of the modern museum). The nineteenth-century collector, in fact, already prefigures an anxiety that would return decades later in a new militant, and militarized, authoritarianism giving political expression to a psychosocial disposition that fears change and fluidity. The fascist's response to the fluidity of modern life that he sees embodied in working-class multitudes and female sexuality, Klaus Theweleit argues, cannot be reduced to the concepts of castration anxiety or incest fear, as it represents "a fear of total annihilation and dismemberment."[9] It is in this sense that museal collecting can be conceived as a precursor to the anarchiving destruction wrought upon Argentine and Brazilian society by the dictatorships of the twentieth century. Like dictatorial politics, collecting is concerned with impeding metamorphosis, but whereas the museum had attempted to achieve this by preserving the self-sameness of things in an object displayed to the gaze, dictatorial policies would remove from view, make "disappear," what threatened to change. Thus the museum, as a spatial arrangement of the objectification of life (nature) and its creative processes ("history," "art"), also looks forward to the camp. It is one of the sites where the rationalist, emancipatory contents of the modern project already announce their eventual falling-over into pure destruction, the moment when biopolitics will turn into thanatopolitics.

## Scopic Rituals

I have been using photography's capture of the museum's scene of display in order to reveal the structural relations between space, materiality, and sovereignty as expressed in the images' formal composition. Rather than as a transparent, aesthetically neutral window, I have taken the photographic picture as a meta-text, which, in turning these relations themselves into a visual object, also tells us something about the production of objects. What the visual mechanics of the camera illuminates, as it reduplicates it, is the museum's character as an optical apparatus. The museum makes the object an object of seeing by bringing it into a particular relation to a subject thus posited as an observer. Neither end of the arrow of this kind of perspectival seeing is ideologically neutral, as Jonathan Crary has pointed out: "Problems of vision are fundamentally questions about the body and the operation of social power." To ask how modernity's optical devices have redeployed people and things in space is to ask "how, beginning early in the nineteenth century, a new set of relations between the body on one hand and forms of institutional and discursive power on the other redefined the status of an observing subject."[10]

The museum thus has to be understood as placed at the very core of this modern opticality. In a sagacious essay, Donald Preziosi argues that

in a very real sense, the modern museum was the most extraordinary optical instrument of all; the veritable summa of opticality, of visuality; an instrument of the scale of the state; a vehicle that at the same time contained the state. It was an instrument for the manufacture, on individual and collective horizons, of societies, ethnicities, races, classes, genders, and individuals; of history, progress, and moralities; of nature itself, and of the future(s) towards which all of what is contained therein might be moving.[11]

The museum, Preziosi suggests, is a multidimensional apparatus in which the paradoxical visuality of the state is spatiotemporally realized. The "museum effect" is the result of an oscillation of the gaze between the different planes of visibility with which the visitor is confronted on entering. On the level of objects, she is invited to see self-contained monads at the same time as these are already inserted in relations of seriality and comparison. On the level of the collection, the museum display provides at once a great allegory of totality ("history," "art," "nature") and a performative, chronological trajectory along which its gradual coming-together can be experienced. Preziosi rightly points us to the radically new, almost hallucinatory, quality of this modern optics, in which a vision of truth is constantly announced as well as deferred. In its anamorphic localization of truth, never entirely resident in the object nor in the collection as a whole, the museum composes a Hegelian spectacle, extending into the material world at large, that it urges us to see in a new, museal light:

What the museum accomplished […] was nothing less than the circulation of modern populations in(to) an ethically refashioned history composed of things transmuted into objects that were object lessons in at least two principal ways—as documentary indices of a history of the world legible as a teleological dramaturgy, as having a direction and a point; and as simulacra of a seemingly endless number of subject positions in social life that might be admired, desired, emulated, escaped, or eschewed. […] The museum became, during the nineteenth century, a "centering device" and in fact a whole optical instrumentality for the positioning, the siting (and the sighting, the rendering visible, the framing) of modern(ized) populations in and for a history that was itself deployed, both museographically and historiographically, as the unfolding of a transcendent truth.[12]

By distributing objects in space, the museum locates the viewing subject in relation to a time that it qualifies as historical, a historicality that the museumgoer is invited to construe both as *other*—as opposed to her own present-ness—and as the very texture of identity, of selfness as bio-graphy, for which the museum visit offers a performative template. Similarly, the viewer is located in relation to a space centered on the (Western European and, somewhat later, North American) platform of observation. As a means of bringing the world into focus, the museum was perhaps the chief visual device of a self-forging modernity authorized through the capture of, and thus the "denial of coevalness" with, the non-European as a space and body of mere materiality, reliant on the ordering gaze of colonial power.[13]

Only in recent years has this centrality of the museum in the emergence of the modern world become the topic of a rapidly growing bibliography of critical and historical studies. Yet while a number of these share a filiation with post-colonial strands of thought, addressing the appropriation and display of non-European artifacts and natural specimens in the imperial centers, little attention has so far been paid to the development of museums in Latin America, which roughly paralleled that in Europe and North America.[14] Indeed, almost from the outset of the museum age and prior to the foundation of many museums in Europe, the presence of Latin American institutions of collecting and display may add more than just a footnote to the history of the modern museum. Their very up-to-dateness was from the outset a key problem that museums in Latin America came up against. They were entrusted with the task of forging coevalness with modern (read: non-Iberian) Europe, through the construction of visual theaters of sovereignty. Yet at the same time, having to bring the material substance of the nation into a perspective tied to the imperial reordering of the world, but locating the point of view within the same space that was simultaneously exposed to this very viewpoint, they could not but reinscribe the *nonsimultaneity* of a (post)colonial location at the very core of the display. European museum scientists visiting their peer institutions in Latin America tended to dismiss them as simply outdated, failing to understand the complex negotiations over issues of perspective, locality, and (non)coevalness in which the American museums had to engage. Rather than as a particular, "abnormal" case in the history of museums, I suggest that the Latin American institutions need to be studied as bringing to the fore certain contradictions underlying the museum form as such, contradictions that in the North Atlantic "center" have become naturalized and thus invisible.

In the chapters that follow I will not attempt to write a history of the museum in Latin America, nor even in Argentina and Brazil. Instead, I want to locate in specific objects and ensembles, and in the event of their display to the gaze, a series of problems related to the interdependence between acts of collecting and displaying and the capture of social relations by an emergent state power. A few general remarks, however, may be useful to anticipate some of the main differences between museums' foundations and organization on both sides of the Atlantic. The most immediate contrast concerns the sequence of disciplinary specialization. Whereas, in Europe, the first museums of fine arts and antiquities were founded right at the beginning of the nineteenth century (either through state appropriation of the aristocracy's belongings or the gradual opening to the public of princely cabinets and galleries), in Latin America artistic and historical museums would only emerge towards the end of the nineteenth century in contexts of cultural nationalism. The first national museums had focused almost exclusively on natural history and, somewhat later, anthropology. They concerned themselves with the symbolic appropriation and reordering of an interior space rendered to the gaze as other, a colonial space of accumulation that, unlike the colonies of the European imperial powers, lay within the territory of the nation-state.

Secondly, museums in nineteenth-century Latin America were not necessarily always about fashioning a public, in a peculiar moral education of the gaze. Well into the second half of the nineteenth century, in their restricted access most national museums in the region continued to resemble the princely cabinets of the eighteenth century rather than their European contemporaries. Admission remained limited to one or two days a week and was often offered only to visitors who could boast the appropriate social and professional credentials. Catering to elite local audiences and visiting dignitaries from abroad rather than the wider population, the Latin American museum over at least two-thirds of the nineteenth century hardly corresponded to its European equivalent, characterized as "a machinery for producing 'progressive subjects,'" or as a means of inducting the self-fashioning of "a voluntarily self-regulating citizenry."[15] While from a sociological point of view this restricted use of the museum apparatus could be taken simply as an indicator of the belated constitution of a bourgeois public sphere, I would argue that it is also intimately tied to the politics of space informing the museums' disciplinary emphasis on "nature." Native populations (and, by extension, their mestizo and mulatto descendants) inhabiting the natural space the museums took as their object were hardly ever empowered to become the subject of observation. Indeed, restricting access to the museum's viewing platform was a crucial means of ensuring that boundaries between self and other, between the beholder and the object, remained clear-cut and beyond appeal. Only towards the end of the century museums' strategies of address gradually shifted towards a visual pedagogy which, I will argue, attempted to turn visitors' performances of spectatorship into a civics lesson.

Finally, the development of Latin American museums in the nineteenth century has to be read against the more general context of insertion into the (visual) economy of capitalism, expressed most notably in the region's presentations at the great universal exhibitions. Both Argentina and Brazil participated assiduously in these "feasts of progress," attempting to woo potential investors and immigrants, but also more generally to inscribe themselves firmly among the "civilized nations" in front of European and U.S. audiences considered to be the legitimate global arbiters. At home, these events were emulated in an endless proliferation of national, provincial, industrial, agricultural, and other exhibitions, culminating in Buenos Aire's Exposición Continental of 1882 (where Brazil presented a sumptuous, much-lauded section of arts and crafts). Exhibitions, in the nineteenth century, were the travelling circus of capital: in their spectacular attempt to make everything a potential object of display, exhibitions contained a promise of social transparency figured in the total accountability of the real, the notion that everything, in principle, could be classified, listed, and receive a price tag. In reality, then, this transparency could only take shape as the universal equivalence of exchange value, that is, as a general obliteration of social relations in their representation as things.

Relations between museums and exhibitions in nineteenth-century Argentina and Brazil were complex, neither entirely competitive nor complementary. Objects often travelled from one space of display into another. Museums used to lend exhibits for display at universal and national exhibitions, as well as offering expertise and display space; collections gathered for presentation at universal exhibitions tended to pass into the ownership of local museums on their return to the country. However, whereas in the 1860s and 1870s museums actively supported the organization of trade and industry exhibitions, towards the end of the century they would increasingly set themselves up as custodians of immaterial, permanent values untouched by the market and its frivolous aesthetic of the ephemeral and spectacular. The museum, parallel to a shift of interest from nature to the heritage of the national past and the spirit of art, became conceived as a refuge from the visual culture of the marketplace, bespeaking a more general process of differentiation between the realms of the state and of capital. Yet even if the museum now attempted to shed its former affinities with capitalist accumulation, nowhere else does the constitutive bond between the state and capital find a more graphic expression than in the museum's material theater of sovereignty.

Below, I will follow the stages of this process through the domains of "nature," "man," and "history." In chapter 1, I compare the development of natural history displays in Argentina and Brazil over the second half of the nineteenth century. My foremost concern here is with the shifting relations between notions of life and national being (*ser nacional*) that are implied in the representation of natural orders past and present. In chapter 2, I move on to the inhabitants of this "natural space," the Amerindian population, as it was represented at the Brazilian Anthropological Exhibition held in 1882 at the National Museum of Rio de Janeiro. Just as the scientific image of nature had always implied a statement on sovereignty and the state, debates on Indians' degree of civilization or savagery in nineteenth-century Brazil also passed judgement on the Imperial state, which had turned a romanticized, virtuous "noble savage" into the centerpiece of its iconography.

In the third chapter, I compare the attempts to gather material testimonies of the Argentine and Brazilian nations' virtuous past, in response to what was perceived, for various reasons, as a crisis of citizenship. In both countries, national history consolidated itself as a discipline around the turn of the century as a means to foster social cohesion. However, in discussing turn-of-the-century debates in both countries on the function and use of remainders from the past, I argue that underneath the veneer of patriotic exaltation lay a deep unsettledness: a fear of the crisis of hegemony that the decaying memorials of national history were already forespelling.

# Empires of Nature

## MUSEUMS, SCIENCE, AND
## THE POLITICS OF BEING

> In the dream in which every epoch sees in images the epoch which is to succeed it, the latter appears coupled with elements of pre-history [...] to give birth to the utopias which leave their traces in a thousand configurations of life from permanent buildings to ephemeral fashions.
>
> —Walter Benjamin, "On the Concept of History"

### Configurations of Life

In 1877, the young Argentine amateur naturalist Estanislao S. Zeballos published an account of a visit he had just paid to the National Museum of Rio de Janeiro in the *Anales de la Sociedad Científica Argentina*, the journal he coedited with Francisco and José María Ramos Mejía. Among their South American sisters, Zeballos asserted, Buenos Aires and Rio were the cities best known for their splendid collections and scientific research:

[T]he Public Museum of Buenos Aires, as the most famous among the temples erected to Paleontology, the science of this century, and the Museum of Rio Janeiro, begin to attract the eyes of the scientific world, thanks to their treasures of natural history. When remembering Burmeister's work in the [Argentine] Republic, it is quite impossible to forget that of Lund in the [Brazilian] Empire, and considering that the spirit of science has taken hold of our youth, we see the same among the young Brazilian scholars, under the command of an eminent South American, Dr. Ladislao Souza de Mello e Netto. [...] Here, then, we have a national body of sages, educated under the inspirations of eminent professors from the Empire and abroad. Congratulating the young Brazilian sages for their progress, and Dr. Netto for the success of his efforts, we can only wish for the Brazilian scientific school to encounter noble rivals in the Argentine Republic.[1]

The most remarkable aspect of Zeballos's chronicle is certainly his claim to an emergent South American science that produces a new global configuration of knowledge. The "world of science," Zeballos notes with satisfaction, is already looking towards South America not merely as a repository of evidence but as a site of knowledge production in its own right: as a "scientific school" capable of contributing its own quota to the universal enterprise of the study of nature and of man. In discussing the Rio museum's reformed displays and publications, Zeballos's text testifies to the emergence, around 1870, of a new scientific idiom among the Argentine and Brazilian lettered elite. This new language took shape in a context of reorganization of the encyclopedic museum cabinets of the first half of the century into institutions dedicated to the study of life in its local manifestations in the space and time of the Argentine and Brazilian nation-state.

Both Rio's Museu Nacional and Buenos Aires's Museo Público had been founded almost immediately after national independence. Arguably, however, only in the final decades of the century would they come to occupy a key position within the wider debate on a "national being" (*ser nacional*) conceived as an emanation of the struggles and successions of forms in the natural world. At the same time, their exclusive authority to collect and display the material evidence of this local modulation of life's universal forces now began to be contested by new institutions. These new spaces of collecting and display were often associated with provincial elites challenging the hegemony of the capital and of federal government. The Museu Paraense of Belém, founded in 1867, the Museu Paranaense of Curitiba (1875), the Museu Botânico do Amazonas of Manaus (1882), and the Museu Paulista of São Paulo (1894), all in Brazil, as well as the Museo de La Plata in Argentina, founded in 1877 as the Anthropological and Archaeological Museum of the Province of Buenos Aires, all testify to a particular urge in late nineteenth-century Argentina and Brazil to collect, classify, display, and speculate on the material evidence of life's unfolding in a regional or national space, thus endowing this space with a new density of meaning.

Histories of science tend to present this process as the more or less belated updating of partial and tributary colonial knowledges to a modern and universal scientific consciousness. Examples of this process are the gradual replacement of mineralogy and botany by zoology, paleontology, and anthropology as core disciplines of the history of nature, and, in the final quarter of the century, a generalized acceptance of the principles of evolution guiding the reclassification and new spatial arrangement of collections. Strategies of display would now change from a merely accumulative and tabular ordering to a monumental and dynamic material spectacle that took the visitor's movement through museum space as a way of inserting narrative and drama into the arrangement of exhibits. Yet in fact, these innovations in museum display were plainly contemporary with similar developments in the great metropolitan museums, several of which had been founded or reorganized around the same time as their South American peers: the new British Museum of Natural History at South Kensington, for instance, opened its doors in 1881, Austria's Naturhistorisches Hofmuseum in 1889, the Bohemian Museum of Prague in 1894, and the Royal Belgian Museum of Brussels in 1903. New York's American Museum of Natural History, established in 1869, had moved into new quarters and reorganized its collections in 1877, two years before the National Museum of Washington, part of the Smithsonian Institution, began construction of a new building to accommodate donations received in the aftermath of the Philadelphia Universal Exhibition of 1876. Perhaps, then, we ought to seek the difference between Argentine and Brazilian scientific museums and those in Europe and North America not in time (as a belated arrival at scientific truth) or space (as a dependent position in the geopolitics of knowledge) but in purpose. For, whereas in the European museum of natural science a universal act of knowing was performatively embodied in the scopic ritual of every single visit, in Argentina and Brazil the museum form, in turning the discontinuous temporality of life into a spatial assemblage, had to forge the reemergence of the local and particular in the figure of national being. Not universal life but national being, we could say, borrowing a concept from Timothy Mitchell, was the museum's "effect of structure." It was the "invisible" that mediated between the real and its representation: a form of truth located neither on the level of the museum object nor on that of the context to which it referred, but, rather, in that which made it possible to represent, in the relay between things and signs.[2]

The universal reorganization of museum displays in the late nineteenth century staged the passage of natural order through life into being that, according to Foucault, led to the emergence of the human sciences.[3] In Latin America, it prompted discourses on race and inheritance that reconceptualized the national question. In both Argentina and in Brazil new strands of social thought more or less directly inspired by Comtian and Spencerian positivism, social Darwinism, and the new physio-psychological disciplines emerging from the Salpêtrière, reinserted "the people" of Romanticism's historical temporality into the time of evolution. This was a new kind of suprahuman historicity uncovered by geology and paleontology, which were now providing the frame of the anthropological time of man. Theorists of national being such as Sílvio Romero, José Veríssimo, Araripe Júnior, and Capistrano de Abreu in Brazil; or José María Ramos Mejía, Carlos Octavio Bunge, José Ingenieros, and the Sarmiento of *Conflicto y armonías de las razas en América* (1883) in Argentina, exchanged ideas and polemics with museum scientists Ladislau Netto, João Baptista de Lacerda, Francisco P. Moreno, and Florentino Ameghino. The evolution of man and his natural environment, as well as the lessons to be derived from it for a politics of state intervention into the life of the people, were common concerns among naturalists and thinkers on the "national question." In this context, arguments in natural history immediately became biopolitical programs, in a particular kind of "double voicing." The identification of biogenetic engineering as the prime task of state politics in late nineteenth- and early twentieth-century discourses of *branqueamento* (whitening) and population control gave political expression to the passage from life to national being that was simultaneously being staged in the museums of natural history. The narrative of evolution, in other words, allowed natural history to become the temporality of state formation.

### Visions of Sovereignty

On August 7, 1812, Bernardino Rivadavia, in the name of the provisional government of the Provinces of the River Plate, decreed the formation of a Museum of Natural History in the city of Buenos Aires, considering that "these investigations [...] will result in useful discoveries." With the support of all citizens of good taste, Rivadavia went on, such a museum would provide the means, "as we approach the moment of our Emancipation," to "ascend to the rank of the civilized nations [*los pueblos cultos*]." Inviting the members of the provisional government, as well as the citizenry at large, to put at the museum's disposition "all the products, proper and foreign to our territory, worth including in this deposit," he signaled a debt that the inhabitants of the newborn (but nonetheless ageless) fatherland had the duty of canceling: "The observation of nature on our continent—the mineral, vegetable and animal kingdom, and all its artifacts—is beyond doubt one of the most dignified occupations of the sages throughout the world [...] who, relishing in the knowledge and acquisition of the precious gifts offered to us by our Fatherland [*Madre Patria*], observe with estrangement that we should have neglected them until now."[4] Eleven years later, with little or no progress having been made in the interim, Rivadavia (now government secretary of Martín Rodríguez) asked the head of the public library, Friar Luis José Chorroarín, who already possessed a small collection of natural history and archaeological samples, to proceed with the creation of a national museum (Museo del País) dedicated "to all the branches of Natural History, Chemistry, Arts and

Industries." For the same purpose, the local Academy of Exact Sciences would form "a representative collection of the country's geology, and another one of its birds," in addition to which the garrison of Carmen de Patagones was instructed to assemble a collection of shells.[5] Carlos de Ferraris, assistant of the Italian pharmacist Pedro Carta, who had been hired by Rivadavia to be professor of experimental physics at the University of Buenos Aires, was put in charge of the taxidermic preparation and arrangement of exhibits. The new museum was officially inaugurated on January 1, 1827.

A similar initiative had been taken in Rio de Janeiro, the capital of the Portuguese Empire since the Royal Court's escape from Lisbon during the French invasion of 1807. Prince Regent João VI in 1818 ordered the transfer of the collections from the moribund Casa de História Natural (a depository for the preparation and storage of animal and plant specimens awaiting shipment to Lisbon and Coimbra, founded in 1784) to a new building on Rio's Campo de Sant'Anna (today's Praça da República). The founding decree echoes Rivadavia's obsession with order and representation as a precondition for the enjoyment and profitable exploitation of nature's gifts, albeit in a rhetoric of continuity rather than of rupture with the colonial past: "Wishing to spread the knowledge and study of the natural sciences in the kingdom of Brazil, which contains thousands of objects worthy of observation and examination, to be employed for the benefit of commerce, industry, and the arts, great sources of wealth which I much desire to develop, I order the establishment of a Royal Museum at this Court, where all existing instruments, machines and cabinets dispersed at other places shall be transferred as quickly as possible."[6] Despite the decree's characterization of the new institution as a museum of the natural sciences, the objects donated by D. João as the museum's original collection were of an exclusively cultural kind: eighty models of machinery, the foot of a Greek statue, a medieval lancet, a silver cup, two iron keys of Roman origin, and several oil paintings. The museum also received a collection of ancient medals donated by the jeweller André Godoy.[7]

A year later, a set of "Instructions for Travelers and Employees in the Colonies on the Means of Collecting, Preservation, and Display of Objects of Natural History," originally issued by the Muséum d'Histoire Naturelle of Paris, was translated and published by order of the Court, extended by numerous comments and annotations on the natural history of Brazil and its exhibition at the museum and botanical garden (annexed to the institution between 1819 and 1822). In these rules of collecting, which Maria Margaret Lopes suggests formulated an "ideal procedure" of natural history institutions, regional mandatories in Brazil as well as in the Portuguese mainland and overseas possessions in Africa and Asia were urged to assemble and send to Rio de Janeiro representative collections of local specimens, which would be classified and catalogued at the Royal Museum.[8] Subsequently, a general catalogue of species (including, where possible, collections of duplicates) would be sent back to the colonies and provinces. The museum and botanical garden, in short, would be the instances of centralization, processing, display, and redistribution of data in a flow of objects and representations that simultaneously reaffirmed Portuguese imperial sovereignty across the globe.

In both cases, then, the establishment of national museums instituted, at least in theory, a two-way traffic that was fundamental to the reaffirmation of territorial sovereignty. On the one hand, it entailed a dislocation of material objects into the synthetic space of the collection; on the other, the visible order of the exhibition supplied the base for the translation of nature into the well-constructed language of Linnaean tabulation. The general nomination of species, in other words, traveled in a direction opposite to the objects it took as its samples, as a form of writing that expanded from the center to the margins. This act of knowing imposed a plane of equivalence on the level of representation that made it possible to introduce "nature" into the system of wealth, as its ingredients could now be exchanged against other objects equally endowed with proper names and, therefore, with calculable value. The museum, in short, is viewed here as what Bruno Latour calls a "centre of calculation": a space of assembly of spatiotemporally distant events, artifacts, and people seized and inscribed, as things, onto a single plane of representation. Collecting was a production of calculability, a "manufacture of equations" that reproduced and guaranteed the stability and combinability of the "immutable mobiles" forged in the passage from periphery to center.[9]

Collecting and exhibiting, as the way to establish a mutual transparency between the orders of nature, language, and wealth, were simultaneously acts of sovereignty, according to the legal tradition of the *res nullius* forged in the seventeenth century by enlightened theorists of colonialism. This theory of colonial sovereignty, contesting Spanish and Portuguese claims to the exclusive possession of the Americas, insisted on the radical exteriority of that which had not yet been named and thus fell to the one who first brought it to language, making it speak itself as a thing.[10] The inscription of the proper name, whose condition of possibility was the "re-cognition" of the place of things in the system of nature, was thus simultaneously an inscription of the law. The first institutions in charge of collecting and displaying objects of natural history in Spanish and Portuguese America—the Gabinete de Historia Natural of Havana, the Casa Botánica of Bogotá, the Casa de História Natural of Rio de Janeiro, and the Museo de Historia Natural of Mexico—had been founded towards the end of the eighteenth century, in the course of the Bourbon and Pombaline reforms, precisely in order to foreclose European territorial claims based on the *res nullius* doctrine. Some of these would provide the initial base of the national museums founded almost immediately after (and sometimes before) the end of the independence wars. Apart from the museums at Buenos Aires and Rio de Janeiro, the new foundations included those of Santiago de Chile (1822), Bogotá (1823), Lima (1826), Guatemala (1831), and Montevideo (1837). Museums were among the first state institutions founded in Hispanic as well as Lusophone America because they were the fundamental expression of a sovereignty hinged on the power of naming.

This fundamental articulation between science, sovereignty, and a particular construction of perspective is often missed by histories of "colonial knowledge." In the spatial imaginary of nineteenth-century natural history, the site of knowledge increasingly ceased to be the anomic wilderness of "the field," where the lonesome *naturaliste-voyageur* wrested order from chaos, coming to reside instead in the places of convergence of objects from distant locations—museums and botanical and zoological gardens. The "centre of calculation" offered the theorist-researcher a synthetic overview that revealed not so much the true image of nature as the invisible structure made up by the empty spaces between one object and the next. Precisely on account of their physical and psychic distance from the multisensory immediacy of the field, sedentary naturalists such as Cuvier and Lamarck would claim an increased truth-value for their (abstract and detached) systematizations of nature over the experience- and context-bound accounts of traveling researchers. As Dorinda Outram proposes, "[i]t was not a big step from the establishment of distance as a cultural value [...] to the production of the idea of objectivity, meaning precisely the placing of 'distance' between the observer and the observed, between the knower and his own responses."[11]

It is precisely this construction of distance, as much an ideological and moral as a geographical dimension, that became a major difficulty for the new museums at Buenos Aires and Rio de Janeiro. At least in the eyes of the foreign naturalists who visited them on their way into the field, these museums were situated too close to their object to provide a clear vision of nature. François de Castelnau summed up his impressions of the Rio museum in 1843: "In a country where nature has so richly gifted the animal kingdom, it was difficult not to be surprised to see such a poor assemblage of its diverse products, a collection which hardly comprised a quarter of the animals of Brazil."[12] And even in 1865, Louis Agassiz, on a data-collecting mission to prove his theory of racial difference, would still dismiss the establishment as *une antiquaille*: "Anyone who knows what a lively and dynamic museum is about, will agree that the collections of this one have remained for years without improvements or additions; the mounted animals, mammals and birds are in decay, and the fish, except for some magnificent specimens from the Amazon, do not give an idea of the variety one finds in the waters of Brazil. You would form a better collection at the city market in a single morning."[13] One does not necessarily have to take these accounts at face value; previous descriptions by French travelers of the 1820s (Bougainville, Thévenet, Denis) written prior to the discursive transformation of museum space into a site of experimental research paint a much more positive picture. The interesting point about Castelnau's and Agassiz's accounts is that they deny the possibility of locating a site of observation within the very space this observation seeks to behold. Regardless of whether or not the museums of the northern hemisphere held more "complete" collections of Brazilian fauna and flora (thanks, in part, to donations of duplicates made by the Rio museum, which its European and North American peers never returned, as director Ladislau Netto complained in 1870),[14] in the view of many foreign visitors a museum located in the tropics was a contradiction in terms. Rather than bringing the stuffed specimens of birds and mammals abounding in the surrounding forest back to life, the decay and rot wrought on the exhibits by the tropical climate highlighted the lack of distance, the pull of a debilitating environment that the museum tried in vain to subordinate to its gaze.

The Royal Museum had been opened to the public—or rather, to "all persons, native or foreign, worthy by their knowledge or qualities," as a royal decree put it—in 1821, displaying a heterodox collection arranged over eight rooms on the first floor.[15] A further two rooms on the ground floor, containing "industrial machinery," had been opened in 1819. A report from 1830, when the institution's name was changed to Museu Imperial e Nacional, lists the following classes of objects in eight rooms: reptiles, serpents, lizards and turtles, woods, and monsters; shells, insects, and fish; monkeys and other mammals; mineralogy; artisanry; birds; indigenous artifacts from Pará and Matto Grosso; Egyptian mummies, numismatica, and paintings.[16] The inventory of what in only a decade had probably become the most important collection on the continent, bespeaks a notable and concerted effort of accumulation, thanks in part to the still active network of colonial exchange operated by the Portuguese Court. The collections of zoology (numbering near five thousand objects, according to the inventory of 1838) and of botany had largely been assembled by Friedrich Sellow and Ricardo Zani, foreign naturalists contracted by the museum in 1820 and 1828, respectively, for expeditions into the interior. Previously, the museum's warden and taxidermist, João de Deus e Mattos, who had already served at the Casa de História Natural, had been sent on hunting sprees into the mountains surrounding the city, preparing animals on the spot. João de Deus, as the city's chronicler Manuel Moreira de Azevedo recalled in a suggestive passage in 1877, "went into the forest and began to hunt; and the bird or animal falling dead was immediately prepared; whatever he killed he preserved. Thus he depopulated the forest to enrich science, and returned laden with different mammals, birds, reptiles, and insects, precious remains of his lethal, yet useful and civilizing, expedition."[17]

Sellow had also helped secure an ornithological collection donated by the Royal Museum of Berlin in 1827, as a means of establishing regular exchanges of duplicates. In 1823, a botanical collection of 2,300 samples, comprising 266 different species, was received from the chief surgeon of the province of Matto Grosso. The mineralogical collection of Abraham Gottlob Werner, purchased in 1805 for the Natural History Museum at Lisbon, had been brought to Rio on the Royal Court's arrival, and was further enriched by subsequent donations from Denmark and Italy, as well as, in 1838, by the personal collection of José Bonifácio de Andrada e Silva, Brazil's first prime minister and a former professor of mining and mineralogy. In 1824, Emperor D. Pedro I had acquired several Egyptian mummies and sarcophagi from the Italian arts merchant Fiengo.[18] Ethnographic objects were also received from North America, the Aleutian and Sandwich Islands, and from Portuguese Africa, in addition to the collections of native ethnographica sent by provincial governors. The museum's first catalogue, published in 1838, grouped the collections into five sections—zoology, botany, mineralogy, fine arts, and customs—following the example of the Muséum de Paris. In 1842, the system was modified and the museum divided into subsections headed by their own directors, following the model of the British Museum's Natural Sciences Department. The new division comprised (1) comparative anatomy and zoology; (2) botany, agriculture and mechanical arts; (3) mineralogy and geology; and (4) numismatics, arts, and customs. The last of these, which included the ethnographic collections, would be directed by important members of the Brazilian Romantic movement, such as the poet Manoel Araújo Porto Alegre and the painter Pedro Américo de Figueiredo e Mello.

The beginnings of the museum of Buenos Aires, known as the Museo Público prior to the federalization of the capital city in 1880, are much more modest in comparison. The key document here is museum secretary Manuel Ricardo Trelles's "Memory on the State of the Museum," delivered in 1856 to the Association of Friends of the Natural History of the River Plate, created two years earlier in an attempt to rescue the museum from the decay into which it had supposedly fallen under Rosas's dictatorship (1829–52). Under Rosas, Trelles suggests, the museum had "reached the lowest rung of decadence and abandon," finding itself transformed into a deposit of trophies from the civil wars. The defeat of Rosas and subsequent foundation of the Association of Friends, resulting in a doubling of the museum's assets in a mere two years, is thus celebrated as the return of a natural order no longer perverted by politics: "We might say that nature has since gathered its possessions and set course for Buenos Aires, to deposit its gifts in the new temple erected to the cult of science."[19] Described as a *museo general* dedicated specifically but not exclusively to the study of nature, the museum (now installed over four rooms at the University on Calle Perú and Potosí, today Alsina) was arranged by Trelles into three sections corresponding to nature's "kingdoms," mirrored by another three comprising numismatics, fine arts, and *"varios ramos"* (miscellanea). The zoological collection, with a total of 2,052 objects, was considered by Trelles as the most important, including, curiously enough, within the subsection "mammals" an Egyptian and two indigenous mummies, as well as numerous human anatomical and teratological samples. The museum also possessed some 700 stuffed birds, 660 molluscs, several monkeys from Africa and Brazil, fish, insects, and reptiles including three specimens of *Boa constrictor* obtained from Brazil. Several recently acquired fossil fragments of *Megatherium, Mylodon, Mastodon,* and *Glyptodon* were awaiting classification by the French paleontologist Auguste Bravard, then in the service of the museum of the Confederate provinces at Paraná. The botanical section, inexistent at the time of the Association's foundation, had since increased to 68 samples, 37 of them already classified, informed Trelles; in mineralogy, the museum had progressed from a previous 736 classified samples to 1,013, with a total of 1,795 pieces thanks to donations representing the geology of Chile, Brazil, Bolivia, Peru, Paraguay, Uruguay, and the Gran Chaco. From the time of Rivadavia, a large numismatic collection comprising 2,641 pieces had survived, purchased from French antiquarians Dufresne and Pousset. The section of fine arts, numbering only 5 objects in 1854, had since grown to 35, most of which, Trelles conceded, were of historical rather than aesthetic importance. The section of miscellanea, finally, consisted of

an Egyptian-style statue presented to the Museum in 1843 by Thomas Gowland, today a member of the Association; mosaic samples from various temples of Herculanaeum and Pompeii, donated by honorary member Dr. D. José María Uriarte; the collection of urns and other objects of the ancient Peruvians, by D. Antonio M. Alvarez; the relief maps, by Mr. von Guelich; the arms and tools of the savages of America, by various members and other gentlemen; and many other objects I will omit so as not to exhaust the attention of the honorable members of the Association.[20]

The list, then, breaks off on the margins of classification. Neither anthropology ("the savages") nor archaeology ("the ancients"), the two disciplines that would occupy center stage towards the end of the century as articulations of nature and history, sufficiently commanded the attention of the "friends of natural history" to merit any mention beyond the status of the curiosity (the unclassifiable, archaic, exotic, monstrous). Yet the division between the "ancient" natives' objects (placed alongside the antiquities of European civilization) and those of the "savages" of the present, a key distinction in the collecting and exhibiting of indigenous life and material culture at the end of the century, is already prefigured here as a temporal divide expressed as space. The relief map is literally the barrier that cuts off the ancients' "prehistory" from the pure present of the "savages."

But then, "man" had to remain on the margins of the collection as long as collecting itself did not involve a totalizing notion of patrimony or heritage based on the nation-state as a spatiotemporal continuum. By midcentury, neither of the two museums, in spite of their relation with questions of sovereignty, was primed on a national territory conceived as a closed spatial envelope framing a particular local order of life. "National being" was not yet a figure of thought, an "invisible," that could organize the display of a collection of objects. But neither was there a notion of continuity in time, of an unbroken genealogical chain linking the forms of nature to the present social order. The museums at Rio de Janeiro and Buenos Aires were national not because they showcased the nation-state but rather because they represented its capacity to represent. They formulated a claim to sovereignty by forging images of order. The collections of coins and medals were as much an expression of this order as those of minerals or birds: an arrangement of dispersed material in a well-constructed language, an order that was both finite and open. In fact, the things that integrated the arrangement mattered less than the tabular space in which they found their place and which, once laid out, allowed in principle for *all* things to be included. If the museum was an expression of sovereignty, of the power to impose the law, it was as a demonstration of the capacity of naming. The sovereignty of the state expressed itself in the collection as the synthesis and articulation of individual donors' paternal claims to particular objects; illustrious citizens' names remained attached to the collection's components in the way sixteenth-century altar paintings used to include images of their patrons. If the museum display served as a synecdoche of the nation-state, it was as an image of social as well as a natural order.

A new relation between collecting, exhibiting, and the nation form would start to emerge after the appointments of the German zoologist Hermann Burmeister in 1862 as director of the Museo Público of Buenos Aires, and of Ladislau Netto, a French-trained botanist, as director of the Museu Nacional of Rio de Janeiro in 1868. Netto had returned to Rio de Janeiro in 1866, following two years of botanical studies at the Jardin des Plantes and the Sorbonne, to occupy the post of subdirector of the museum's botanical section. Between 1868 and 1870 he served as interim director of the museum and in 1876 was appointed to the post of general director, which he held until 1893, a year before his death. Burmeister, who at the time had already published an influential account of scientific travel in Brazil, was appointed to the post of director of the Public Museum of Buenos Aires in 1862, on invitation of Juan María Gutiérrez, at the time rector of the University of Buenos Aires, and recommended by Juan B. Alberdi. The previous candidate, the French paleontologist Auguste Bravard (then in the service of the museum of the Argentine Confederation at Paraná) had died in the Mendoza earthquake of 1861. Burmeister held the directorship of the museum until his death in 1892, also coordinating, between 1870 and 1875, the establishment of a Faculty of Exact Sciences and the creation of a National Academy of Sciences at the University of Córdoba, staffed, on his indication, by fellow naturalists from Germany.

Museum chroniclers in both cities concur in describing Netto's and Burmeister's arrival as the moment of true foundation, as a new beginning that relegated all previous developments to the stage of prehistory. Burmeister, his successor Carlos Berg claimed, "created a scientific institution out of a curiosity cabinet,"[21] while Netto, in the words of Moreira de Azevedo, "gave life and animation to this house of science."[22] He initiated "the most fecund, active, and intense period in the history of the Natural Museum," as his colleague, rival, and eventual successor João Baptista de Lacerda conceded: "The collections were revised, replacing old decayed specimens by recently prepared ones; showcases were extended; dispersed bones were joined to compose skeletons, preserving the skins; the collections were given an aesthetic appearance; new labels were attached and the old generic names replaced by modern ones."[23]

Quite literally, the museums were now brought to life as the new governing principle of the collections' reorganization: a general reclassification that corresponded to a new arrangement of objects in space, and indeed of the spaces containing them, so as to allow for discontinuity to become visible in the distance between one exhibit and the next. What took place, then, was a reordering of nature, which dismissed the previous arrangement as pure chaos. In Burmeister's words,

[s]ince assuming my post, I have almost completely reorganized the establishment, removing from the showrooms many objects too insignificant to figure in a public and scientific museum of any kind, and arranging others in a more natural order, in keeping

with their specific qualities. You no longer see minerals mingling with shells on one and the same shelf, trophies with mammals, nor birds in total confusion, which the first curator had arranged, apparently, by order of the size and color of the individual specimens. Today the objects of each branch are united on their own shelves, and the birds and mammals classified scientifically.[24]

This rearrangement of objects "in a more natural order" implied, at the same time, a new demarcation of the collection's limits. Burmeister insisted, throughout his tenure, on loaning or donating artistic and historical pieces to other institutions so as to make room for the display of a natural history cleansed of all traces of human intervention. Nature itself needed, in turn, to be restricted to an ideal domain of representativity: "Removed from our Museum, to be deposited in the new collection created at the Faculty of Medicine, were the phenomena and products of illness, which *de jure* belong to that establishment rather than to a public Museum dedicated [...] to the cult of the Muses, embellishing human life without hurting the gaze by exposing it to public displays of deformities and illnesses of the animal body."[25] Removed, then, were the aberrant and singular, the "monster" that, under the previous rationale, had defined the natural system from outside as a manifestation of pure difference that made specification possible inside the limits of the natural order. Now, on the contrary, the excess and disorder of monstrosity is deemed too dangerous for a public gaze in need of instruction. And it was through this shift from the singular to the exemplary, from variety to normativity, that museum space entered into a metonymic relation with a territory defined, from that point on, as an internally coherent space for a particular order of life: "once all the birds and mammals are prepared, I will dedicate myself to the arrangement of the national species [*especies del país*], in particular [those] of the River Plate and of the other rivers and lagoons of the interior."[26] This change of focus, in which the museum becomes the Ark of Life in its national variety, runs parallel to an infusion of temporality. Paleontology now moves to the fore of the museum's areas of collecting:

This is the richest part of the Museum of Buenos Aires, the territory of this Province being the most abundant deposit of this kind of object in the entire world. Therefore Buenos Aires is the best placed to form the most precious collection known in this part of the world. The most curious and complete skeletons of antediluvian animals on display at the museums of London, Paris, Madrid, Turin, etc., are all from the Province of Buenos Aires. However, today, thanks to the wisdom of the provincial government, disposed to prohibit the export of fossil bones, the Museum of Buenos Aires will see its collections grow day by day. It is a patriotic duty for the children of this country to preserve these treasures on their own soil, and to deposit them in the Museum of their Fatherland.[27]

Undoubtedly Burmeister's invocation of "patriotic duty" strategically posited his own scientific interests as a matter of national emancipation. On his arrival at Buenos Aires, finding the Association of Friends of Natural History practically defunct, he immediately proceeded to create a Paleontological Society of Buenos Aires aimed principally at funding excavations and publishing paleontological research in the *Anales del Museo Público*, an almost entirely single-authored journal to be distributed among peer institutions in Europe and the Americas. Yet whether or not Burmeister's equation of paleontological progress with national emancipation was purely opportunistic is beside the point: its discursive effect, of major importance for the scientific imagination of the late nineteenth century, was the notion of a national territory containing, as in a reliquary, the past of nature, the space from which life on earth had originated, and which was therefore called upon to solve its enigmas. Burmeister never renounced his catastrophist theory of volcanic revolutions transforming life's spatial environment, and his interest in collecting the fossil past never included the search for the "origins of man" that would obsess the following generation of naturalists. His museum was not yet the unbroken continuity of a "narrative of objects" stretching from the remotest forms of life to the masterpieces of contemporary art, and his interest in anthropology and archaeology as linking the histories of nature and of man was, consequently, almost absent. Yet the mounted fossil skeletons, reconstructed through an analysis of the anatomical functions of dispersed fragments, made visible a history of life that had moved from the surface into the entrails of beings and from the domain of a universal taxonomic order into that of a discontinuous, organic structure.

A new relation, then, appeared between the visible and the invisible that imposed new challenges and difficulties on museum display. Although by 1889 the museum had extended its space over eleven rooms in the university building (including offices and library), Burmeister continued to complain about the lack of exhibition space to cope with the size and number of fossil exhibits, especially after the conquest of Patagonia and the southern Pampas had opened up new fossil deposits.[28] A collection of thirty-two huge boxes remitted from Chubut by traveling naturalist Enrique de Carles had not even been unpacked, Burmeister informed the Minister of Public Education in 1888, "as the Museum lacks sufficient space to either study or display these objects to the gaze of the public."[29] In the following year, he reported that "scarce progress has been made by the National Museum due to its ongoing state of lethargy, motivated by the lack of space in the showrooms the establishment currently possesses."[30] Visiting the establishment in 1889, the taxidermist and international trader in natural history samples Henry A. Ward confirmed Burmeister's impression, after praising the elderly director for his descriptions and drawings, which "have made us as familiar with these monsters from other areas as if they were modern animals." However, he concluded, "it is sad that a museum of such importance, for its intrinsic value as well as for its tradition, should have to display its treasures in small and poorly lit rooms with low ceilings, accessible only through a large and tiresome wooden staircase and a narrow corridor; the locality destroys all the effect this invaluable collection would produce if conveniently displayed in an adequate building."[31]

If a building could now destroy a collection, the collection itself was no longer conceived merely as made up of material things. Rather, it had now become a *relation* of detached viewing that made the beholder see the inner workings of an object and the place it occupied in the series of "life." The object's place was no longer determined by its surface affinities with other objects but by the functional equivalences between anatomical details highlighted by the mise-en-scène of the fossil fragment in mounted skeletons. Objects were now "to be looked not at, but *into*," as Dorinda Outram puts it.[32] If Burmeister's museum, according to Ward's account, failed to visualize the invisible history of extinct forms, it was because it lacked the means to put its exhibits at a distance, to install between the object and its beholder an emptiness saturated with meaning.

The new history of life forged by the natural science museum of the late nineteenth century was a complex spatiotemporal arrangement that sent its visitor on an "organized walkway" towards her own future as she immersed herself in an immemorial past.[33] Life, as it addressed the museum visitor, was first and foremost an *event* in the present, a performative encounter with the remote past forged in a new articulation between architectural space and the space of the collection. While the glass and steel carcasses of the new metropolitan museums of Europe and the United States made possible the opening up of a space between viewers and objects for the tangible manifestation of evolutionary time, Latin America's national museums founded in the aftermath of independence remained literally caught in colonial inner-city buildings. Thus, once again they were being accused of an excessive proximity to their object (though now in a historical rather than territorial sense: a lack of modernity, and an excess of coloniality).

At Rio de Janeiro, Ladislau Netto had already identified the problem in 1870. His solution proposed to turn scarcity into virtue by opening museum space towards the surrounding space of "nature," thus turning the porous border between the collection and tropical nature into a center of experimentation:

> Those who have had the opportunity to visit some of the natural history museums of the Old World cannot but consider inappropriate and insufficient the quarters occupied by our own Museum. [...] It is inappropriate for its location in the heart of the city, where it is impossible to obtain gardens in the vicinity. Therefore, this institution despite its ample scope and utility has had to renounce its most elevated and beneficent tasks, namely the physiological and anatomical study of the two organic kingdoms of Creation. How shall we establish, in the actual circumstances, at the immediate service of the museum, an experimental botanical-zoological school, in which biological phenomena [...] can be studied on a daily basis in all their phases and varieties?[34]

It was in this direction signaled by Netto that Brazilian museums of the turn of the century ventured, with varying degrees of success: a notion of "experimentation" that differed fundamentally from Burmeister's model of a closed space of specialist research. Despite Burmeister's demands for extended display space, the Buenos Aires museum remained a material reservoir sustaining the production of texts, such as the encyclopedias of native flora and fauna he submitted for display at international exhibitions.[35] As the foundation of new scientific museums at nearby La Plata or at São Paulo and Belém in the 1880s and 1890s showed, to update the spaces of science in turn-of-the-century Argentina and Brazil was not altogether impossible. If the Museo Público remained caught in a mode of display that was now deemed lethargic and lifeless, it was because it had chiefly remained an instrument of inscription, a generator of illustrations that sustained a (written) discourse of knowledge. Visuality, for Burmeister, remained in a subservient relation with language—a conception that would be radically inverted at the institution's new provincial rival, the Museum of La Plata.

### Life's Disputes

The paleontological, botanical, and zoological findings made in Argentina and Brazil over the last third of the nineteenth century speak to a growing capacity of the state to appropriate and subordinate local situations. To "discover" past and present species and artifacts always involved the capture and translation of local beliefs and memories: in order to make a museum object from a bone fragment one relied on the expertise of native guides, local politicians and landowners, amateur collectors, and so forth. The centralization of local "evidence" by national museums, in short, was a manifestation of a form of power based on the capacity, validated by the universal idiom of science, to "objectively" represent the local. To turn the local into an object of seeing in turn posited a nonlocational point of view occupied by a transcendental subject of observation. Yet this empowerment of a single sovereign gaze was in fact as much a conflictive and contested process as the properly political one of state consolidation. Towards the end of the century a series of new museums emerged as an expression of local elites' attempts to partake in, as well as to challenge, the "objective" representations of life's space and time forged in the national capitals. Although based on different rhetorics and forms of display, the new museums at La Plata, São Paulo, and Belém all participated in a politics of being that articulated the past of nature with the future of society.

At Rio de Janeiro, the National Museum had considerably extended its activities under Ladislau Netto's directorship. In 1875, a cycle of public lectures in botany, agriculture, geology, anthropology, mineralogy, and zoology was started, followed the next year by the publication of a trimestral journal, *Archivos do Museu Nacional*, containing original research undertaken by museum staff. A physiological laboratory—the first of its kind in Latin America, dedicated particularly to the study of tropical venoms and illnesses and the physiological characteristics of native plants—was annexed to the museum in 1880, a mere fifteen years after the foundation of Pasteur's and Bernard's laboratories in Paris. Following the museum's removal in 1892 to the Quinta de Boa Vista, the former Imperial palace at São Cristóvão (fig. 6), the institution also finally acquired its own

FIGURE 6. Anonymous (possibly Marc Ferrez), Museu Nacional, Sala Blainville. Illustration from João Baptista de Lacerda, *Fastos do Museu Nacional* (1906). Museu Nacional / UFRJ, Rio de Janeiro.

park and garden. Upon assuming the post of general director, Netto had reorganized the collection into three sections: anthropology, zoology, comparative anatomy, and animal paleontology; botany and plant paleontology; and physics, mineralogy, geology, and general paleontology. The collection of native ethnography and archaeology (superior to any other of its kind in the world, Netto claimed) needed to be relocated into a museum of its own, he suggested, but for the meantime it remained attached to the National Museum.[36] Upon the failure of his initiative, Netto reincorporated the collections of indigenous artifacts in 1888 to form a fourth section, together with the "anthropological" samples of human remains: a new science of man that had gained autonomy both from its zoological and historical neighbors to occupy an intermediate position between the history of nature and that of the nation.

Unlike at Buenos Aires, the reform of Rio's National Museum did not result in paleontology's promotion to become the master science of a national history of nature. The fossil record was an area where Brazilians, as Netto's successor Lacerda recognized in 1906, could not compete with their Argentine peers because "in Brazil, the conditions under which the ossuaries of extinct species were formed, are very different from those that have occurred in Argentina."[37] The focus came to be instead on the origins and future of "Brazilian man," a debate that must be read against the background of wider disputes over issues of race, miscegenation, and nationality surrounding the abolition of slavery in 1888.

In fact, the new anthropological section's intermediate position between the history of nature and history proper allowed for the recasting of the entire collection's meaning as a lesson in national development. The museum, rather than merely a means for displaying to visitors' eyes an extant "natural order," would now become a prescriptive indicator of future measures of biopolitical intervention. The display of human remains and of artifacts of indigenous culture alongside collections of rocks, plants, and animals imposed on the former a logic of classification that promised a positive knowledge of "racial development." It thus opened the possibility, as Louis Couty, head of the museum's Physiological Laboratory put it, of a "Brazilian science [*Ciência do Brasil*]" destined to solve the problems of life, "in particular, the life of the complex organisms that constitute a people," a science of miscegenation, then, which would nonetheless avoid the gloomy conclusions reached by contemporary European racial thought (Buckle, Gobineau, Haeckel, etc.).[38] The display only implicitly referred to Brazil's black population by exhibiting, alongside objects belonging to the "cannibals" and "barbarians" of New Zealand and the Aleutian Islands, "several vestiges of the uncultivated peoples of Africa [...], proof of the barbarism in which many of [them] still find themselves today," thus symbolically placing Africans at the dawn of humanity.[39] Yet at the same time, in the physiological laboratory museum scientists carried out experimental research on their potential genetic contribution to a future "Brazilian type." The museum, then, was at once a means of salvage and a catalyst of transformation of racial others. In Lacerda's words:

Civilization is entering the *sertões* of Brazil: in less than a century the indigenous tribes will have disappeared, and it will be difficult to find in their descendants a trace of the primitive race. Cross-breeding between Indian and white is rare among us compared to that of white and black. [...] As a worker, the Indian is unquestionably inferior to the black; he is more agile than the latter but his physical resistance and muscular strength are sensibly less. We have measured with a dynamometer the muscular strength of adult individuals belonging to the Bororó, Botocudo, and Xerente tribes, and the instrument showed a force below that observed in white and black individuals.[40]

Whereas the attempts to reform the National Museum paralleled those of reforming the Imperial state, the new regional museums of Belém and São Paulo were founded immediately after the overthrow of the monarchy in 1889 and the turbulent years of Deodoro da Fonseca and Floriano Peixoto's military governments. Controversy over the meaning and content of modernity in Brazil enveloped the new institutions both from the outside—their very foundation implying a claim to self-representation on behalf of regional elites—and from the inside of the natural sciences, as a debate on museums' objects and modes of classification and display.[41] In 1894, the foreign zoologists Emil August Goeldi, at the Museu Paraense, and Hermann von Ihering, at the Museu Paulista, both of whom had recently renounced their positions as correspondent researchers at the National Museum, assumed the directorship of heterodox collections assembled by local amateurs. The museum at Belém, founded under the auspices of the local Sociedade Filomática, had been in existence since 1867, run largely by the writer and aficionado archaeologist Domingos Ferreira Penna. The Museu Paulista's collections originated in the donation, in 1890, of the private museum of Colonel Joaquim Sertório, a wealthy collector of *naturalia* and *exotica*, to the state of São Paulo. A year after Ihering's appointment, the collection was transferred to the still vacant Ipiranga monument, a neoclassical palace designed by Italian architect Tommaso Gaudenzio Bezzi at the site of Emperor Pedro I's proclamation of independence in 1822 (fig. 7). Ironically or not, the monument commemorating the role of the thriving immigrant state of São Paulo in the foundation of the nation-state was to contain not history but nature. Or rather, the foundation of the state—captured in Pedro Américo's monumental painting *The Cry of Ypiranga*, displayed on the premises—was articulated not with a material narrative of the formation of the Brazilian people but one of the evolution of

FIGURE 7. W. A. Meyn, *Museu Paulista*. Lithograph, cover page of *Revista do Museu Paulista* 1 (1895). Museu Paulista, São Paulo.

natural species. The space of the social was indicated by an absence, a void that only a properly instructed future citizenry would eventually come to fill.

Similarly, Goeldi, in his first annual report to the governor of Pará state, insisted on the need to withdraw those objects now considered "incompatible with the character and spirit of the Museum": coins and medals, weaponry, newspapers and other historical documents, portraits of the imperial family, and so on. At the same time, he transferred the institution into new quarters on the city's outskirts to make room for a botanical and zoological garden. In 1900, the latter had grown to house more than five hundred animals, and Goeldi had to reassure local authorities that his collecting mania would not continue indefinitely but only until a representative overview of the local fauna and flora had been assembled.

Both Goeldi and Ihering took pains to advertise their arrival as a general watershed between the "savage collecting" of the local amateurs they succeeded and a new era of "serious" science that was dawning, not just at Belém and São Paulo, but in Brazil at large, "a kind of borderline separating the past from the future of the Museum," as Goeldi put it, "a visible borderline drawn once and for all."[42] Ihering, in the same year, further raised the stakes by proclaiming in the first issue of the Museu Paulista's journal that, in all of Brazil, only the two new museums satisfied the requirements "of museums organized on scientific foundations and with competent staff," alongside those of Buenos Aires, La Plata, and Santiago de Chile.[43] Unlike the National Museum, Ihering claimed, his and Goeldi's institutions were not involved in the vain emulation of an encyclopedic and metropolitan model which disciplinary specialization had long left behind. Rather, "the purpose of these collections is to give a good, instructive idea of the rich and interesting nature of South America, particularly Brazil, and of South American man and his history. Therefore, we have a good representation of Brazil from the different groups of the animal kingdom, accepting only a few characteristic samples from other regions of the globe."[44] Eventually, Ihering would further radicalize this idea of augmenting the scientific value of the museum by reducing its scope. He even went so far as to propose turning the Museu Paulista into an institution exclusively dedicated to the study of molluscs. Goeldi, meanwhile, toyed with the idea of breaking up his museum's spatial integrity by distributing small research pavilions in the museum's gardens: "If each of the sections of which the Museum is currently comprised obtained its own pavilion, such that a 'Botanical Institute' would appear here, there a 'Mineralogical-Geological Institute,' and still further on an 'Ethnographic Institute,' I would gladly sacrifice the idea of a single monumental building."[45] In both cases, we perceive the same crisis of museum space as an arena of totalizing visuality—a crisis that nonetheless opened an opportunity for local and particular insights into the multilayered evolution of nature, while questioning the possibility of a unifying vision such as that offered by the museum of the federal capital.

Both Goeldi and Ihering adopted the new "principle of sparseness" first formulated in 1878 by Agassiz at Harvard's Museum of Comparative Zoology and in 1884 by William Henry Flower at London's new Museum of Natural History at South Kensington. According to this new museology, the public exhibition had to be kept separate from collections destined exclusively for research purposes. This system "currently adopted by the majority of modern museums," Ihering explained, "consists in selecting only the most important and well-prepared pieces, such that, in the modern system, less is exhibited, and only the best examples. It is obvious that in this system the collections become more valuable, useful, and satisfactory as a means of instruction."[46] As Tony Bennett has pointed out, this new principle of sparseness signified a definite break with the principle of curiosity proper to eighteenth-century displays of natural history, which until the 1870s had still allowed the measuring of a collection's value on the base of its singularity.[47] Under the new rationale, by contrast, objects in the public collection would be selected for their commonality, their lack of individual features, which meant, at the same time, that the label would take precedence over the object. If meaning now came to rest exclusively on the exemplarity of exhibits, it was because the objects merely pointed to the scientific narrative that framed them. The object became a signifier, the label a referent.

The new distinction between the museum's tasks of scientific research and

FIGURE 8. Anonymous, Museo de La Plata, botanical garden with birdcages and front façade of the museum. Silver gelatin print from original glass negative (ca. 1910). Archivo General de la Nación, Buenos Aires.

public instruction as a spatial separation between different ways of seeing also invented a new interiority of science: a few spectacularly arranged items in the space accessible to the general public; plenty of material kept in drawers, boxes, and shelves for the attention of specialists. The empty spaces separating the public collection's exemplary displays referred to something that was visible elsewhere, albeit exclusively to an expert gaze capable of deciphering it. It is no mere coincidence, I think, that this new economy of the visible in the space of "knowledge" coincided with the consolidation of a liberal ideology of representation in the political sphere. Liberalism, in the Argentine Order of 1880 as much as in the Brazilian Old Republic, simultaneously invoked "the people" as the collective subject of sovereignty and excluded the majority of the population from any form of political participation. This does not mean that the space of science was merely the ideological reflection of the state form, or vice versa. Rather, both participated in a mode of representation, the transparency of which contained its own opacity. Its very legibility was sustained by a hieroglyphics only accessible to those endowed with a power to speak. If, in short, Linnaean natural history's "empire of nature" had been sustained by a conception of order that the Brazilian constitutional monarchy had expressed on a different plane, the new "economy of nature" (a concept dear to Darwin) was likewise involved, in a relation of mutual validation, with bourgeois liberal conceptions of the social and its representation, staged and performed in the museums' rituals of showing and of spectatorship.

## Passages of National Being

Accompanied by the noise of construction work, roads being paved and neoclassical buildings raised from the flat soil of the pampas, the visitor approached the imposing temple of science designed by architects Friedrich Heynemann and Henrik Aberg, "standing in a park, amid splendid avenues and groves of tall eucalyptus and other trees, which, in the course of a few years, will form a veritable forest." Richard Lydekker, a British paleontologist invited to La Plata in 1893 by museum director Francisco Pascasio Moreno to help classify a series of fossils, described the building:

[H]aving passed the well-proportioned Grecian portico, the visitor [...] finds himself in a rotunda, with a gallery and roof supported by two tiers of iron columns, and lighted above by a large skylight; its walls being decorated with frescos representing the scenery, native life, and some of the wonderful extinct mammals of Argentina. From this rotunda, which occupies the center of the front of the building, there diverge, on the ground floor, two galleries on opposite sides, which, after running a straight course for some distance, curve round so as to form a pair of apses at the two extremities, which are again connected by a straight gallery running parallel to the one in front, both back and front galleries being connected by cross-galleries and chambers, so that the whole edifice forms a continuous block of building. [...] On the ground floor the central chambers are, in the main, devoted to anthropology and ethnology; while the galleries on the right of the entrance contain the geological and paleontological exhibits and those on the opposite side the animals of the present epoch.[48]

The first purpose-built natural history museum on the continent, the Museo de La Plata, constructed between 1884 and 1888, offered its visitors a synthetic and monumental experience of "organized walking through evolutionary time" and across national space (fig. 9).[49] Dedicated exclusively to the material belongings of "the great Argentine Republic," the museum "expresse[d] and illustrate[d] from the most remote times until today" the natural and human histories of the nation, as another foreign visitor put it.[50] Rather than in the state appropriation of amateur collections, as practiced by its Brazilian peers, the museum had its origin in a concerted effort of a new generation of Argentine naturalists. Foremost among these were Moreno himself, the paleontologist

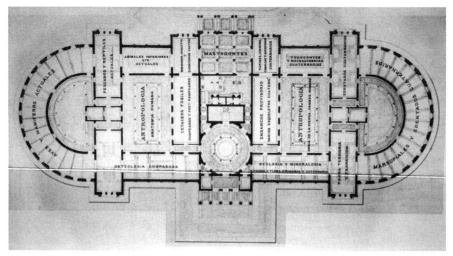

FIGURE 9. Friedrich Heynemann and Henrik Aberg, Plan of the ground floor of the La Plata Museum. Illustration from *Revista del Museo de La Plata* 1, no. 1 (1890–91). Museo de La Plata, La Plata, Argentina.

Florentino Ameghino and his brother Carlos, and Estanislao Zeballos, who in 1889 donated his collection of "some hundred indigenous skulls, ancient and modern, among them several renowned chiefs" to the La Plata museum.[51] The arrangement of rocks, fossils, animal and human skeletons, native crafts, paintings, sculptures, and photographs composed a monumental allegory of the state of 1880 that had become consolidated after the conquest of the former frontiers of Tierra Adentro. Visitors were to observe the gradual coming together of this totalizing image in an itinerary that advanced, in Moreno's words, "in an unbroken continuity from the most simple and primitive organism to the book that describes it."[52] Visitors advanced through museum space in an ascending spiral imitating the movement of evolutionary time. The narrative laid out by the museum, in fact, juxtaposed the theory of the evolution of species with the history of state formation and the biographies of the museum's own founders. It offered a new, ambitious, and unprecedented articulation of life, national being, and state power that addressed its visitors in the moral language of an initiation rite. Sarmiento, in his speech of 1885 on the occasion of the opening of the first galleries to the public, fully understood this ritual dimension of the display of prehistoric life:

I imagine one of these rural folk of old, born and raised not far from here where, not so long ago, his herds had been grazing, taken from his *estancia* like an Asian patriarch, invited by his sons [...] to attend [this] celebration. What a surprise if they showed him, with an air of satisfaction, [...] a city entirely of their own creation, whilst he was busy raising his cattle, and crowned by a treasure of riches like the Museum we inaugurate today. Nonetheless, this same surprise is on the face of everyone present, given our Spanish American, colonial, Argentine mode of being, since everything we see here is foreign to our habits and customs [...] so vast that it has visibly been constructed not for the present, but for a coming generation.[53]

The museum, he concluded, in salvaging the vestiges of the archaic past of the Pampas, was at the same time a monumental commemoration of those who had only recently "raised her from her pristine state of barbarism." Safeguarding the relics of the past was a way of opening towards the future a space that had until recently dwelled outside time, in the monotonous present of "prehistory."

Let us follow Lydekker somewhat further on his "first walk through the seemingly endless galleries," during which, he confessed, "I was absolutely lost in astonishment and admiration."[54] The Corinthian columns of the portico, crowned by a bas-relief allegory of science in the form of an angel of knowledge, the work of Venetian sculptor Víctor del Pol, were joined on either side by rows of busts invoking an intellectual ancestry from Aristotle and Lucretius to Lamarck, Cuvier, Darwin, and Burmeister. On entering the building, the circular vestibule decorated with alfresco paintings of scenes from "the prehistoric life in the pampas" offered a synthetic visual prologue to the principal themes of the exhibition (fig. 10). On the first floor, the series continued with landscape vignettes of the cardinal points of the Republic, in a kind of incipient Argentine muralism that reiterated the centrality of Buenos Aires as the vantage point, the non-landscape from whose point of view nature became a visual object. Of the commissioned artists, several were fast acquiring a reputation as members of the so-called Generation of 1880, gaining recognition through the exhibitions of the Sociedad Auxiliadora de Bellas Artes, which eventually led to the foundation of a National Museum of Fine Arts in 1896. The visual idiom of their frescos looks forward, in its sombre, crepuscular tones, to the Pampean eulogies painted by Angel Della Valle or Eduardo Sívori in the following decade. If pictures such as *El rancho índio* (*The Indian Hut*) by Reynaldo Giúdice, *La caza del guanaco* (*The Guanaco Hunt*) by Emilio Speroni, and *La vuelta del malón* (*Return of the Raiding Party*) by José Bouchet—anticipating Della Valle's homologous work from 1896—depicted scenes of contemporary native culture, their display alongside Emilio Coutaret's *Smylodon* and E. Matzel's *Mastodon and Glyptodons* posited them within a prehistoric temporality, as survivors of an extinct age. The point was brought home by Giúdice's *Una caza prehistórica* (*A Prehistoric Hunt*) and Luis

FIGURE 10. Anonymous, Museo de La Plata, entrance hall. Illustration (Lámina 3) from *Revista del Museo de La Plata* 1, no. 1 (1890–91). Museo de La Plata, La Plata, Argentina.

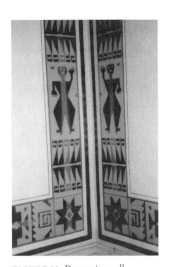

FIGURE 11. Decorative wall ornaments on the ground floor of the La Plata Museum. Photograph by the author.

de Servi's *Descuartizando un gliptodonte* (*Dismembering a Glyptodon*), visual anticipations of the museum's central hypothesis on the aboriginal origins of American man in the era of the great fossil mammals.

The walls and ceilings, meanwhile, were painted in decorative patterns that continued those of the front façade's lower frontispiece, running over into the rooms in the form of decorative bands that imitated glyphs and other Aztecan, Mayan, and Incaic visual motifs found at the temples of Palenque and Tihuanaco (fig. 11). The museum's decoration, then, suggested yet another layer of "evolutionary continuity," this time from the "origins of American man" in the Argentine South to the Amerindian civilizations of Peru and Mexico.[55] "I have tried," Moreno explained in his guide to the exhibition, "to give the decoration an ancient American character, which would nonetheless match [the building's] Greek lines."[56] Together, then, the languages of decoration, architecture, and the visual arts manufactured a spatial envelope that inscribed the material objects in a cycle whose beginning and end was national being. Civilization, the exhibition suggested, had finally reconquered its own cradle.

"The building," Moreno had explained in 1886 in a letter to the Minister of Public Works,

is of a new kind; in order to quickly understand the majestic harmony of life, it allows a grasp, in an uninterrupted continuity of perception, of everything from the first beings emerging from imponderable seeds to the human organism; the visitor will see there his entire genealogical tree. The ring of a physical perspective represented by the longitudinal galleries [...] is completed by the transversal galleries, destined to preserve the vestiges of South American moral evolution across the ages.[57]

The evolutionary sequence of the outer "biological ring," then, provided visitors with the key to read the "moral history of man," the chapters of which, from the skulls and skeletons of indigenous "ancestors" through native material culture to the collection of fine arts and the library, situated on the first floor, formed the inner patios. Nature's and man's evolution interrelated in museum space in a series of entries and exits, the one serving as a material and visual commentary on the other. The galleries of palaeontology and comparative anatomy featured huge numbers of mounted skeletons, especially large fossil and contemporary mammals such as glyptodons and whales, in a conscious attempt to impress visitors by the sheer scale and number of exhibits (figs. 12–13). This strategy of the spectacle was harshly criticized by overseas museologists such as Lydekker, for whom the museum's accumulation of vernacular species prevented it from acquiring an adequate variety of exhibits through exchanges with peer institutions abroad. Ameghino, the museum's principal collector of paleontological material, had resigned from his post as vice-director in 1887, disgusted by the "vulgar impostor" Moreno's policy of "mounting in costly assemblages enormous pieces that are not even worth throwing into the rubbish," a mercenary exploitation of science, he claimed, for sheer visual effect.[58] But if Moreno had readily sacrificed the principle of sparseness of late nineteenth-century museology for an aesthetic of the gigantic, seeking to overwhelm visitors without the mediation of labels and other pedagogical devices, this was because a museum, for him, was an instrument of wonder rather than of resonance, to quote Stephen Greenblatt's distinction between forms of display based on singularity or on contextualization.[59] The silent, frozen dance of skeletons aligned in the direction of

FIGURE 12. Anonymous, Museo de La Plata, glyptodons, room 3. Albumin print (1891). Archivo General de la Nación, Buenos Aires.

FIGURE 13. Anonymous, Museo de La Plata, section of comparative anatomy, room 15. Illustration (Lámina 6) from *Revista del Museo de La Plata* 1, no. 1 (1890–91). Museo de La Plata, La Plata, Argentina.

the visitor's itinerary—the spectral revival of dead bodies moving into a future that only held for them a fate of extinction—commanded a gaze of reverence and awe that would eventually turn into curiosity and, finally, knowledge.

The spatial arrangement of the museum—the unbroken evolutionary chain from the beginnings of life to the triumph of science—thus also provided a model of moral instruction: an evolution of consciousness that would gradually take shape in the process of walking through the exhibition and letting the initial bewilderment settle into a new form of certainty. Moreno always opposed the academicism of the Buenos Aires museum, and he resigned from his post as director when, in 1906, his own institution was incorporated into the new University of La Plata. For him, the museum form was a means to communicate with the illiterate, popular mind, producing consciousness in a passage through illusion. "The impression the common, little-instructed visitor begets from these objects," he explained in the first volume of the museum's journal,

at least from those his understanding can process, is subsequently transmitted to his friends, encouraging them to see for themselves; then they interpret and comment on them, and from one commentary to the next the first impressions shed the false ideas in which they had been steeped before, and a conscious interest for the museum is born. [...] I have observed that many visitors to this establishment return frequently, some of them visiting it every Sunday to spend hours in the rooms already open to the public which, even so, are not the most interesting ones. To the uneducated folk the museum has become a pleasant meeting place; respectfully they observe its contents, enthuse over a hen with chicks, a wildcat catching a partridge, etc., and forget the tavern, which might lead them into crime. [...] Thus, slowly, the spirit of the people becomes cultivated by what they learn with their eyes.[60]

The museum's role as a moral antidote to lower-class vice (in particular, the vice of socialism) was a common trope in the writings of late nineteenth-century museum educators, with whom Moreno had become acquainted during his sojourn at Paris and London in 1880–81. However, his museum of Argentine evolution extended the exercise of public self-fashioning, a key element of the European museum's role as a mass educator, into a dramatic, ritual restaging of the founding scenes of the nation-state. The museum offered a way of experiencing once again the foundational experience of nationality: the emergence, in the "wilderness" on the borders of national territory, of a new, modern form of subjectivity associated with knowledge. Thus the Conquest of the Desert as the founding myth of the late nineteenth-century Argentine state was reimagined here not as the effect of military might but of the emergence, in the face of "wild," "prehistoric" nature, of modern, progressive reason. The viewers' gradual advance from bewilderment to knowledge was therefore at the same time a formation of national consciousness, emulating at the level of the individual subject the spiritual foundation of the state form itself. The violence of conquest that had allowed the formation of the museum's collection was thus simultaneously disavowed and restaged in the encounter with a "dead" nature.

An assiduous contributor to newspapers and journals, Moreno never tired of presenting the museum's foundation and his own evolution from juvenile collector to museum scientist as a moral narrative of initiation that every single visitor to the Museo de La Plata could reenact in the dreamtime of his passage through the ages of Argentine evolution.[61] "Evolution," he wrote in his museum guide of 1890,

is found in all forms of thought, and everything is linked with one another. [...] The origin of this Museum of La Plata was, among other objects of equal importance, an earthenware imitation of a mock-Chinese idol, a few little stones of sparkling colors, some "petrified seeds," actually the internal molds of Tertiary molluscs, and a conglomerate of shells I had classified, back then, as a "petrified tiger paw." These pieces, a quarter of a century later, are interpreted in their true value and occupy their place in our galleries, stripped of their primitive meaning, which nonetheless had given them their merit. Probably, without this unconscious imitation of the Tradescants by a fourteen-year-old, the Museum of La Plata would not exist, and when I think of its origins, I smile on hearing it being treated as a simple "bazaar."[62]

From the boy's fantasies of possessing the curious and exotic to the adult's establishment of the proper scale of values, then, collecting is for Moreno a form of moral education of a progressive subject, an experience of knowledge-gathering through material accumulation that can and must be repeated by museumgoers of the popular classes in their gradual passage from wonder to understanding. The museum visit as an experience of initiation is thus the equivalent of the naturalist's journey that had provided the space-time of passage between the child's curiosity cabinet and the adult's scientific museum. This liminal realm between the age of fantasy and the time of the real, Moreno suggests, can now be ritually revisited in the well-ordered space of the exhibition, its primal wilderness having been tamed into an order of classification. The museum visit as a performative ritual of spectatorship restages the state's foundational myth of the imposition of sovereignty through knowledge. As it had supposedly come to the state, this knowledge comes to the spectators in a way that is completely devoid of violence: the objects themselves speak to them their proper names. Yet if Moreno ironically acknowledges the origin of the museum in the narcissistic fantasy objects of preadolescence, one wonders to what extent the "pieces interpreted in their true value" are not still inscribed—and in even more powerful ways—in the same logic of aggressive retention. In fact, if collecting, as I have argued in the introduction to this section, offers a fetishistic alternative to genital sexuality, it is striking that Moreno should advertise it as a model for individual and collective maturity. Perhaps the continuous references to the infant collector are, rather, a way of preserving the innocence of natural history, disavowing its complicity with conquering violence and capitalist accumulation, a move that is characteristic of the attitude Mary Louise Pratt has aptly called "anti-conquest."[63]

The beginnings of the La Plata Museum hark back to the "Museo Moreno" young Francisco had begun to assemble in 1871, when he was sent to stay with relatives in the south of Buenos Aires province during the yellow fever epidemic. Installed in a small garden pavilion on his father's estate, the museum featured samples of fossils and indigenous human skulls, a description of which Moreno, with Burmeister's encouragement, sent to Paul Broca in 1874. Broca, a leading figure in the physical anthropology of the time, published the piece in his prestigious *Révue d'Anthropologie*, highlighting the importance of Moreno's craniological findings for the periodization of human life on the American continent. Moreno's collection of Amerindian skulls attracted the attention of Europe's leading osteologists (Broca, Quatrefages, and Virchow, among others), as they seemed to disprove the position of the North American school, captained by George Samuel Morton, of multiple human types in prehistoric America, which led the Americans to cast doubt on the unity of the human species. Moreno's skulls, by contrast, showed marked similarities with the fossil findings at Neanderthal, discovered in 1857 but not definitely recognized as a distinctive human type until the late 1860s, and at Cro-Magnon (1868). Thus, they considerably strengthened the evidence in favor of a single "prehistoric man" in general and in America in particular, where human life had been assumed to be of a much more recent date.[64]

Following several journeys to Patagonia between 1873 and 1877, during which Moreno succeeded, for the first time, in reaching Lake Nahuel Huapí and the sources of the Santa Cruz River from the Atlantic, he offered his collection to the province of Buenos Aires in return for a lifelong appointment as director of the Anthropological and Archaeological Museum to be founded by the province. His proposal having been accepted, the museum opened in August 1878 in provisional quarters on the fourth floor of Buenos Aires's Teatro Colón with a public lecture by Moreno on "The Study of South American Man." Following the federalization of the capital city in 1880, controversy ensued over the separation of provincial from state institutions. A group of young naturalists, including Moreno's cousin Eduardo Holmberg, future director of Buenos Aires's zoological garden, and Florentino Ameghino, on return from Paris where he had exhibited his own collection of Pampean fossils at the Exhibition of 1878 and published his book *La antigüedad del hombre en El Plata*, pushed for the nationalization of Moreno's museum, to the detriment of the old Museo Público, which would pass to the province. Despite receiving support from congress and senate in 1881, Moreno's project was shelved by the federal government, and he eventually approached the governor of Buenos Aires province, Carlos D'Amico, who in 1884 decreed the construction of a new museum at La Plata, the recently founded provincial capital.

In addition to its enthusiastic embrace of an evolutionary model of nature and a material pedagogy directed at the popular sectors, the Museo de La Plata also diverged from Burmeister's museum in the national capital in its emphasis on human life within the wider frame of natural history, and on the recently conquered "deserts" of the south as its principal reservoir of collectibles. Sarmiento, in a piece written on the occasion of the museum's first inauguration at the Teatro Colón (at a time when he himself was busy working on *Conflict and Harmonies of the Races in America*) praised Moreno as a youthful Virgil guiding the elderly polymath through the inferno of Argentina's barbarian prehistory. Moreno, Sarmiento asserted, had crafted a new kind of poetry through the alignment of skulls on the museum's shelves: "What a history do these skulls tell us! Every group represents a human age. The form of the skull is a chapter in a narrative, counted not in centuries but in millennia! [...] And Patagonia turns out to be the Ultima Thule sung by the poets, which geographers have so long failed to locate [...], since every finding had always pointed to another one still further in the past."[65]

Moreno's frantic accumulation of human skulls and skeletons articulated the violent imposition of a state biopolitics over the formerly autonomous frontier regions with a scientific mind-set in which the outer margins of the imperial order were supposed to hold the key to unlock the mysterious origins of Man and indeed of the Earth. Darwin, during the voyage of the *Beagle*, had already called attention to Patagonia as "a privileged reservoir for the advancement of science" where "living fossils" could still be found among its native inhabitants, human and nonhuman. Accompanying the advance of "civilization," the museum was called upon to perform an act of salvage, of preservation of the body parts left behind by the massacres attributed by scientific knowledge to the fatal course of the struggle for life. "American man," Moreno explained, "is rapidly becoming extinct, and soon we will only be able with great difficulty to decipher the secrets our predecessors, on vanishing, took along with them." Hence, he concluded, "we need to study the tribes still living in a state of savagery, so that, comparing them with the vestiges [of prehistoric man], we will encounter infinite analogies that will permit us to reconstruct the history of our fossil grandfathers. [...] [A]n immense museum exists in the surface layers of the national soil: let us bring it to light."[66]

Precisely the violent elimination of coevalness, produces the evidence that allows the construction of a mythical genealogy, inscribing the "extinction" of the native inhabitants that is the Argentine state's genocidal condition of sovereignty within evolution's serialization of discontinuities: that is, at the core of national being. In the time of evolution, continuity of descent is set equivalent with the violent erasure of the previous echelon by the subsequent one: discontinuity becomes the only true continuity. Particularly eloquent in this regard is the story of Inacayal, a Tehuelche chief "rescued" by Moreno in 1884, along with several members of his clan, from the prison camp in the Tigre delta where they had been deported after General Roca's Desert Campaign. Lodged at the museum, where staff unsuccessfully encouraged them to help prepare exhibits and produce "ethnographic materials," the natives were submitted to anthropometric measurements and photographic sessions, so as to collect the anatomical evidence of their evolutionary proximity to "prehistoric man." On entering the museum, Inacayal, whose dwellings Moreno had visited only a few years earlier (describing in his travel narrative the negotiations he had maintained with him over peace treaties and food rations) had become a specimen, a living sample of the *hombre fósil* (fossil man). Upon his death in 1888, his skeleton, brain, scalp, and death mask were preserved and put on display alongside the other exhibits of "indigenous anatomy" whose assembly he had witnessed in his final years.[67] It is precisely this hijacking of the other's life into the space of the museum— the transformation of his slow suicide, this ultimate act of resistance, into a case study of extinction—that allows the completion of the evolutionary series through the verification of discontinuity. The vanishing of the last representative of an archaic phase of man's evolution in turn posited the emergent Argentine nation as its legitimate successor, to the extent that it became conscious of this "prehistoric" ancestry, thanks to science's labor of salvage and preservation. Both physically and symbolically, the gallery of anthropological anatomy constituted the core of the museum: at once mausoleum and mass grave, containing "almost a thousand skulls and eighty skeletons [...] from the witnesses of the ice age until the recently defeated Indian," this crypt of science was the site of the emergence of national being from a space of death.[68]

The arrangement of exhibits, as shown in the first issue of the museum's journal (fig. 14), is centered on the large two-story showcase of mounted skel-

FIGURE 14. Anonymous, Museo de La Plata, anthropological section. Illustration (Lámina 7) from *Revista del Museo de La Plata* 1, no. 1 (1890–91). Museo de La Plata, La Plata, Argentina.

etons, literally resuscitated from their graves to enter the purgatory of a spectral afterlife. They are surrounded, on the ground floor, by the collection of skulls on top of which, hung on the wall like hunting trophies, are exhibited the death masks of the natives who died in captivity at the museum. On the upper gallery, indigenous material culture, including a large number of funerary objects, completes the display with the "vestiges of another age." Some of these had, in fact, been produced in parallel to the museum's own construction by the native detainees: a "prehistoric" production that could be observed, as in a time machine, in the glass box of museum space. Yet the true symbolic center of the room, at once the source and site of confluence of meaning, are the busts of the pioneers of anthropology—Blumenbach, Broca, Virchow—placed on top of the showcase, literally dominating the scene. In contrast to the indigenous death masks facing them from the walls, they bear no indexical trace of a vanished body; rather, they stand for the self-transcending eternity of "spirit." Cast in stone, they incarnate history's triumph over prehistory's space of death, transformed into visual order by the supreme force of thought rather than murderous violence. In fact, though, this space of death at the core of the museum display is at once a condensation of the violence of collecting and the point from which it explodes into the entire space of the exhibition. As it disavows violence, the museum also works violence on the gaze itself, making it complicit with what it beholds and reminding us that spectatorship and objectness are questions of life and death. It not only plays on the violence of the radical otherness (and objectness) that it places before its visitors' eyes, but also on the violence of exhibiting itself: the superior violence of the museum apparatus that has contained the excess of otherness in its image of order. However, as an external frame of the performance of seeing (of seeing things as objects), this apparatus also addresses its visitors as submitted to its gaze and thus as potentially in the position of absolute exposure, of "bare life," in which they contemplate the collection of corpses. This is the silent threat implied in the museum's visual pedagogy, the fact that, as one is turned into an eye that beholds the object world from a position of scopic authority, one nonetheless never ceases to be a body that might itself become the object of an immaterial, disembodied gaze. It is this threat implied in the way the museum of nature addresses the gaze that I shall explore further in the following chapter, the way the power and authority of the museum are continuously based on the possibility that it might be a trap.

# Spectacles of Sacrifice

## INSIDE THE BRAZILIAN ANTHROPOLOGICAL EXHIBITION

> But who would have said! These cannibals were the ones to be frightened of being devoured by public curiosity!
>
> —Angelo Agostini, *Uma visita à Exposição Anthropologica*

### Grand Opening

July 29, 1882—Marching bands parade through the streets and fireworks light up the skies of Rio de Janeiro in celebration of Princess Isabel's birthday, a public holiday in the entire Empire of Brazil. The princess herself is the guest of honor tonight at the National Museum on Campo de Sant'Anna, where the cream of Carioca society celebrates the opening of another of the season's great exhibitions. The Emperor D. Pedro II himself, renowned for his zealous patronage of the arts and sciences, is in attendance with his wife, Empress Teresa Cristina; also attending are most of the city's leading literati, some of whom have donated exhibits or contributed pieces to the exhibition's lavish *Revista Illustrada*, edited by Mello Morães Filho, to be distributed among visitors in the course of the event. Still awaiting completion is a seventy-page catalogue listing the objects on display, which spread across eight large rooms on the museum's upper floor, redecorated and baptised for the occasion with the names of famous travellers and explorers from the past: from Portuguese and French chroniclers Vaz de Caminha, Rodrigues Ferreira, and Jean de Léry to the missionaries Gabriel Soares and José de Anchieta and modern-day scientists Martius, Hartt, and Lund. Correspondents of the city's principal dailies as well as the renowned (and widely feared) caricaturist Angelo Agostini and the photographer Marc Ferrez are reportedly present to record the event for the wider public. Also in attendance, finally, is a small band of Botocudo Indians from Espírito Santo and three Xerente from Minas Gerais, who have been brought to the capital to live on the exhibition's premises for the length of the show. "The arts and sciences," Ladislau Netto, the museum's director, tells this multifarious audience in his opening speech, "are to be congratulated for having conceived and realized this most national of events, in the aim of raising the Empire of Brazil to the level of universal intellectual progress. […] This grandiose crowning of our efforts, the moment we have been longing for, the public consensus and support of the learned societies, and the barely contained amazement of everyone present, are witnesses to the great jubilee of Brazilian anthropology which we are inaugurating today at the Museum."[1]

The Brazilian Anthropological Exhibition, whose inauguration ceremony I am evoking here, was primarily an attempt on behalf of the National Museum to recover some of its formerly exclusive authority to display the national patrimony in the face of an increasing number of contenders. Regular provincial and national exhibitions had been held since 1861 to select the country's displays at the world fairs, exhibitions of fine arts were organized by the Imperial Academy, and yearly horticultural exhibitions had taken place since 1879 at the replica Crystal Palace, which the Count d'Eu, Princess Isabel's husband, had himself built at the royal family's summer retreat of Petrópolis. Only the previous year, moreover, the National Library had organized the first large-scale exhibition of Brazilian history, while at the Ministry of Agriculture and Commerce next to Paço Imperial square a National Exhibition of Industries opened in preparation for the forthcoming Continental Exhibition at Buenos Aires. If the struggle against dispersion, according to Walter Benjamin, is the secret driving force of collecting, the Anthropological Exhibition of 1882 could be seen as occupying a crucial place in this "exhibitionary complex." Its principal concern was with the salvage and reassessment of the Empire's Romantic iconography, which was increasingly considered redundant. Rather than as a celebration of the richness and diversity of Brazil's indigenous population, its crafts and symbols past and present, the event was intended to be what the museum's resident physiologist and future director João Baptista de Lacerda described as "a popular celebration of science," the spectacular rehearsal of a detached, "objective" perspective on an internal other who not long ago had embodied the monarchical state in its literary and artistic manifestations. Material evidence of "real" indigenous life called for a reappraisal of the Indian's suitability as an emblem of the modern nation.

Yet at the same time, I will argue, science's re-enunciation of indigenous as bare life (to quote Giorgio Agamben's concept, which I will use here to analyze anthropology's reformulation of ethnic otherness) actually repeated in its own way the foundational gesture of the literary and artistic Indianism it was challenging. Indeed, if Brazilian Indianism could be conceived as a discursive and iconographic variation on the theme of sacrifice, thus providing an imaginary arena in which the social and political contradictions of a slaveholding liberal monarchy could be spelled out and dramatized, anthropology sought to reformulate the sacrificial bond in the terms of a sovereign ban. This dramatic shift in the construction of internal otherness roughly paralleled the political and legal transition from a colonial and mercantile to a genuinely capitalist mode of production, in which "life is more and more clearly placed at the center of State politics (which now becomes, in Foucault's terms, biopolitics)."[2]

However, the reassessment of otherness carried out at the exhibition, I shall argue, in fact inscribed the biopolitical itself within the mytho-logic of sacrifice it was ostensibly leaving behind. As John Manuel Monteiro suggests, the scientific display of the Indian that was supposed to replace previous literary and artistic myths in fact plainly reinstated traditional dichotomies between noble and ignoble savages, Tupís and Tapuias, mythical past and "degenerate" present.[3] Here I want to chart the emerging field of anthropology as a symbolic arena in which the tensions over the identity and status of self and other in late nineteenth-century Brazilian society could be played out.

### Objects of Alterity

Exhibiting alterity—the collection, classification, and display of the material culture, human remains, and living bodies of non-Occidental peoples—was a key element in the wider process of reconceptualizing human diversity in European post-Renaissance thought. Although it still retained the single-origin paradigm inherited from the Biblical tradition, the enlightened notion of "race" was at least partly derived from colonial travellers' observation of non-Europeans as innately different from themselves. The French naturalist François Bernier's *Nouvelle Division de la Terre par les différentes Espèces ou Races d'Hommes qui l'habitent* (1684), for instance, proposed a quadripartite distinction of human races that was taken up in the following century by Linnaeus, who would additionally assign them different "humours" or physiopsychological inclinations (Europeans were "sanguine," Americans "choleric," Asians "melancholic," and Africans "bilious"). Later in the century, the comparative study of crania developed by Blumenbach shifted the category of race firmly towards physical determinism, also introducing the idea of a progressive degeneration of the Caucasian type the farther mankind had spread out from its original dwellings in the temperate regions, under the malignant influence of unsuitable climates and environments. This narrative effectively rephrased, albeit in secular terms, the biblical sequence of the expulsion from Eden and the dispersion of mankind after the fall of Babel. Although polygenetic counterhypotheses to the scientific mainstream remained influential well into the nineteenth century, archaeological discoveries of "prehistoric" sites (confirming an extended periodization of humanity well beyond the limits of biblical time) and the gradual acceptance throughout the second half of the century of the Darwinian theory of evolution would eventually establish sociocultural developmentalism as the paradigm for explaining human diversity. Even though, from a biological point of view, the evolution of the species might have taken place thousands of years ago, social organization itself was now seen to obey the laws of selection and inheritance, progressing slowly and univocally from savagery through barbarism to civilization. Indeed, as George W. Stocking explains, while deciding the controversy over the origins of mankind definitely in favor of monogeneticism, the new paradigm nevertheless allowed accommodating much of the ideological baggage of polygeneticism:

[I]n the new expanse of evolutionary time, one might assume a single human origin and an evolving human nature, and at the same time regard the differences between existing human races as so deeply rooted as to be virtually polygenic in character. Thus it was that in the diffusely evolutionary milieu of later nineteenth-century European colonial expansion, the traditional developmental sequences of savagery, barbarism, and civilization (color-coded as black, brown/yellow, and white) took on a systematic biological significance. Contemporary savages were commonly assumed to be closer—in cultural behavior, in mental capacity and brain size, and in bodily characteristics and skeletal structure—to the apelike ancestors of *Homo sapiens*, and it was widely thought that, like those ancestors, they too would soon become extinct.[4]

Museums were the physical and ideological sites in the imperial metropolises where spatiotemporally distant "evidence" was arranged visually into a single synthetic image, thus allowing scientific narratives to span otherwise insurmountable distances and temporalities. The material documentation and display of non-Western peoples and their cultures became a means of sustaining the archival fiction of colonial and imperial power as based on the central administration of knowledge.

As Johannes Fabian has pointed out, "cultural preservation" in the museum invariably constructs the object in a temporality of disappearance rather than of emergence. The pastness of the object as set against the present and the presence of the observer is at the core of a set of antithetical oppositions (subject/object; civilized/uncivilized) which "had congealed into a 'science' [...] *before* field research became institutionalized as a requirement for professional certification."[5] Authenticity is thus simultaneously decomposed and recomposed in the anthropological object: since the object has already travelled into "our" space, its original purity has been irreparably damaged by foreign intervention—yet by building a spatiotemporal carcass around it, by confining it to the heterotopic space of the museum, the object is restored to an anthropological no-time in which otherness can once again be experienced as if it were still intact and complete. The detachment between viewers and objects that allows for this imaginary rescue of a doomed alterity is inversely proportional to the real extent of colonial intervention and subjugation of communities and cultures: a poetics of disavowal is at the heart of ethnographic collecting and exhibiting.

Barbara Kirshenblatt-Gimblett distinguishes between two different strategies of anthropological display that she calls the "in-situ" and "in-context" approaches. The first of these attempts to recreate cultural environments (native villages) in the space of the museum, the second to surround the object with paratextual devices that stand in for its absent context (labels, tours, guides, spatial arrangement, lighting, and so forth). Necessarily, both approaches always appear in combination and compromise formations at the level of actual displays, as do the geographic or typological principles of classification to which they can to some extent be related. Rather than opposing each other, the relation between in situ and in context displays is one of mutual confirmation. While the former promises a surrogate experience of native everyday life, it is only once the other has been put at a distance by means of classification that he can be safely approached in the voyeuristic ubiquity of panoptic vision. Exhibiting alterity, then, amounts to something very similar to an autopsy: not only does it confirm the death of "primitive society," it also shows it to have been self-inflicted, the result not of imperial violence but of "primitivity" itself.

### The Indianist Controversy

As the genealogical series implicitly inscribed in the sequence of rooms at the Anthropological Exhibition suggested, the observation of native societies, customs, and physical traits in Brazil had started immediately upon the arrival of the Portuguese, in the colonial chronicles of Vaz de Caminha, Soares, and others, continuing through the works of the European travellers and naturalists of the eighteenth and early nineteenth centuries, to gradually reach the scientific maturity to which the exhibition itself testified. The tradition of anthropology, in other words, was in a sense the very tradition of Brazilian lettered culture, which had constituted itself as a body of discourse in writing about, and thus overwriting, native Amerindian culture. Early nineteenth-century travellers such as Spix and Martius, Saint-Hilaire, Wallace, and Bates had concentrated their anthropological research on the "origin of American man," searching for evidence that would confirm one of the several evolutionist or degenerationist hypotheses on human diversity discussed at the time. As Lilia Moritz Schwarcz has argued, the rising interest in the second half of the century in race as a biological rather than historical or cultural phenomenon was closely tied to the process of abolition. At the same time, the paradigmatic shift in scientific institutions towards positivist and evolutionist ideas on race creatively adapted these to make viable the perspective of a mestizo nation (*nação mestiça*), all the while subscribing to a theoretical framework that condemned miscegenation as a form of colonial contagion (Buckle, Gobineau, Galton).[6]

The end of direct colonial rule in Brazil did not improve but rather worsened the already desperate situation of most indigenous groups. As Manuela Carneiro da Cunha explains, over the nineteenth century the "Indian question" largely ceased to be one of the coercion of labor and became one of the expansion of landed property into the interior. Following the expulsion of the Jesuits in 1759, in 1808 the Portuguese court arrived and subsequently aligned itself with local planters' and landowners' interests. Thus the diversity of players of the colonial era, which had provided Amerindians with minimal spaces of negotiation, had vanished by 1822.[7] Even though the Constitutive Assembly in 1823 recommended coordinating provincial policies with a view towards a "General Plan of Civilization," in the end no measures whatsoever were adopted, leaving colonial missionary law in place as the only legal framework that acknowledged the existence of a native population. While a discourse of "peaceful conquest" prevailed on the level of national government, the absence of clearly defined policies allowed provinces to carry out their own military advances (as did Ceará and Goiás in the 1830s, a period of feeble central authority) and establish fortified outposts, so-called *presídios*, in charge of policing indigenous groups. Forced settlement accelerated the process of transforming communal lands recognized by colonial law into exchangeable property. Unsurprisingly, passive resistance to settlement and desertion from state-imposed villages (*aldéias*) remained frequent throughout the century, providing "modernizers" with further evidence, if any was needed, of the Indians' indolence and incapacity to raise themselves to the level of civilization.

In the sequence of legal and administrative figures that accompanied the advance of "civilization," an increasingly biopolitical reason emerged. If, as Agamben argues, abandonment is the originary relation of law to life, we could say that indigenous life entered state law in the form of a founding exclusion that related it to the state in exclusively negative terms, as life that would be stripped of its former rights of exception. In this purely negative relation to the law, then, which is the equivalent to the biological trope of extinction, indigenous life became bare life, a life literally and immediately placed at the mercy of the state, which sustained a continuous power of decision over its prolongation or termination. The question of how to relate racial to legal discourse was even more explicitly discussed with respect to the Afro-Brazilian population following the abolition of slavery in 1889. A new biopolitical knowledge would now claim a direct bearing on the law, as in the Bahian psychiatrist and anthropologist Raimundo Nina Rodrigues's 1894 study *The Human Races and Penal Responsibility in Brazil*, which attempted to quantify the different levels of guilt that could be allocated for certain crimes under the premise of an inherent psycho-physiological inferiority of blacks and mulattos as compared to whites.

It is against this biopolitical production of bare life in late nineteenth-century Brazil that we must set the analysis of the Anthropological Exhibition's relations of continuity and rupture with regard to the Indianist tradition. The Imperial state had made the Indian into a centerpiece of its political iconography, cast in fantasy headgear and capes and conforming to Greco-Roman conventions of beauty and proportion. Allegorical Indian figures were used as a territorial marker, as on Louis Rochet's equestrian statue of D. Pedro I (1862), where Indians representing the nation's four great rivers occupy the four sides of the pedestal (see fig. 2). Indeed, the same iconography still decorated the entrance to the Empire's pavilion in Carlos André Gomes's design for the Universal Exhibition of Paris in 1889.

Yet while much of Indianist literature undoubtedly constituted a fiction of the state, the tragedies of Indians and mestizos could, in the hands of authors such as Gonçalves Dias or Teixeira e Sousa, themselves of mixed-race descent, also decry racial exclusion and violence in the present. As David Brookshaw argues, on its more critical edge Indianism can be read as a denunciation of capitalist modernization from the point of view of a betrayed rural Eden: "It is a literature of betrayal: the betrayal of a native American paradise, and the betrayal of the paradise which was supposed to replace it—that of an agrarian utopia—by other envisioned paradises, all of them built on the more efficient exploitation of nature and men."[8]

Both the official and critical strands of Indianist fiction, however, referred to one and the same trope to manufacture the discontinuity proper to all mythical tales of origin ("how has *then* become *now?*"): the figure of sacrifice. It was as a sacrificial victim that the indigenous other could be projected as engendering Brazilian nationality. In one of its most famous versions, José de Alencar's

*Iracema* (1865), sacrifice appears as the price to be paid for the original sin of miscegenation. Despite opening a new space and time for the nation, miscegenation destroys ancestral bonds and drives the lovers into exile. The feminized American continent, in its lascivious and potentially (self-)destructive sexuality—a trope that naturalist novels such as Aluísio Azevedo's *O cortiço* (The Slum, 1890) would extend to the black urban proletariat—has to be symbolically exorcized through the sacrificial self-purging of the seducer herself. Her erotic body functions as a liminal space of the state: a necessary locus of initiation that needs to be immediately foreclosed and overwritten by the law of the widower-father, who imposes, over her dead body, a family morale. Notably, Indianism's decline in literature coincided with its zenith in the visual and performing arts. *O Guarani*, in Carlos Gomes's state-sponsored opera adaptation, premiered at the Scala di Milano in March 1870 to widespread acclaim and travelled on to Rio in December of the same year. A painterly adaptation of *Iracema* by José Maria de Medeiros (fig. 15) was unveiled in 1881, depicting the nude female figure exiting the dark forest and curiously observing Martim Soares Moreno's sword planted on the beach, in an allegorical synthesis of territorial and sexual conquest.

It was literary and artistic Indianism, in fact, that had sparked scientific interest in the native population. Romantic poet Gonçalves Dias had provided the National Museum with some of its earliest ethnographic collections when travelling, in 1859, through the interior of Pará as a member of the first all-Brazilian

FIGURE 15. José María de Medeiros, *Iracema*. Oil on canvas (1881). Museu Nacional de Belas Artes, Rio de Janeiro.

scientific expedition. The year after, Gonçalves de Magalhães published in the *Revista do Instituto Histórico e Geográfico Brasileiro* an essay on "The Indians of Brazil from the View of History," in reply to Francisco Adolfo Varnhagen's dismissal of the noble savages invented by a literature that the latter, in his *História Geral do Brasil* (1855–57), had sarcastically referred to as "*caboclismo*." Both Domingos Soares Fereira Penna, the first director of Pará's provincial museum, and João Barbosa Rodrigues, director of Rio's Botanical Garden and of the short-lived Museu do Amazonas, undertook archaeological excavations and compiled legends and songs of the Tapuio communities of the Amazon.

The emergent anthropology, offering a detached knowledge of rather than imaginative empathy with and desire for the Indian, challenged Indianism's sacrificial myth of foundation. However, the generation of writers and scholars emerging around 1870 at institutions such as Recife's Faculty of Law and Rio's Military Academy continued to search, in the new scientific realism's idiom of race and inheritance, for ways of conceiving the absorption of difference. Unsurprisingly, they came up with figures of thought not so radically distinct from the sacrificial myths of their predecessors. In fact, the very ideology of *branqueamento*—the gradual "whitening" of the Brazilian population through the prevalence of the stronger over the weaker ethnical component—was in many ways a translation of Indianism's myth of nationality as an absorption of difference into identity. The Anthropological Exhibition, in this wider context, appears as one of the earliest and most ambitious attempts to re-ritualize the biopolitical capture of bare life as a scene of national initiation. The contradictions and tensions this attempt produced are therefore to some extent illustrative of those the Imperial state at large experienced in its struggle to find a proper entrance into modernity.

One of the first synthetic attempts to collate the emerging body of archaeological, linguistic, and anatomical scholarship was José Vieira Couto de Magalhães's *O selvagem* (The Savage). Written between 1874 and 1875 at the request of the organizing committee of that year's National Exhibition, presided over by the Emperor Pedro II himself, the work was subsequently displayed at the Brazilian pavilion of the Philadelphia World's Fair. The greater part of this text—itself almost a synthetic, portable anthropological exhibition spanning palaeontology, archaeology, linguistics, physical and social anthropology, philology, and geography—consists of a hands-on course in Tupí-Guaraní, in keeping with the author's belief in linguistic interaction as a means of pacific conquest. In the accompanying essay, Couto de Magalhães attempts to fuse literary Indianism's political edge of rural utopianism with some of the most "advanced" scientific paradigms, outlining the contours of a miscegenated modernity. "Many of us ask: what good has come from those savages?" he admits in the introduction, and goes on to reply:

No less than half of Brazil's actual population—not the one that occupies high office in the public function, in the salons, the theaters and the cities, but the population which extracts thousands of products from the soil, which we export or consume, this almost unique population which operates the cattle industry, the population which to this day has had to pay the highest toll of lives, for it is the descendant of the Indian, the mestizo of Indian, white and black who almost exclusively provides the recruits for the army and navy. Your Royal Highness, president of this commission, while commanding our forces in the Paraguayan War, have seen in the men of color who composed nearly the entire body of our troops, a transposition of the working population of Brazil.[9]

What Magalhães urges the monarch—and president of the National Exhibition—to see, then, is precisely the bare life that underlies the sacrificial myth of the Imperial state, the original division of "the people" into "the population holding high office" and the excluded, fragmentary multiplicity of bodies marked not by office but race (a life identified not in its political function but by mere nativity, an immediately biological life). Such an exclusion, he argues, has turned into an obstacle since it conflicts with the recruitment of "the actual population" (the people) for a function that is clearly political—warfare—hence the need to politicize bare life. As a way of achieving such an articulation, he yokes Darwinian evolutionism to his analysis of rural folk culture, presenting the latter as an expression of the gradual process of adaptation to the natural environment, in which only the racial traits most functional to the survival and strengthening of the national organism prevail. Thus in fact there is, in accordance with the very principle of natural selection, no *a priori* superior or inferior race, only ones more or less adapted to the diversity of local environments: "The only transformation that succeeds and becomes predominant is the one in greatest harmony with the local circumstances in which the multiple functions of life are exercised. This is what occurs to mankind and to animals everywhere, and this is what will occur in Brazil."[10]

Despite its evolutionist argument, *O selvagem* was quickly dismissed by the young positivists who disputed its promotion of *mestiçagem* (racial mixing) as a biopolitics of national integration. Instead, they insisted on the need for a break with both Indianism and its object as a precondition for Brazil's entry into modernity. Sílvio Romero, spokesman of the Recife School, criticized Magalhães's complicity with the official "indio-mania" that had turned Brazil into the most self-indulgent and backward nation of the Americas, idealizing an indigenous population that was among the least developed in the world. Instead of contributing to a deluded fiction of native origins, studies of popular expression in Brazil should dedicate themselves to its particular Luso-African blend: "It is not, as Dr. Couto de Magalhães and all the other exaggerated Indianists maintain, just *Tupy* that transforms the Portuguese language; it is also the many African languages spoken in Brazil for three and a half centuries."[11] More to Romero's liking was a study published in the same year as *O selvagem* in the first volume of the National Museum's new journal, which had inaugurated a quickly expanding interest in physical anthropology over the last decades of the nineteenth century. Its authors, Rodrigues Peixoto and Lacerda, were based at the museum's new physiological laboratory and were correspondents of leading European osteologists, whom they supplied with skulls from indigenous gravesites for the comparative study of human anatomy. Craniology, the measurement of human skulls to deduce the intellectual and moral properties of individuals and races, was also the subject of Peixoto and Lacerda's text, profusely illustrated with skulls in profile and full frontal view, alternating with long tables of anthropometric measurements. Having examined both "prehistoric" specimens and the remains of Indians recently killed in a punitive military campaign in Minas Gerais, the two physiologists arrived at the foregone conclusion that their subjects occupied, along with the Eskimos and the Patagonians, the lowest scale of human evolution in the Americas, a state of savagery that had remained unchanged over three thousand years: "On account of their small cranial capacity the Botocudos need to be placed alongside the New Caledonians and the Australians, in other words, among those races most notable for their degree of intellectual inferiority. Their capacities are, effectively, quite limited, and it will be difficult to make them take the road to civilization."[12]

Peixoto and Lacerda's article, then, called for a radical break with the Indianist archive, which archaeologists and ethnographers such as Couto de Magalhães still took as their frame of reference. Medically trained physiologists such as Lacerda, in contrast, advocated unconditional allegiance to the new biological and militantly racist strands in European scientific discourse, promoted by the new anthropological societies that challenged the humanist and monogeneticist "prejudice" of their ethnological counterparts. The open and boldly utilitarian stance of this new physical anthropology, its systematic pathologizing of cultural traits that could not be subsumed under imperial capitalism's mode of production, responded in the first place to a rising demand for raw materials that called for spatial expansion of the production zone and the maintenance of low labor costs. Scientific assessment of the capacities of particular groups to "take the road to civilization," in this context, directly resulted in recommendations of whether priority should be given to the coercion of a native workforce or to the repopulation of an area with immigrant laborers. The latter was suggested, for instance, by the zoologist and director of the Museu Paulista, Hermann von Ihering, for the interior of São Paulo state. Ihering's article "A antropologia do Estado de São Paulo," first published in São Paulo's bulletin for the Louisiana Purchase Exhibition of St. Louis, 1905, where the museum also displayed some of its archaeological and ethnographic collections, boldly recommended the extermination of the state's remaining Amerindian population:

The Indians of the State of São Paulo do not represent an element of labor and progress. As in other states of Brazil, no serious and continuous work can be expected from civilized Indians, and since the Caingan[g] are an obstacle for colonizing the backland regions they presently occupy, it seems there is no other means at hand than to exterminate them. [...] It is my conviction that it is due to these circumstances that the State of São Paulo needs to introduce thousands of immigrants, as the services of the indigenous population can not be counted on in an efficient and reliable way when it comes to the kinds of labor required by agriculture.[13]

While championing their real-life extermination, however, the Museu Paulista nonetheless contributed to the National Exhibition of 1908 with a life group display of the very communities its director considered obsolete. The catalogue mentions "3 rude huts of the Caingangs or Coroados, Cayuás, and

FIGURE 16. Marc Ferrez, Brazilian Anthropological Exhibition. Illustration from João Baptista de Lacerda, *Fastos do Museu Nacional* (1906). Museu Nacional / UFRJ, Rio de Janeiro.

Chavantes Indians. The first constructed in the shrubs and the latter at the base of Urca hill, in a natural cave. Each of them features a savage home in natural size, with its corresponding utensils and gear for war, fishing, and hunting."[14] Photographs of the exhibits were published in the *Catálogo do Estado de São Paulo*. Visual simulation of indigenous village life, then, constituted the evidence for a negative assessment of its aptitude for survival.

At the Anthropological Exhibition of 1882, these conflicting strands within scientific discourse, competing to succeed Romantic Indianism, were present both on the level of display itself and in the labels, commentaries, and other writings that framed them. Whatever their ideological differences, however, all of them were concerned with reformulating the sacrificial myth at the core of literary and artistic Indianism. Ironically (or not) in its claim to succeed literature as a truth-teller for the nation, the exhibition referred to indigenous life more than ever in sacrificial terms, in a ritual offering of otherness through which a new national self was magically called to the scene.

### Rites of Passage

A forest of spears. Fanning out around shields and bows, hanging from walls and ceilings in abstract geometrical patterns, atavistic energies streaming off some mystic, empty center. Hearts of darkness, pitched against the clarity of the white wall; high, classicist ceilings towering above the chaotic excess of savagery, where things and bodies repeat themselves, in strange angles, as on the shattered pieces of a broken mirror. Marc Ferrez's photograph of the Anthropological Exhibition (fig. 16), part of a series taken at the event, underscores the specular effect of the display through a careful arrangement of planes. In the foreground, surrounded by two waterbirds and treading on a soil of weeds and dry earth, an indigenous woman wearing a hat and skirt walks by, carrying a basket, while farther back, men in canoes laden with rods go out fishing. They bear an uncanny resemblance to one another. Still farther towards the background, two female figures wearing pearls or feathers stand beside a hut. We cannot be entirely sure about these last (different from the boatsmen in stature and costume), but photographs taken from other angles of the room confirm that the ones in the foreground are in fact statues, plaster casts taken of the Xerente by the sculptor Léon Deprès and dressed in clothes collected among the native communities. Lacerda, in a guide of the National Museum published in 1906, when he had succeeded Netto as director, describes the arrangement like this:

In the exhibition rooms, huts containing the hammocks and utensils of the Indian were put up, canoes and rods such as they use for fishing; figures of Indians hunting, all taken from the natural. The beautiful collections of garments and frocks made from feathers which the Museum already possessed, were brought into a more artistic order; arms, arrows, *maracás*, trumpets, blowpipes, bows, occupied a great extension of the room; the stone axes, grinders, tamping tools, *tembetás*, etc., in their regular distribution formed tables worthy of comparison. The *curare* venom in pumpkin flasks and earthen cooking pans, the arrows and arrow-cages, hunting weapons, with their tips cooked in venom, composed a group of objects especially attractive to the physiologist. Exhibits of charcoal paintings, remains of birds and fish extracted from the *sambaqui* gravesites, a topographical sketch of these exquisite formations of caves, human skulls and skeletons found in them, stone tools and arrowheads, composed another group which attracted the attention of visitors. [...] Each exhibit belonged to a particular tribe, thus facilitating comparison between artifacts of one and the same kind, but from different tribes.[15]

Of the exhibition rooms, three were dedicated to "ethnography," featuring in situ displays of native village life and showcases with tools and weaponry. "Archaeology" occupied a further two rooms, featuring the collections of ceramics and stoneware from the Amazon, assembled by Netto on a recent expedition to the province of Pará, as well as similar collections made by Domingos Ferreira Penna and Orville Derby, and pieces unearthed from the *sambaqui* mounds in the south by Charles Frederick Hartt. A further room, designated as "Ethnography and Archaeology," contained pieces of pottery and a large number of garments, in particular a magnificent collection of feather capes and headgear from numerous tribes both "ancient and modern." The section on "anthropology," also occupying one room, held skeletons and skulls exhumed from native gravesites, mostly by Netto himself among the Temembé of the upper Rio Capim, though almost certainly the human remains described by Lacerda and Rodrigues Peixoto in their article of 1876 would also have been shown. The final room—the Sala Anchieta—had been reserved for scholarly and artistic representations of the Indian: studies in the Tupí language and in American ethnography and anthropology, donated by the National Library; oil paintings of indigenous types, specially commissioned from artists Aurélio de Figueiredo e Melo and Décio Villares; and photographs, prints, and watercolors from the Emperor's personal collection. All documented a national Indianist tradition that the exhibition acknowledged as well as claimed to depart from.[16]

For, indeed, the event could be, and claimed to be, read as a monumental reassessment of the status and value of the exhibits in the Sala Anchieta in the light of a scientific discourse sustained by the hard evidence of material objects. However, controversy persisted over what exactly this new discourse had to say. To begin with, the name of the event poses a series of questions: why an "anthropological exhibition," if archaeological and ethnographic, even literary and artistic, material prevailed over that of a properly anthropological character (a term reserved, at the time, for the physiological study of non-European races), and although Netto himself, in previous publications where he attempted to persuade the government to fund a new museum dedicated to Brazil's Amerindian populations, had consistently employed the nomenclature of "archaeology" or "ethnography"? While physiologists such as Lacerda clearly took the choice of "anthropology" as an invitation to expound on the political implications of their scientific agenda (the question, Lacerda argues in his contribution to the journal of the exhibition, was to compare the utility of Indians and blacks for prolonged physical labors, in which the latter widely outperformed the former), other contributors such as J. Serra sharply opposed "yankee utilitarianism" and upheld the "Latin" tradition of "Ramiros, Palma, Vicuña [Mackenna] and other South American writers who esteem the Indian's services, recommending their catechesis and civilization by gentle and persuasive means."[17]

If the terms of engagement with the native other—charitable empathy or detached objectivity—thus remained a matter of controversy, the point of view that produced objects and their viewers could not but be an ambiguous, multifocal montage of visual forms that often seemed mutually exclusive. From the evidence that has remained, we can discern at least four different modes of display: first and foremost, the life groups of plaster figures which, as in an open diorama, dramatized the ethnographic objects in a kind of three-dimensional photograph, staging a frozen instant of native village life. In situ displays, although familiar from wax cabinets and other popular entertainments in European cities, had only become a regular exhibition device with the extensive use of life scenes at the world's fairs and great department stores of the second half of the century, both to simulate the exotic and to stimulate interest in the latest fashion trend. The Swedish folklorist Arthur Hazelius adopted them in 1873 for his Museum of Scandinavian Ethnography, whose innovations in life group composition had a huge impact on German and, via Franz Boas, U.S. displays of ethnography and popular traditions. Unlike Hazelius and Boas, however, who championed life groups as a context-bound alternative to the typological tradition of classifying objects on account of their formal similarities, Netto freely juxtaposed life groups and typological showcases such as that of musical instruments (fig. 17), likewise photographed by Marc Ferrez. Typological arrangement also seems to have governed the display of archaeological materials, judging from illustrations in the museum journal's special issue on the exhibition.

In a circular to museum staff from 1890, Netto explained the principles on which he had organized these "families of objects," distinguishing eight different "classes."[18] In addition to "hunting and fishing tools" and "festive and musical objects," further classes were composed of religious and funerary items, domestic utensils, feathers and other adornments, model reconstructions of native villages, as well as what we could call "linguistic traces" (a class containing native vocabularies, legends, inscriptions, manuscripts, and published material on indigenous themes). In this classifying scheme modelled on the material assets of the 1882 exhibition, the life groups, books, and paintings were imaginarily placed into another glass box and, there, appeared to be subsumable under a general paradigm of typological classification. However, the juxtaposition of display strategies at the exhibition disavows Netto's claim to a homogeneous organization.

FIGURE 17. Marc Ferrez, Brazilian Anthropological Exhibition, artifacts and aspects of indigenous life (musical instruments). Silver gelatin print from original glass negative (ca. 1882). Biblioteca Nacional Brasileira, Rio de Janeiro.

In fact, in situ displays as well as paintings and prints offered the visitor visual alternatives to the typological comparison suggested by the displays of tools and weapons. On yet another plane, we have to locate the properly "anthropological" displays of human remains: to my knowledge, no visual record survives of these, but from Lacerda's description and the exhibition catalogue, we can infer that at least some of them must have been exhibited in reconstructed gravesites, while other skulls and skeletons were shown in glass boxes, facilitating physiological comparison between different "racial types."

And finally, what of the Xerente and Botocudo men and women who were staying on the premises and, press coverage suggests, quickly became the event's most popular attraction? All we seem to be left with are traces, pictures of replicas, representations of representations. Were they really there? I would argue that our difficulty in recovering their presence, wresting evidence of their passage from the exhibition's images and objects, is due not so much to the loss and fading that goes with the passing of time, but with a politics of concealment already at work in the exhibition itself, a disappearing act of museum magic. The exhibition worked on the bodies of the indigenous men and women a noncoevalness that converted them into simulacra, imitations of themselves. Plaster casts that could actually move: in fact, Ferrez's images of the life groups—freezing a movement that was already static, photographing what was already photographic and thereby bringing it alive in an uncanny, spectral afterlife—show us the making of the object in reverse mode, as it were. As ghosts, Ferrez's Indians once more set free the moving bodies the exhibition had reduced to eternal poses and to the self-sameness of racial types.

Perhaps one of the most striking aspects of the Anthropological Exhibition is the speed with which it was planned, assembled, and opened. Even though Netto claims to have conceived the idea of an anthropological and ethnographic show in 1880, after it dawned on him that the government would not fund a permanent Anthropological Museum, as late as January 1882 we can still see him heading north in search of material to put on display.[19] He spends a few weeks on the island of Marajó, province of Pará, digging up pottery and stoneware from funerary mounds. Having thus covered archaeology, he reserves the remaining two weeks before taking the steamer back to Rio on February 26 for an ethnographic and anthropological expedition up the River Capim. From Belém, where he drops off his archaeological findings before moving on, he reports: "Now, leaving archeology with rest, I will dedicate myself to anthropology and ethnography and travel inland for two days, to make contact with three savage tribes, whose attire I want to study in real life and from close up, and whose cemeteries I will rummage through, to exhume the bones of these primitive sons of our forests."[20]

Three tribes in two weeks. And very savage. Real life, cemeteries. For Netto, it seems, the interior is a great reservoir of material, living and dead, which needs to be "rummaged through" to come upon the most striking pieces, stones and bones to which the museum has already allocated the empty slots they will eventually come to fill. Their destination is clear prior to their discovery.

It took Netto less than four months to classify and prepare his findings for display at the exhibition, where they provided a substantial portion of exhibits and were later passed on into the museum's ethnographic, archaeological, and anthropological collections. The ethnographic encounter with Indians still "unspoiled by cultural mixing," as Netto puts it, takes up less than two pages of his travel account and seems to have left no mark whatsoever on his scientific ideas and practice, perhaps because an encounter had never properly occurred in the first place. That is to say, for Netto, the collector, the indigenous other exists solely as the keeper of materials that need to be wrested from him so as to be put in their rightful place, the museum: "Of all the booty I had so peacefully acquired in these latitudes, I took most pleasure from the skeletons and skulls I had taken away with me, employing ruses I would not call pious, but which were justified for the good of science."[21] The aim of ethnography, for Netto, is not to understand cultural difference but to illustrate it, as difference is merely a form of noncoevalness, a backwardness in time. Archaeology and anatomy, the two disciplinary practices between which Netto's "fieldwork" takes place, have always already marked its temporality as one of irrecoverable nonsimultaneity:

All the questions of anthropology can be summarized, as you know, into two essential problems: the first seeks to determine the genesis of humanity; the second, which is intimately linked to the first, consists in the discussion of the monogeneticist and polygeneticist hypotheses, regarding the laws of evolution on the zoological level. [...] The doubt of reason, troubled by the famous *to be or not to be*, the anxiety of a brain battling against itself in the abysses of the unknown, is what expresses best the mood of those who apply themselves to the study of the ancient peoples of our continent.[22]

This slip from anthropology into autobiography, from the origins of American man to the scientist's Shakespearean quest for truth, is hardly a surprise when set against the effect of noncoevalness this narrative is constantly manufacturing. If the native represents the dawn of humanity, the mental backtracking of the anthropologist becomes indeed a cerebral rite of initiation, a journey into the liminal space where humanity and animality collapse into one another. "Initiation," in fact, is revealed in this passage to be the emerging discipline of anthropology's own form of self-reflexivity, the way in which it allows subjectivity to constitute itself against the primitive through whose space it must nonetheless pass.

In Netto's writings, however, the liminal space of Brazilian indigenous cultures is set against another space of travel and initiation, that of the European universities where he first comes into contact with an archaeological interest in Brazilian prehistory: "It is true that, ever since 1867, inspired by the work of Louis Lautet, who was then encouraging me to undertake a comparative study of Celt-Iberian and Brazilian primitive pottery, I found myself almost involuntarily engaged in this kind of effort. I was acting rather as a simple collector of dispersed material than as a properly entitled and experimented researcher."[23] Yet, once he had been confirmed as museum director and gathered copious amounts of indigenous objects, following public appeals for donations, Netto would assume the voice of a full-fledged anthropologist, eventually even daring to challenge the "restricted views" of his European and North American peers:

In 1880 my ideas were already very different from what they had been. Charles Hartt was then beginning to impress me with the sobriety and discretion with which he treated the ethnological questions of our continent. However, [...] I could not entirely subscribe to the restricted views of so many North American ethnologists. What did not allow me to do so was the countless evidence placed before my eyes, demanding a reason for its analogies and resemblance to the antiquities of other primitive peoples, if not from the Old World, then at least from our own continent. [...] It was under the influence of these new ideas and under pressure from these doubts that I resolved to organize an Anthropological Exhibition.[24]

The exhibition, then, was to make visible what Netto had already suspected; namely, the filiation between "primitive Brazilian" and other civilizations of old—Amerindian and possibly even European and Asian. The simultaneous encounter on his journey to the field, of "primitive savages" and "beautiful relics" of classical resemblances, lead Netto to deduce that the connection between both had to be at best remote. Having thus bracketed savagery (in an argumentative turn that simultaneously emancipated him from his French and North American mentors) Netto could reclaim the remnants of his newfound Brazilian Golden Age as the Imperial state's own antiquity: "the men of the *sambaquis* were the degenerate offspring of very advanced nations, of whom they preserved as their last relics, like the ancient oriental peoples in exile, the sacred urns and penates..."[25]

Although much ridiculed at the time for his urge to establish a classical parentage for his native golden age, Netto managed, through his formula of a virtuous yet vanished indigenous empire, to simultaneously dismiss and reinvent the colonial myth of Romantic Indianism. The exhibition was a monumental version of the modern subject's liminal experience of self-forging, simultaneously recognizing and distinguishing himself from external and internal others, from his celestial and infernal mirror images facing him from above and from below. Transformed into spectacle, science itself produces the dreamspace of alterity in which the observing subject can momentarily lose herself in a flight of fancy, only to reenter the plane of consciousness by way of the museal order of classification. Knowledge, then, comes to the observer in an almost hypnotic trance, reencountering her own body and soul after having, if only for an instant, become other, gone primitive:

On entering these rooms, every one of us will find himself as if suddenly thrown, against his will, onto a hitherto unknown plane of existence. The imagination, guided and marvelled by what is displayed to us in this place, flies across the insurmountable forests of the great Amazon's estuary defeating space, settling on the shores of the hospitable

Ipurinãs, on the margins of the vast Aquiri or in the sad huts of the last descendants of the noble Turinarás and Temembés, in the valley of the upper Capim. Next, it enters the depths of the sacred tombs of the valiant Aruãs on the island of Marajó, as if cancelling out the passing of centuries, to witness the grave and solemn ceremony of burying a sumptuously ornate funerary urn that carries the remains of the bravest of chiefs, or the oldest warrior of the tribe.[26]

This flight of the imagination to the ancient origins of Brazilian man was of course essentially the same as the fantasy that Romantic Indianism had offered to a previous generation of readers. Science, in fact, only succeeded literature by restaging its foundational myth of an identity that emerged in its passage through difference. Brazil, for Netto, could become modern only to the extent that it was dreaming its own antiquity.

## Pictures of an Exhibition

To provide visitors with this surrogate experience of liminality, the Anthropological Exhibition drew on a wide range of visual forms. Images were crucial to the enframing of the indigenous object. Yet just as the strategies of material display shifted between different exhibitionary aesthetics and the disciplinary discourses that underwrote them, visual representations at and of the Anthropological Exhibition spanned numerous genres, from Deprès's statues to paintings and photographs, which both integrated and documented the display. Popular caricaturists such as Agostini, who visited the event, also produced their own, satirical versions, which can be seen as a visual commentary on the exhibition's iconography: a theater of mirrors reflecting one another, drawing attention to the stains and cracks in the glass.

Let us begin with what would seem to be the most discrete and neutral plane of visuality, Marc Ferrez's photographs of the showcases we have already seen above. Material artifacts had been among the earliest subjects to attract the camera's attention, testifying to the affinity between photography's and the museum's technology of immobilizing the material world. Daguerre himself, between 1837 and 1839, reproduced an "Arrangement of Fossil Shells"; among Fox Talbot's first pictures were "Articles of China" and "The Milliner's Shop" (ca. 1844). The filiation between natural history and the commodity form, which Benjamin would notice in his investigations of nineteenth-century Paris, is already fully unfolded here. Yet, as Elizabeth Edwards observes, while photography was regularly employed since midcentury as a curatorial device in the fine arts and archaeology, facilitating comparison between distant pieces and thus contributing to the emergence and formalization of scholarly disciplines, systematic incorporation of the medium into ethnographic museum practice did not begin until the 1890s. This lateness is all the more puzzling since, as Edwards notes, photography had shaped ethnographic practices in the field from very early on, closing "the space between the site of observation on the colonial periphery and the site of metropolitan interpretation."[27] Ethnographic object photography was only standardized by the turn of the century, the graphic conventions of natural science illustration clearly prevailing over those of an emerging visual dialect for reproducing artworks and luxury goods, due perhaps to the background of many anthropologists in medicine or natural history. Instead of the emphatic use of lighting and angle in photographs of sculptures and monuments, enhancing subjective engagement, ethnographic documentation favored detachment and aesthetic self-restraint, indicating an object's belonging to a series rather than its individual traits. In encouraging visual comparison, ethnographic object photography intensified the museum effect in its discrete deployment of "techniques for the management of attention, for imposing homogeneity," and helped forge a visual economy founded on a system of equivalence.[28]

Ferrez, however, was neither an ethnographer nor a naturalist, but a commercial photographer (perhaps the finest in nineteenth-century Brazil) specializing in landscape views. Trained at the studio of the court's preferred photographer Georges Leuzinger, Ferrez, the son of a French artist teaching at the local academy, set up his own company in 1867 and regularly exhibited at national and international exhibitions, where he collected numerous awards. In 1889, the Brazilian commission for the Universal Exhibition at Paris entrusted him with the production of an album of views of the country, which appeared as an appendix to the Baron of Rio Branco's *Le Brésil*, itself a part of Levasseur's *Grande Encyclopédie*. Ferrez had already photographed indigenous men and women on numerous occasions, at least once on commission to produce material for anthropometric research, and several of these portraits were included in the album of Brazil on display at his Rio de Janeiro studio (fig. 18).

Ferrez's series of the exhibition is divided into two groups of pictures: panoramic shots of the exhibition rooms, highlighting the life group displays (figs. 16, 20), and close-ups of showcases, which emphasize the patterns of arrangement rather than individual objects (figs. 17, 19). At first glance, the latter merely seem to add yet another frame to those already supplied by the showcases themselves. In this succession of framing devices, David Jenkins has suggested, a gradual narrowing of meaning takes place, as "the reduction of three-dimensional objects to inscriptions on paper, result in the simplification of the symbolic and conceptual management of objects which stabilized meanings."[29] Yet we must not forget that this "three-dimensional object" had already been reduced and sta-

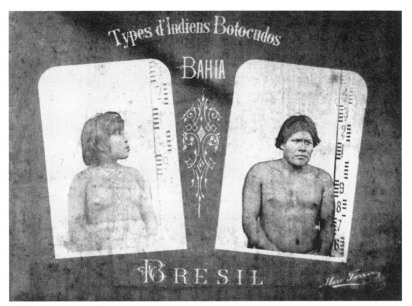

FIGURE 18. Marc Ferrez, Native Botocudo types. Albumin print (ca. 1874). Ibero-Amerikanisches Institut, Berlin.

bilized as an object of museum display. In fact, its tangible three-dimensionality was itself the expression of the loss of use-value it had suffered in being offered up to the visitors' gaze. It is, then, not necessarily in terms of reduction alone that the passage from museum object to photograph can be fully grasped. Why should photography not also work, voluntarily or not, in the exposure of the previous operation performed on the artifact in order to constitute it as object? There is no reason why photographs of objects, and perhaps museum objects in particular, should lack a *punctum*, as Roland Barthes has called the incisive point of clarity in which the immanence of the image collapses. Take Ferrez's print of percussion instruments and blowpipes (fig. 19), where the detemporalized, geometrical arrangement of the display is both emphasized and subverted by the photographer's dramatic use of light and shadow, a visual signature that, rather than erasing all traces of subjective engagement, locates the objects in the space and time of the museum encounter. If photographs and museum showcases are means of appropriating things, of "putting oneself into a certain relation to the world that feels like knowledge—and, therefore, like power," as Susan Sontag has noted, their juxtaposition may draw our attention, curiously, to the very opposite, the way things slip away from us, or begin to look, as do the bristled cane sticks of Ferrez's photograph, like driftwood or booty—wounded objects cut off from a practice they can only call forth as absence, in a language of mourning.[30]

FIGURE 19. Marc Ferrez, Brazilian Anthropological Exhibition, artifacts and aspects of indigenous life (musical instruments). Silver gelatin print from original glass negative (ca. 1882). Biblioteca Nacional Brasileira, Rio de Janeiro.

FIGURE 20. (*below*) Marc Ferrez, Brazilian Anthropological Exhibition, artifacts and aspects of indigenous life. Silver gelatin print from original glass negative (ca. 1882). Biblioteca Nacional Brasileira, Rio de Janeiro.

Of course, Ferrez may not have actively intended a critique of the violence of collecting and material display. Yet the way in which his pictures turn the display of objects into a new visual object brings to the fore something that is already at work in the exhibition itself but is naturalized, made invisible, by the museum apparatus. Photography, by contrast, brings the object and the museum's framing devices onto one and the same plane, *it objectifies objectification*. The classic horror movie plot of the museum object coming back to life is but another version of the spectral effect I am trying to grasp here: in the object's becoming an image and in the apparatus of its capture alike, in their common seizure by yet another device of spectral mimesis the devices and agents of objectification are more affected than that which has already been objectified. The photograph, in this sense, is implicitly carrying out a kind of revenge of the object. More importantly, it restores a sense of historical contingency to the frozen time of the museum display, precisely as it uncovers the instantaneity of its manifestations.

By instantaneity I mean a kind of objective notation of the tensions, contradictions, and struggles involved in the making of objects, "forgotten" precisely as these are laid to rest in their objectness, as museum pieces. In another picture of the showroom that contains the plaster casts of the Xerente fishermen, for instance, Ferrez reproduces the juxtaposition of life group and trophy displays through the planar structuring of the photographic frame, choosing a focal length that reproduces both levels of the display, as well as the classicist architecture that envelops them, in the same degree of resolution (fig. 20). The image is thus traversed by a tension between the self-contained village scene—natives going peacefully about their everyday tasks—and the spears, clubs, and shields surrounding them in ornamental patterns, tokens of a violence that literally hangs above their heads, threatening to disrupt yet also contained in the rectangular frame of the museum's neoclassical interior. An image of native life in the museum, it is at the same time an image of science as superseding the other's excess, the ferocity that the other wields against civilization, by the disciplinary order of classification. The heraldic arrangements of weaponry, which form a kind of screen between the life groups and the museum architecture, are thus the site where the atavistic force of the other is both invoked and contained. An exteriority that is constitutive of the interiority of science, a fetish of anthropology, the trophy display more than anything points to the colonial violence of the objects' acquisition.

Whereas photography was enlisted at the exhibition to document and highlight the illusionism of the display, the task of visualizing the exhibition's physiological agenda fell to painting. Several portraits of indigenous types (using as models the Indians who had been brought to Rio) were commissioned from Aurélio de Figueiredo e Melo, Pedro Américo's younger brother, and Décio Villares, a young painter and sculptor who would soon become the official artist of the Republic. Judging from the works still in the museum's possession, the result was heterogeneous. Aurélio's life-size portrait of a feather-clad Walpes Indian, reminiscent of Albert Eckhout's seventeenth-century paintings of native types still on display in the museum's vestibule, carries a notable influence of Romantic Indianism's idealization of the chivalric warrior. Villares's series of small-size portraits, executed in a more soberly "scientific" mood, far exceed the limits of typification and turn into complex visual engagements with their subjects. In keeping with their phrenological agenda, Villares's paintings focus exclusively on the sitters' heads and busts, in profile or half-profile, shown in front of a neutral monochrome background from which any reference to locality has been removed. Similarly, items of clothing are, unlike on Aurélio's painting, stripped of any colorful exoticism, leaving viewers with a self-explaining physiognomy that supposedly denotes the degrees of moral development that separate the semi-civilized *caboclo* (mestizo, or half-breed) (fig. 21) from a pure-blooded Xerente (fig. 22) or, at the very bottom of the scale, a Botocudo woman with her artificially extended lower lip (fig. 23). The austerity of the visual frame exposes the sitters completely to a physiological gaze, no longer distracted by any narrative or allegorical elements, a gaze that is not returned. (In this the portraits differ sharply from the ones of republican dignitaries that Villares was entrusted with before and after the coup of 1889, in which the gaze returned sternly to the viewer asserts political authority and charisma.) Yet while biology clearly determines the terms of engagement with the indigenous other, a similar effect of aesthetic excess as on Ferrez's photographs is at work on Villares's paintings, ultimately unsettling their ideological agenda.

The portrait of the Botocuda woman (fig. 23), a particularly intriguing image that avoids the temptation of facile freakishness, from a critical perspective becomes a site of visual self-reflexivity on the production of bare life. Clearly the painting is more actively staged than the others of the series, allowing the gaze to stray from the sitter's face to the string of stones and jaguar claws around her neck and indeed her bare shoulder, adding to the image an unexpectedly sensual dimension that reconnects it with Indianism's erotic investment in the indigenous body. Yet here the partial baring of a female body adorned with the tokens of ferocity, which, in images such as José Maria de Medeiros's *Iracema* (fig. 15), had served to underscore the sensual excess and desirability of this body, turns into the radical opposite of a sexual offering. Hers is a "toothed body," a body that rejects the beholder's gaze. Where Iracema's sensual forms had dialogued with the lush volumes and colors of Medeiros's Romantic landscape, Villares's

FIGURE 21. (*above, left*) Décio Villares, *Caboclo.* Portrait from series *Tipos indigenas*. Oil on wood (ca. 1882). Museu Nacional / UFRJ, Rio de Janeiro.

FIGURE 22. (*left*) Décio Villares, *Xerente Indian*. Portrait from series *Tipos indigenas*. Oil on wood (ca. 1882). Museu Nacional / UFRJ, Rio de Janeiro.

FIGURE 23. (*above, right*) Décio Villares, *Botocuda Indian*. Portrait from series *Tipos indigenas*. Oil on wood (ca. 1882). Museu Nacional / UFRJ, Rio de Janeiro.

image denounces the utter incommensurability of the physiognomy captured in the visual language of painterly naturalism. The gulf between an aesthetic form hinged on a positivist notion of the real and the body-aesthetic of its subject has become too vast here to allow for the erotic approach suggested by Indianism, as Villares seems only too aware in simultaneously citing and dismissing the option of sensualist fantasy. The Botocuda woman's mouth with lower teeth exposed by the bucal disk literally turns into the sign and the site of a prohibition that interdicts the consumption of visual pleasure offered in the trope of partial exposure. What is exposed in the interdiction of erotic investment is bare life, a life that cannot be invested and that representation can therefore only grasp in terms of its own impossibility, by making visible the impropriety of another representation. But in this way, too, Villares's paintings become self-critical in a similar fashion to Ferrez's photographs. At the same time, this signature of misencounter functions as a negative assertion of coevalness: physiognomy, indeed, turns from a phenotypal signifier of racial evolution into the enigmatic bearer of a biography (enigmatic because the life it refers to is absent from the sphere of *bios*, or qualified life). Whereas Ferrez's photographs render visible the silent frame of ethnography's arrangement of indigenous material culture, Villares's portraits defy the noncoevalness worked onto the cultural objects and indeed the very body of the native other precisely by stressing the impossibility of representing bare life, exposing the lack that turns the spectacle of otherness into an illusion of presence.

### The Cannibal's Kiss

The noncoevalness between modernity and the primitive, which the Anthropological Exhibition enunciated as mutually constitutive attributes of science and its object, was an easy prey for satirists such as Angelo Agostini, whose cartoon published in August 1882 in the *Revista Illustrada* draws on the comic potential of anachronism. Indeed, his visual commentary on the event already looks forward to the playful juxtaposition between the modern and the archaic that would spark off Brazilian modernism almost half a century later at São Paulo's Modern Art Week of 1922.

In the first box we see Agostini's alter ego, a little Pierrot, sneaking into the museum where the Emperor is inspecting some pottery figurines he is offered by Netto in the manner of a greengrocer praising his merchandise. "It is to be suspected [the caption informs] that H. M. pronounced some considerations on the subject of State religion."[31] Next, we see the little clown staring at an ornamental arrangement of spears and clubs, which, he suggests, are far more splendorous than the emperor's civilian waistcoat: why not add to his ceremonial toucan cape, he proposes, a headdress and skirt such as the ones on display at the exhibition, and he might make a most showy cacique?

The second part of the cartoon (fig. 24) is inspired by Villares's portrait of the Botocuda woman (which Agostini copies) and imagines the amorous encounters of a native couple with their ceremonially extended lips, the suitability of which for cannibalistic feasts does not escape the cartoonist. Unlike Villares, then, Agostini takes the native other's excessive body, organized around the devouring, cannibalistic mouth, not as a site of interdiction that preempts

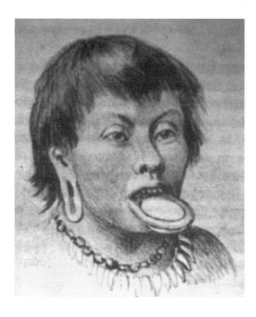

FIGURE 24. Angelo Agostini, *A Visit to the Anthropological Exhibition* (detail). Illustration from *Revista Illustrada* (1882). Biblioteca da Casa de Rui Barbosa, Rio de Janeiro.

Romantic fantasy but as one of carnivalization of the narratives of origin put forward by Indianism and anthropology alike. Agostini, in other words, ignores the prohibition Villares had located in the monstrous mouth that overcoded the erotic body of Indianism as a toothed, impenetrable body of alterity, and instead reinserts it into a parodic Golden Age, in which Indianist romance turns into the grotesque. By refusing to acknowledge their difference, Agostini ridicules both Indianism and the scientific discourse that claims to have succeeded it. The grotesque mouth, then, in which Villares's painterly realism embodied the unbridgeable gap between the virtuous and desirable Indian of novelistic fantasy and the unrepresentable otherness of bare life, in Agostini's cartoon shows what is its real threat: juxtaposition. The Botocuda woman, who infringes the oral interdiction and crosses back into Indianist romance, ridicules the truth claims of the new, scientific representations of otherness, constituted precisely upon their separation from Indianism's sentimental tradition. Just as it would, almost half a century later, in Oswald de Andrade's "Anthropophagic Manifesto," the grotesque, devouring mouth in Agostini's cartoon becomes a site of the unmaking of the discursive regulations and conventions through which Western science had made the other into an object. In showing his little clown threatened with cannibalistic ingestion, Agostini's cartoon inverts the museum exhibit's relations of size, objectness, and power vis-à-vis the observer. It is the museum itself, in fact, which is unmasked here as the true anthropophagy: a devouring of bare life on behalf of a "curiosity" that feeds off its remains.

# Antiques and Archives

## FINDING A HOME FOR HISTORY

Since we lack founding fathers, we shall invent them, as others have done; and since a people is easier to impress than an individual, the people will convince themselves that they have founding fathers. Once convinced of their existence, they will believe in their heroic deeds, too; poets will write hymns in their honor, and sculptors will cast their physiognomies in marble and bronze.

—Eduardo L. Holmberg, *Olimpio Pitango de Monalía* (1915)

### Times of Remembrance

The final decades of the nineteenth century saw increasing attempts in Argentina and Brazil to unify and standardize the curriculum of national history under the aegis of state institutions such as public schools, archives, and museums, as well as to select and classify the documentary and material basis sustaining the official narrative of the past. The Brazilian Historical Exhibition of 1881, celebrated at the National Library, produced a three-volume catalogue listing over 20,000 items, a monumental compilation that, as José Honório Rodrigues claims, was larger than any existing national bibliography of its time.[1] Eight years earlier, in his *Noções de coreografia brasileira*, distributed at the Universal Exhibition of Vienna in 1873, Joaquim Manuel de Macedo had already summarized the mythological repertoire from which the exhibition of 1881 would still draw its principles of classification: the natural exuberance of tropical nature; the Portuguese colonizers' heroic foundation of the nation; the benign, civilizing mission of the monarchy; the political wisdom of the ruling elite that prevented the Empire from falling into the anarchic state of its republican neighbors. After the republican coup of 1889, this courtly historiography, which was forged around midcentury by Francisco Adolfo Varnhagen and other affiliates of the Historical-Geographical Institute (founded in 1838), was gradually replaced by a new emphasis on the formation of national society, echoed by a new interest in the teaching of history as a way of disseminating patriotic sentiment. José Veríssimo's *A educação nacional* (1890) sparked a movement of educational reform focused on the increase of Brazilian geographical and historical subjects in the curriculum. Textbooks were composed by some of the country's leading intellectuals: *A história do Brasil ensinada pela biografia dos seus heróis* (The History of Brazil as Seen Through the Biographies of Its Heroes, 1890) by Sílvio Romero; *Contos pátrios* (Stories of the Fatherland, 1900) by Olavo Bilac and Henrique M. Coelho Neto; or *Através do Brasil* (Across Brazil, 1910) by Bilac and Manoel Bomfim; and the popular publishing house Livraria do Povo launched a pedagogical series Biblioteca Infantil in 1894.

In Argentina, historical research and writing, previously the domain of erudite journals, culminated in the 1880s and 1890s in a series of weighty monographs, foremost among which are the final editions of Bartolomé Mitre's *Historia de Belgrano* (1887) and *Historia de San Martín* (1887–90), and Vicente Fidel López's ten-volume *Historia de la República Argentina* (1883–93). A National Archive was created in 1884, inheriting the collections of the archive of the province of Buenos Aires, organized in 1874 by the collectors and polymaths Andrés Lamas, Manuel Trelles, and Juan María Gutiérrez. In 1889, historian Vicente Fidel López was entrusted by the mayor Francisco Seeber with the selection of spots in the city of Buenos Aires to which commemorative plaques of historical events and heroes should be affixed. In the same year, Seeber ordered the creation of a municipal historical museum, which soon afterwards was turned by presidential decree into the Museo Histórico Nacional. Throughout the closing decades of the century, student associations organized patriotic pilgrimages to founding sites of the nation-state, such as the meeting place of the Congress of Tucumán, and all major (and some minor) cities were gripped by a statue fever of previously unseen dimensions. Monuments of civil war commanders Lavalle and Paz were erected in Buenos Aires and Córdoba in 1887; the following year National Congress approved projects for a memorial of the *Ejército de los Andes* at Mendoza, statues of Narciso Laprida and Fray Justo Santa María de Oro at San Juan, and a commemorative column of the battle of San Lorenzo. In 1889, a monument to commemorate the first anniversary of Sarmiento's death was projected and a contest for a national pantheon advertised. In 1890, the year a massive financial crisis put an abrupt end to lavish public spending, the mayor of Buenos Aires had asked permission from congress to erect monuments in honor of Juan de Garay, the city's founder; the viceroys Vértiz and Liniers; independence heroes Alvear, Las Heras, and Brown; governors Saavedra and Dorrego; and the writer Vicente López.

The archive and the museum (the state collection of national antiques) were the two forms of repossessing the past that opened up the space into which history could be inscribed. Historiography is a writing that inscribes into the fold between antiques and archives, referring the one to the other yet also always reinscribing their irreducible difference. For, between the archive and the museum, there is a difference that is not merely about the nature of the objects both keep in storage. An archive is not a museum of documents, nor is a museum a material archive, a database of objects: rather, there is an archive wherever a collection of documents is established, and a museum where a gathering of antiques—which are a particular kind of monument—takes place. While certain objects seem to carry in themselves an inclination to be stored in one form or the other, the question is nonetheless not so much about the "nature" of collectibles as it is about the aesthetics and politics of preservation to which they are being submitted. Alvaro Fernández Bravo has shown how, in turn-of-the-century Argentina, there were heated debates about the ownership of certain manuscripts of the heroes of independence, claimed both by the National Archive and the Museum of National History as their rightful possessions.[2] In fact, every document can be exposed in its monumentality by the gaze of the archaeologist; every monument can be reinscribed in the archive's thread of documents. The point, then, is not that memory always opposes and resists the archive, as Andreas Huyssen claims, but rather that "museum memory" and "archive memory" propose different, and to an extent antagonistic, economies of remembrance and forgetting.[3]

### Performing the Archive

A strange effect of self-effacing memory was reported in December 1881 by "Junio," the chronicler of Rio de Janeiro's satirical journal *Revista Illustrada*, on having visited the Brazilian Historical Exhibition at the National Library. "I entered the first room," he wrote, "then left to enter the second, from the second on to the third … from the first to the second floor, from the second to the third where, unable to climb any further, I descended, turning back on my own footsteps, from one floor to the other and from one room to the next until I had regained the street. I had seen everything. Yet when I tried to remember what I'd seen, I couldn't remember a thing."[4] Multiplicity engenders nothingness: like an inverted Ireneo Funes (Borges's famous memorialist who suffers from a hypertrophy of recollections, which consequently remain unclassified, disconnected from one another, radically singular) Junio announces his utter inability to represent, that is, to select, reorder, and synthesize his sensations and impressions from the exhibition visit. The trope of a loss of legibility of the material world, due to the very overabundance and overexposure of its contents, is widespread in the closing decades of the nineteenth century. This overabundance generates a "fatigue of the eyes" where a transparent, well-ordered totality should have been laid out, as Philippe Hamon explains in a beautiful essay on architecture, writing, and exhibitions.[5] The inventory collapses into the jumble of the flea market, the very form of display modern exhibitions had sought to leave behind but into which, as Walter Benjamin insisted, the unredeemed, failed material of the capitalist age must inexorably fall back. The contrast between the weighty catalogue—"two volumes, each of which weighs six kilos, imagine!"—useless precisely because it faithfully replicates the limitless array of objects at the exhibition, and the inability to narrate, to *chronicle*, the show, is also the critical edge of Junio's review. Dispatched to inform his readers about an exhibition of national history, the reporter comes up against the incompatibility between his writing and that which he is invited to see, in other words, his incapacity to *historicize the exhibition*. In fact, his review can be read as a subtle critique of the archive from the point of view of narrative; an ironic, prescient demonstration of the contradictions implied in the late nineteenth-century collectionism of national pasts. The question Junio poses is about the relation between memory and the exhibition; about the manufacture of amnesia through antiquarianism and archiving; about the loss of the past precisely when it is taken as a possession.

Fortunately for us, though, Junio returned to the exhibition the next day, considering it his duty to leave his readers with more tangible impressions and thus allowing us in turn to gain an impression of the order of display, even though, Junio announced, "this time I was committed not to continue beyond a single showroom, which is the only way to see something." What Junio saw in the Sala Pedro II were mainly portraits and busts of the two emperors and their families, as well as of some of the major politicians and writers of Imperial Brazil (Gonçalves Dias, José Clemente, José Bonifácio), historical paintings such as Víctor Meirelles's already canonical *Primeira missa no Brazil* (1860), and prints by Debret representing views of the port city on the occasion of the arrival of princess Carolina Leopoldina, Pedro the First's wife. As a reencounter with the dynastic iconography of the Imperial state, offered as history and to history, the exhibition consecrated a set of faces, poses, and landscapes from the previous half-century as already pertaining to history's domain, as well as indicating the detached point of view from which to behold a self-enclosed past.

For, indeed, the exhibition proposed an itinerary that, while reaching far beyond the short history of the Brazilian Empire, was modelled not so much on the organized path through chronological time of the museum of natural evolution as on the simultaneity of commodities at the industrial fair. Objects were divided into sections (literary, artistic) and classes, each of them in turn divided into several layers of sub-rubrics. The exhibition thus constructed a spatial image of historical time, modelled precisely on the geographical space it posited on the other end of history proper. Geography formed the "Classe I" of the subsection "Preliminares," further divided into: (1) general geography; (2) rivers; (3) coast and ports; (4) provincial geographies; (5) itineraries; (6) travel, with subclasses (a) general collections, and (b) particular journeys in chronological order; and (7) geographical, hydrographical, and topographical maps, subdivided into (a) general maps and atlases, (b) partial maps, (c) coastal maps, (d) fluvial maps in alphabetical order, (e) borders, subdivided as (i) general maps, (ii) particular maps (northern borders, western borders, southern borders), and (f) provincial maps.[6] The same pattern of classes, subclasses, and sub-subclasses applied to the section on Brazilian history (actually the second subsection of the exhibition's literary section), subdivided into classes of civil, administrative, ecclesiastical, constitutional, diplomatic, and military history, natural history, history of literature and the arts, economic history, biography, and history of currency. The artistic section contained the following classes: views, landscapes, and port scenes; history (subdivided chronologically into six subclasses and another one of portraits); social types, customs, and dress; geneology and heraldry; portraits, statues, and busts; and natural history.

A mania of classification, indeed—and we have only mentioned the principal classes without entering the intricate web of subsections and subclasses, with their particular combinations of chronological and categorial names—which in its ramifications, juxtapositions, and internal contradictions recalls the labyrinthine architecture of Borges's Library of Babel. The association is not altogether haphazard, for in fact, as in Borges's fictions, the logic of the display juxtaposed on one and the same plane the spatial orders of the exhibition and that of the archive, and both of these with the sequential one of the catalogue. That is, it attempted to make coincide, in one and the same representation, an architectural and epistemological space of storage with one of monumental exposure. On the level of writing, this coincidence was both duplicated and completed by the one between the catalogue, the serialized inventory of the past, and the sequential historical narrative it both presupposed and promised. Organized on the initiative of the library's director, Benjamin Franklin Ramiz Galvão, the Exhibition of Brazilian History was a spectacular experiment on and with the past, an experiment in specularizing the archive and in archiving the spectacle, so as to bring history itself into the form of an event that would produce, in the same breath, a definite closure and a radical opening.

Ramiz Galvão (1846–1938) had participated as a military surgeon in the Paraguayan War before being appointed professor at the Colégio Pedro II on his return to Rio de Janeiro. Soon afterwards he was appointed to direct the National Library, where he initiated the series *Annaes da Biblioteca Nacional*. A friend of Benjamin Constant Botelho de Magalhães, minister of public education after the republican coup of 1889, he was named director of primary and secondary education of the federal capital in 1890, a post he would occupy once again in 1912, the year in which he also became an orator at the Instituto Histórico e Geográfico Brasileiro, of which he had been a member since 1872. In 1922, he organized a *Dicionário Histórico e Geográfico Brasileiro* on occasion of the centenary of independence, and in 1928 he was elected a member of the Academia Brasileira de Letras.

In his annual report of 1874, four years after his appointment as director, Ramiz Galvão had already called attention to the existence among the library's possessions of "a very rich and numerous collection of prints from all the schools and by the most famous masters of the craft," and the need to think about ways of "recovering from the dust of oblivion those most valuable collections of rare prints" (fig. 25).[7] Seven years later, having served, in the meantime, as coordinator and juror at several national exhibitions, Ramiz Galvão had come up with

FIGURE 25. Antônio Luiz Ferreira, The section of prints at the National Library of Rio de Janeiro. Albumin print (1902). Biblioteca Nacional Brasileira, Rio de Janeiro.

the form of a great historical show modelled on the universal exhibitions. In the course of the show speeches on historical subjects would be given, books and papers on historical subjects presented, and prizes and medals awarded. An invitation was circulated to provincial governments and municipal councils in January 1881 requesting the submission of relevant material (books, documents, maps, paintings, prints, statues, and so on). Shipments of memorabilia were subsequently received from Pará, Pernambuco, Bahia, Rio de Janeiro, and Minas Gerais, while the thriving immigrant states of the south, despite the strong presence of southern themes at the exhibition, appear to have ignored the call. Emperor Pedro II put his personal library at the Paço Imperial square (which was opened to the public for the duration of the event) at Ramiz Galvão's disposal.

The exhibition was inaugurated on December 2, the Emperor's birthday, and continued until January 2, 1882. It took up almost the entire space of the library, whose reading rooms were baptised for the occasion with the names of the patron saints of national historiography (Francisco Adolfo Varnhagen, the geographer Manoel Ayres de Casal, the chronicler Balthasar da Silva Lisboa, and the naturalist José Mariano da Conceição Velloso). Library services for readers were suspended. Not content with exhibiting the visual treasures he had "discovered," Ramiz Galvão had seized the occasion to attempt something far more ambitious, namely, to turn the entire library into an exhibition. "History," at the Exposição de História do Brasil, was the becoming-exhibition of the archive. A documentary corpus originally destined for the deciphering gaze of readers who would arrange it into threads of documents, series, and narratives was now being arranged for the visual purchase of a beholder. As visual object, the archive was supposed to have encountered its definite, ultimate form. At the same time, the model of the industry fair allowed the presentation of this "objective" arrangement of the past as the state of the art, a preliminary balance in the great march of progress, and thus as a point of departure rather than an ending. "A resurrection of the past and a preview of the future," as Ramiz Galvão put it in his opening speech, the exhibition was also a self-celebration of historiography as the progressive self-fashioning of a national consciousness:

Sir, the idea that generated this solemn event was a highly patriotic one, but the Brazilians who designed and realized it, albeit in modest proportions, had something bigger in mind than merely to render a deservedly exalted homage to the Fatherland. For the first time in America, and perhaps in the entire world, a group of workers have put together an exhibition of everything concerning the national history, offering their fellow citizens in one single and large picture, a rich source of study of what has been, and a warm encouragement for what is yet to come. […] A people without a history is a passing shadow, not a lasting trace; it is a confused multitude, [...] not a compact, invincible regiment [...]; it is a doubt, not a sociological fact; a vague sketch, not an immortal canvas. Let us welcome, then, the splendid light of historical writings, which are preparing and ensuring the glorification of the future by evoking the past![8]

History, then, was at once an object and a process, the production of the "workers" whose labor in and with the archive ensured the survival of the collective ("the people"), always under the threat of dispersion that comes with oblivion. Ramiz Galvão had planned to accompany the event with a series of public speeches on historical topics, the selection of which was entrusted to a commission of thirty notables including Ladislau Netto, Machado de Assis, and Víctor Meirelles. The commission would also serve as jury to award prizes for best essay in various categories; a call for papers was circulated, in an edition of one thousand copies, among the Empire's foremost men of letters. A second series of speeches would be held, according to Ramiz Galvão's plans, three years after the event, so as to register its impact on the progress of historical research in Brazil. As the inauguration approached, however, the small number of submissions received forced Ramiz Galvão to suspend the entire program until the publication of the exhibition catalogue, with its indications of hitherto unknown sources, would have sufficiently stimulated historiographic production, as he explained in a letter to the government. Published in two tomes as volume 9 of the *Annaes da Bibliotheca Nacional*, with a supplementary volume following in 1883, the catalogue listed 20,337 exhibits on a total of 1,758 pages.

Ramiz Galvão's expectations were further frustrated, however, by the rather reserved public response to his pet project. The number of visitors only amounted to a modest total of 7,601, whereas the National Exhibition of 1873 had attracted 8,500 visitors in a single day (the total number of visitors at the national exhibitions of the 1870s, usually open for two months, varied between 40,000 and 80,000).[9] In the press, the exhibition was widely criticized for the confusing, incomprehensible order of display, increased by the disparities between the catalogue (which in any case it was impossible to bring along because of its bulkiness) and the material distribution of exhibits, which featured only a selection of the objects listed. Unfortunately for Ramiz Galvão, the show happened to coincide with the first Brazilian Industrial Exhibition, held at the neighboring Ministry of Agriculture in order to select materials for display at Buenos Aires' Continental Exhibition the following year. The comparison drawn by observers between the two events was usually unfavorable to the National Library exhibition: commentators such as the implacable Angelo Agostini of the *Revista Illustrada* or Félix Ferreira of *O Cruzeiro* contrasted the vigorous modernism of the industrial fair with the bookish and outdated vision of an imperial state whose very anachronism was underscored by the history show's fixation with a pompous dynastic past.

If historical debates from around 1870, following the interventions of a new generation of intellectuals such as Sílvio Romero and Capistrano de Abreu (who was among Ramiz Galvão's collaborators in preparing the 1881 exhibition), had shifted from the emergence and consolidation of the imperial state towards the question of the sociocultural and "racial" process of the formation of a people, the Exhibition of Brazilian History only included an oblique reference to the issue under subsection 9 (*elemento servil*, "the servant class") of class 12 (economic history), ranking below items such as roads and navigation, telegraphs and postal services; charitable institutions, societies, masonry; or penitentiaries. Like the Anthropological Exhibition half a year later, the National Library's show of Brazilian history at once disavowed and revealed what had been its condition of possibility in the present, namely, the apogee of the Imperial state. In the very gesture that had been intended as a monumental confirmation of its success, the exhibition forespelled the final crisis of the Imperial state. What had been intended as a source of permanence turned out to be the most acute sign of transience.

Ironically, the catalogue of the show was displayed at Buenos Aires's Continental Exhibition a year later, where it promptly received the grand prize. Ernesto Quesada, writing on the Argentine Historical Museum in 1900, praised the Brazilian exhibition as a model for the arrangement of national history displays in the Americas, contrasting it favorably to the cluster of material at the Argentine museum while lamenting the ephemeral nature of the Brazilian event:

No country in America [...] has surpassed Brazil in that most noble task of reconstructing the past: the only regret is that it has been a passing effort, since all the collections required to celebrate a model exhibition of history were assembled in 1881 in Rio de Janeiro, but thereafter these treasures became dispersed again. The only lasting remainder of this effort is an impressive catalogue in whose two heavy volumes an abundance of sources for all kinds of investigations can be found. [...] And all this material is admirably and methodically classified.[10]

Ramiz Galvão, however, frustrated by the public disapproval of his project, had resigned from his post as director of the National Library in July 1882. The project of a permanent exhibition of Brazilian history would only be taken up again in 1922, on the occasion of the centenary of independence, with the foundation of the Museu Histórico Nacional. A small historical collection was already kept for the exclusive use of its members on the premises of the Instituto

Histórico e Geográfico Brasileiro, first mentioned in 1850 in the annual report of secretary Joaquim Manuel de Macedo. In 1883, Joaquim Pires Machado Portella, director of the National Archive, had created the Museu Histórico do Arquivo Nacional, containing mostly numismatic materials and written documents. In 1917, the annual report of director Luiz Gastão Escragnolle Dória announced the comprehensive reorganization of the museum, whose collections in 1922 would become the core of the new Museu Histórico Nacional. Installed in old colonial quarters restored in neocolonial style (the former Casa do Trem e Arsenal), the new museum would be directed by Gustavo Barroso from 1922 and 1930, and after 1933 onward, managed in the interim by Rodolfo Garcia.[11]

## The Truth of Time

Three years before the Brazilian Historical Exhibition, an attempt to recollect and expose the national past had already been made in Buenos Aires. Andrés Lamas, the Uruguayan polymath and collector, resident in the country since 1863, was showing a selection of his "antiquities'" at the Exhibition of the Charitable Ladies, one of the main social events of the season inaugurated on October 6, 1878, in the upper galleries of the Teatro de la Ópera. A veteran journalist and political agitator during the time of Rosas, Lamas (1817–91) had founded the short-lived, Montevideo-based Historical-Geographical Institute of the River Plate in 1843 and compiled an (unpublished) geographical and historical dictionary of the region. After brief stays in Uruguayan government in 1872 and 1875, he moved definitively to Buenos Aires, where he dedicated himself to historical research and writing, including studies on the May Revolution, the life of Rivadavia, and the roots of the Latin American independence movement. Lamas's importance in the final decades of the century, however, lay chiefly in his role as a collector and archivist, keeping in his home on Calle Piedad (today's Bartolomé Mitre) a vast collection of memorabilia, artworks, numismatica, and historical documents, dispersed after his death through public auction.

The show at the Teatro de la Ópera featured a small number of "American antiquities," principally Peruvian pottery and Brazilian feather garments and collars. The section of Argentine antiquities had been restricted to seven copper and stone figurines, since, as Lamas argued in the catalogue, the parallel exhibition of Estanislao Zeballos's anthropological collection, later to be donated to the La Plata museum, would have made redundant a greater number of objects. An equally small section on the "era of discovery" contained miniature portraits of Columbus, Vespucci, and the Catholic Kings in marble, gold, and silver; a section on the colonial era actually comprised mostly objects wrested from the last viceroys and colonial bureaucracy immediately before independence, as well as trophies from the time of the British invasions. The subsequent section on the Rosas period—by far the largest, with sixty-one objects in total—contained portraits of the dictator and most of his pantheon of relatives and dignitaries, weapons and torture instruments belonging to Rosas's secret police, the Mazorca, and all kinds of federalist devotionalia. Exhibits from the Paraguayan War (the second largest section, with forty-three objects) included trophies conquered from the enemy forces as well as seals, medals, coins, and other symbols of Solano López's government ransacked by the occupying troops. Throughout the exhibition, portraits of colonial governors and other historical personalities, as well as a small collection of colonial furniture, flanked the showcases.[12]

A year later, as vice president of the organizing committee of the Continental Exhibition (by then still planned for 1880, but eventually postponed to 1882 due to the three-month civil war over the presidential succession), Lamas drafted a proposal for another historical show to be held on the exhibition's premises. This time, the history show would contain mainly items from the independence struggles, a period completely absent from the 1878 exhibition. Thus Lamas suggested requesting from government agencies and from private lenders the uniforms and coats of arms of the regiments that had defended the city of Buenos Aires against the British; the famous Oruro shield and garland of Potosí, given to general Manuel Belgrano by local residents to celebrate his victories over the Spaniards; flags of the patriotic armies; and facsimiles of the declaration of independence and the manuscript of the national anthem. "In such an exhibition," he wrote, "what most immediately represents the glories of the country must take first place, and an attempt should be made to gather the greatest possible number of objects; secondly, the exhibition must be designed with the utmost decorum."[13] In the long term, he continued, "to gather in one place all those precious objects now dispersed over the entire territory, and in some parts—as is the case in this very capital—out of the milieu in which they belong, would be to avoid more painful losses and to acquire the fundamental base for a national institution dedicated to preserving them with the veneration they deserve."

Something, then, had changed between 1878 and 1879, not merely regarding the topics and periods represented in the display but also regarding the values associated with them and the attitudes with which they were supposed to be contemplated. There had been a change, in short, of the relations between present and past as manifested in the encounter between material remnants and the gaze of a beholder. The past had changed from a foreign place into a refuge of the self. The objects gathered in the 1878 exhibition still commanded the bewilderment and awe of a beholder who would thus establish her own fundamental difference and distance with respect to them. The project of 1879, in contrast, sought to represent to the empathic gaze of the present the remainders of a past that, despite its increasing retreat into time, had to be kept near and dear to its beholder, who was supposed to recognize in them her own image. If the exhibition of 1878 had been focused on trophies wrested from defeated enemies (Rosas, Solano López, the Spaniards, the Indians), this was because the past was, literally, a foreign country: a hostile, and inhospitable, "other time." To exhibit history was to confirm its pastness and to exorcise its spell over the present. As a trophy, the historical object celebrated and confirmed the triumph of the present, its liberation from history. Initially a revolutionary mode of historical display, which had its origins in the French Revolution's public exhibition of the spoils wrested from the aristocracy, this aesthetic of confrontation that depicted even the immediate past as freakish and distant was used in the second half of the century by Argentine liberal historians to vilify the populist regime of Juan Manuel de Rosas and the "anarchy" of the federalist caudillos. At the turn of the century, this tendency would culminate in the political gothic of Adolfo Saldías's *Historia de la Confederación Argentina* (1888/92) or in Lucio V. Mansilla's and José María Ramos Mejía's mass-psychological speculations on the forms of mental contagion and collective neurosis during Rosas's dictatorship.

Lamas's project of 1879, by contrast, acknowledged the need to resignify the past as an affective resource and a repository of the fundamental values on which national society was supposedly grounded: a patrimony, a heritage to be protected, revered, and preserved by the community of sons and daughters. Yet at the same time, this new, devotional attitude towards the past also reinscribed elements of the previous exorcising ritual, since to exhibit history still implied containing and pacifying the epic turmoil of foundation it both invoked and, literally, put to rest. As Nicolás Avellaneda, ex-president and honorary chairman of the show put it in his opening speech in 1882: "The people of San Martín have become the people of the first Continental Exhibition."[14]

By the time the Continental Exhibition opened its doors, however, Lamas's initial sketch for the historical section had undergone several modifications, first by Lamas himself, who, in a letter of February 22, 1882, had requested from the provincial government of Buenos Aires a series of items representing not only the struggles of independence but also the colonial era and the Paraguayan War of 1865–70, thus notably extending the initial scope of the project and reintroducing into it elements from the previous, confrontational pattern of display employed at the exhibition of 1878. Following complaints from the organizing committee of the Continental Exhibition, concerned that references to military confrontations with neighboring countries might offend prospective exhibitors, a commission chaired by Lamas and integrated by Manuel Ricardo Trelles (ex-secretary of the Museo Público), Angel Justiniano Carranza (with Lamas, the most important collector of national antiques), and Estanislao Zeballos (founder and ex-president of the Sociedad Científica and the Instituto Geográfico Argentino), among others, finally agreed on a display focused on the development of science, arts and crafts, and the printing press: a history more in tune with the general character of the event. The show was divided into eight sections and several subsections (archaeology, painting and sculpture, manuscripts, typography, historical geography, and numismatics).

Rather than a radical change in Lamas's conception of national history, then, the shift in the selection of objects between the exhibitions of 1878 and 1882 expressed a more general ambiguity. In fact, the ebullient triumphalism with which the Creole establishment welcomed President Roca's regime of "peace and administration" as a definite break with the past and as the successful arrival in modernity sat uncomfortably alongside the new concern with preserving the national memory. Historiography, in fact, became the arena in which a new discourse of cultural conservatism was beginning to take shape, mobilizing the weight of tradition to limit the social effects of the transformations in production, infrastructure, and the demographic composition of society following spectacular rises in immigration. Those who perceived modernity at once as a promise and as a threat, José Luis Romero argues, "are the ones who have a tradition, considerable economic interests, a common mode of life, and, above all, a profound belief in being the legitimate historical heirs of those who had laid out the foundations" of the nation.[15] The unshaken faith in the unfolding of the liberal state that had still underpinned the work of Bartolomé Mitre was now giving way to an anxiety about the decadence of the ancient virtues, along with a nostalgic longing for the still recent but already incommensurably distant past that expressed, as Oscar Terán suggests, a crisis of legitimacy. The 1880s, he argues, saw a gradual replacement of liberal Romanticism's "imitative and universalist nationalism" by "one of a diacritical, essentialist and culturalist nature."[16] Federico Tobar, on reviewing a key work of the new conservative historiography, Vicente Fidel López's La Revolución Argentina (1889), formulated one of the most radical versions of this programmatic break with the old liberal program of "populating the desert": "Those who, like the illustrious Sarmiento, have proclaimed, in their theories rather than by their own example, an aberration as singular and harmful as this one, have forgotten history's secular lessons in the evolution and development of nations. These misgivings have spoiled the purity of our national sense of judgment and our American ideal, morally and economically hindered our development, inserting into our organism repulsive elements that slowly tear it apart."[17]

Even Sarmiento himself, however, who in 1845 had still identified the "evil of extent" to be Argentina's principal and all-encompassing problem, would now confess to a feeling of claustrophobia in a city "overflowing" with multitudes from overseas: "When we see thousands arriving day by day, everyone feels the discomfort of the situation, like a threat of suffocation, as if the air and space were lacking for masses like these."[18] In a city whose streets, Estanislao Zeballos exclaimed in congress in 1887, were increasingly becoming colored in the banners of foreign countries, forging a sense of national belonging had become a question of ensuring public order. But if, as Lucio V. López, minister of the interior and the son of historian Vicente Fidel put it in a speech at the Faculty of Law's graduation ceremony of 1890, "to return to the past means to reread our history, […] to demolish cosmopolitanism and to trace once and for all and with a firm hand, the definite shape of our Fatherland,"[19] the challenge lay in transforming into a source of popular patriotic sentiment the very process of constructing the liberal state—that is, the subjugation and extirpation of native and popular forms of social practice. In other words, the "spiritual essence" to be imposed on the newly arrived residents from overseas was the very same "Creole way of life" these same immigrants had been called to make redundant. As Lilia Ana Bertoni points out, towards the end of the decade, in the discourse of the Creole elite "the image of the hard-working and vigorous immigrant, the decisive agent of the transformation of reality, was being seen in a more critical light, relativized and even associated with negative implications."[20] In 1888, future president Roque Saenz Peña, at the South American Congress of International Civil Law, invoked the right of the South American republics to "select from the anonymous mass" of immigrants those "elements" beneficial to their own progress. The year after, *El Diario* recommended the immediate deportation of Russian Jews who had arrived aboard the steamer *Welser*, given their innate tendency towards vagrancy, vice, and prostitution. In 1899, on the initiative of Miguel Cané, founder and first dean of the Faculty of Philosophy and Letters, congress passed the so-called Residence Law allowing federal government to deport convicts and politically undesirable immigrants alike.

The turn (or return) towards a presumably homogeneous Creole past prior to the emergence of a mass society implied at one and the same time the search for new pedagogical contents to which to submit the increasingly heterogeneous and dangerously volatile populace, and a desire to withdraw from the complexities of the present into the safe haven of an imaginary harmony. History provided a spiritual refuge where the troubled patrician mind could forget about the ills of the street and the marketplace. Here, in history, was the longed-for place where, as Cané put it, the sons and grandsons of the founding fathers could exchange the material splendors of their own fin de siècle for the harmonious, rustic simplicity of old:

Where, where have those old, faithful servants gone that I saw in my parents' house during my first years? Where are those freed slaves who would treat us like little princes; where their sons, born as free men and raised side by side with ourselves, companions of childhood games, their lives laid out before them with nothing to worry about but to serve well and faithfully? The movement of ideas, the influence of the cities, the flow of fortunes and the vanishing of the old, solid homes, have changed all that. Today, we are served by a European butler who steals from us, is better dressed than we are, and reminds us of his status as a free man whenever he receives a stern gaze.[21]

But if, for Cané and his generation, the time of their own childhood after Caseros—the already remote past of the *gran aldea*, the big village, as the title of Lucio V. López's novel put it—could become an object of nostalgia, cultivated in tender anecdotes, souvenirs, and curiosities, the past that was being offered up to old and new citizens as an object of devotion and reverence was the time of independence. Though only marginally further removed in time, this epic of foundation had already attained the dimensions of myth. Following the educational reform of 1884, the ratio of hours in the middle school curriculum dedicated to history at large and to Argentine and American history was inverted in favor of the latter. In 1874, eight hours per week were being dedicated to world history and four hours to national and South American history; in 1893, the former had been reduced to four hours and the latter extended to eight and a half hours.[22] After 1881, the May celebrations of independence, traditionally a popular feast with bonfires and public games, were seized by the national government and turned into military parades. A particular success was the formation of battalions of children who, dressed up in uniforms emulating those of the federal army, would march onto the Plaza de Mayo and intone the national anthem.

The new central square had also been the object, in 1884, of a major controversy among members of the lettered elite about the ways to remember the heroic past, and about the relations between modernity, monumentality, and heritage in the rapidly changing urban space of the capital. In the context of ambitious urban reforms, Torcuato de Alvear, the modernist mayor, had already started to modify the city's central public space by razing the colonial archway that had separated the Plaza de la Victoria from the Plaza 25 de Mayo to create one single, monumental square between the municipal *cabildo* (town hall) and federal government's Casa Rosada: an empty space of power commanding the humility of passersby and an ideal stage for mass gatherings and parades: the symbolic and ritual center of a thriving nation-state (fig. 26).

FIGURE 26. Anonymous, Plaza de la Victoria (today Plaza de Mayo). Photographic print from *Album de vistas y costumbres de Buenos Aires y de la República Argentina* (Buenos Aires: Guillermo Kraft / Engelbert, Hert & Cia., 1889). Museo Mitre, Buenos Aires.

Alvear's original plans had also foreseen the replacement of the original independence monument, erected in 1811 and modified by Pridiliano Pueyrredón in the 1850s, by a more contemporary and "tasteful" memorial; a plan that was eventually dropped after a poll of historians, archivists, and antiquarians had revealed widespread opposition. The debate, whose principal contributions were reprinted in the *Revista Nacional* (the journal edited by Adolfo P. Carranza, future director of the National Historical Museum), provides an important insight into the conceptions of historicity and monumentality held by different sectors of the Creole elite. The decisive piece was a long essay by Andrés Lamas insisting on the patriotic duty to preserve the original monument and offering, en route, an ad hoc theory of monumentality. It is here, I suggest, that we have to look for the rationale that underpinned not only Lamas's exhibition projects of the late 1870s and early 1880s but also the Historical Museum founded in 1889.

The independence memorial, or Pirámide de Mayo, originally installed on the first anniversary of the insurgency against the colonial authorities in Buenos Aires but subsequently altered after the overthrow of Rosas, posed questions not only of authenticity versus representation, but also about the present's relation with its various pasts, and about the ways of unmaking previous acts of forgetting without endangering the possibility of reinstating an increasingly distant and fragile core of values the monument was supposed to emblematize. If the present monument was in fact but a modified version of the original, was it not the duty of the present to restore its ancient meaning, precisely by rebuilding it wholesale and within the architectural context of the new square that signified the fulfillment of the dream of 1810? This was the position of the modernizing faction integrated by Bartolomé Mitre, Vicente Fidel López, Angel Justiniano Carranza, Manuel Ricardo Trelles, and Domingo Faustino Sarmiento, who, in his response to the survey, compared the relation between the new monument and the original to that between a funerary urn and the ashes it contained. Updating the outer casket, the reliquary, he argued, would not alter the essence it carried, and the sacredness it bestowed on the ritual meeting place of the nation, as long as the original bricks of 1810 were used as foundation for the new monument:

[N]o national tradition is violated by removing the dead pyramid's ashes to the mausoleum that is being prepared for them, situated where the widening of the square requires it [...], as long as the bricks (the genuine ones) enclosed by the new layers of plaster and marble are used for its foundations. We are not entitled, in a city as refined as this one, to build in 1883 cardboard simulacra instead of monuments, nor to leave to posterity constructions that, while lacking the merit of antiquity, are in breach of the immutable laws of the plastic arts, dedicated to the cult of Glory and of Divinity.[23]

Sarmiento and his fellow modernizers brought into play the monument's responsibility not only vis-à-vis the past but also the future. As part of the new design of the square, it would turn into a memorial not just of the revolutionary decade of 1810 but also of the 1880s as the definitive, triumphant closure of state formation. In this light, preserving the Pueyrredón version of the 1850s would have been aesthetically and politically incongruous, as it would have enshrined a precocious, false point of arrival. In López's words,

to pretend to preserve today this pyramid, altered and deformed as it is by ridiculous accessories of later, much later fabrication, would be to respect the ephemeral and unauthorized fancy of posterity, rather than the aspirations, the decrees and the laws of those who had been authors of the great act which they themselves ordered to commemorate. [...] But since the new monument will be embellished by the extension and adornments applied to this very square, by no means will it offend the nature of the *sacred terrain* that was the theater and cradle of our republican history. On the contrary, this same, beautified soil will transmit in artistic and grandiose forms the progress of our culture, and it will be a testimony of the results achieved by the events it commemorates, that is, a vivid image of the justice and benefits brought about by the May revolution.[24]

Interestingly enough, it was Trelles and Carranza, both collectors of national antiques, who went furthest in their support for the monument's replacement, arguing that, even if the pyramid had been the original one (which it was not) it would not have been worth preserving since, in its humbleness, it would have transmitted an erroneous image of the revolution's greatness and glory. Thus, argued Trelles, "if, to show our respect for their antiquity or for the memory of our founding fathers, we had preserved our primitive churches with their earthen walls and their straw or tile roofs, rather than replacing them with the present constructions, we would give an improper idea of Christian civilization."[25] The truth of the past, Trelles and Carranza suggested, was a question of perspective, therefore as it faded into the distance its image had to be constantly refashioned according to the proportions and standards of the viewer's own present: "The more grandiose a monument, the greater the cult it inspires," as Carranza pragmatically put it.[26]

Despite minor differences, then, the modernizers agreed about the irrefutable nature of progress and, hence, the right and duty of the present to remake the leftovers of the past according to its own scale and forms. Archival rather than antiquarian in character, their position emphasized the simultaneously preservational *and* constituent character of any public enshrinement of the past, the fact that, as Derrida puts it, "archivization produces as much as it records the event."[27] Precisely in order to return to the past its true spiritual dimension, they suggested, its modest material remains had to be removed, or at least hidden from view.

By contrast, the conservative or antiquarian faction, unable to share their opponents' unambiguous faith in history's successful culmination in the present, worried about the "spiritual decay" provoked by relentless materialism and expressed in the false, self-indulgent pomp of the modernized city: "Our traditional historical monuments are disappearing," warned Lamas, "perhaps because we have not yet become conscious of the importance of historical filiation."[28] On the moderate end, José Manuel Estrada and Nicolás Avellaneda recommended preserving the old pyramid on the grounds of its authenticity, insisting on the categorical difference between artistic and historic monuments and that the latter could not be judged on the criteria of the former. The substance of the historic monument was not beauty but time, which a new monument, for all its merits, could never reinstate. More categorically, Miguel Esteves Sagui declared: "A monument contemporary to the events themselves cannot be made redundant [*subrogado*]."[29] In openly moral terms, Esteves Sagui contrasted the elders' virtuous poverty with the ostentatious but spiritually impoverished present, where the "religion of the Fatherland" was dying out under the nefarious impact of positivism and the "idols" of other nations were replacing people's allegiance to their native Argentine soil.

In a less alarmist mode, but nonetheless profoundly skeptical about the achievements that supposedly entitled the present to reconstruct the work of the past, Andrés Lamas agreed with Avellaneda on the distinctiveness of the historical monument singled out precisely on account of its inalterability. Its sole function was to remain; therefore, even the slightest modification betrayed its very essence, its pure pastness. Having time itself as its substance, the historical monument was by nature irreplaceable. It could not be disputed in the way it represented the past, for it only did so inasmuch as it was of the same time as that which it commemorated, as it was *out of its time*. Hence, the historical monument represented, in the present, the truth of its time, *the truth of time*, which it preserved in its materiality:

the monument represents *the truth of its time*. Under every aspect one considers it— socially, politically, morally—the representation of truth is what constitutes the authority and usefulness of historical monuments. […] You can erect the most magnificent monument as a substitute for the modest one our glorious ancestors have left us; but neither today nor ever will it be the May Monument, because it will not be the one the May insurgents have built, because it will not represent the ideas, nor the resources, nor the art of the time in which it was built. The richer, the more artistic the new monument, the less will it be the monument of the May insurgents.[30]

As a collector rather than a historian, Lamas not only posited an ontological difference between the historical object and the discourse of historiography or between representation and the materiality of the remainder, but even came close to questioning the very possibility of apprehending the past. Monumentality, for him, is the incommensurability of the past that both demands and refutes supplementation. Ultimately, against the mute self-sameness of the material remainder—the *ruin*—every historical narrative is a priori condemned to the status of fiction. Curiously, however, his insistence on the prevalence of the material, tactile dimension of the historical object's presence over its character as a sign, drove Lamas to the most radical conclusion of all those polled, denying altogether the possibility of exhibiting history. Instead of demolishing the monument, he proposed, it should be stripped of its later alterations and enclosed in a bronze or iron casket—a coffin—only to be opened on ritual occasions such as independence celebrations. The only way to preserve the purity of the past, he seemed to suggest, was to shelter it from the eyes of posterity, to put it to rest, indeed, to bury it.

## The Armies of the Dead

Every weekend, the Calle Defensa in the neighborhood of San Telmo turns into the Paseo del Anticuario: street musicians and artisans of various crafts line up with human statues and tango couples, while legions of tourists from overseas are invited by the local merchants to exchange their precious euros, dollars, and yen for the material leftovers of the Argentine bourgeoisie's moment of splendor, shipment costs and customs duties included. Yet while the spread of this anti-quarianism for export, which has turned the once derelict quarter into a tourist hotspot, ironically confirms the definite, irrevocable end of the liberal cycle nostalgically evoked by gentrified urban reconstruction, few visitors dare to venture on into the orange palazzo beyond Avenida Brasil that houses the National Historical Museum. Founded in 1889 and inaugurated the year after, the museum bravely attempts to compete with its wealthier neighbors, the antiquarians, holding fast, in its ramshackle display of dusty portraits, moth-eaten uniforms, weaponry, and period furniture once belonging to some famous founding father, to an image of national grandeur that has long turned into an oddity, an anachronism, indeed into *Urgeschichte* in its properly Benjaminian sense: a vision, not so much of the nineteenth century, to which the entire exhibition remains confined, but of the phantasmic anticipation of a twentieth century that never occurred. No mention, for sure, of speeches from the balcony and feet in the fountain, of torture chambers, clandestine obstetric wards, and bodies thrown from airplanes. On entering the *Quinta de Lezama* building, on the edge of the park of the same name that separates San Telmo from the popular quarters of Barracas and La Boca, one moves forth into the false eternity of a bygone present's ephemeral attempt to project itself into the future by way of the commemoration and enshrinement of a particular image of the past, presented as final, beyond appeal, at one with itself.

Yet, I will argue, already at the time of its foundation the museum had been haunted by the same anxiety about the irrecoverability of the past it was attempting to salvage as Lamas's proposal for the independence memorial had been a few years earlier. Not content with being merely a site for the storage and display of objects of memory, the museum actively tried to forge a public culture of remembrance, promoting the repatriation of the remains of national "founding fathers" who had died in exile, or organizing the centenary celebrations of their birthdays. Where possible, these rituals of memory would include transferring their remains to their native provinces, as well as installing plaques and medals on their graves and homes, and publishing short biographical sketches in the press. Reproductions of the portraits of San Martín, Rodríguez Peña, and the

Junta of 1810 from the museum's own collection were printed in editions of up to 20,000 copies and distributed among schools and state institutions, or handed out to visitors on public holidays. On the initiative of museum director Adolfo P. Carranza, minor towns of the interior were renamed in memory of "great Argentines."[31] Under Carranza's supervision, too, four profusely illustrated volumes of the journal *El Museo Histórico* were published, containing short notes on items from the collection, as well as reports on the museum's proceedings and acquisitions. Carranza also published three volumes of *Memoirs and Autobiographies* and another two dedicated to the participation of ordained priests in the May revolution. In 1908, in the wake of the national centenary celebrations, a new journal particularly designed for use in the school classroom, *La Ilustración Histórica*, was launched; and booklets on, among many other topics, names of streets and squares in Buenos Aires, "Notables of Independence," "Traditions and Legends," "Great Citizens," and "Patrician Ladies of Argentina," were published by the museum on request from state institutions and private societies. From 1903, Carranza also supervised the distribution of commemorative plaques in the capital and advised artists employed to produce material for the centenary exhibition of 1910 on historical subjects. Where objects to commemorate past occasions and protagonists were lacking, the museum itself commissioned them, rescuing history from the invisible, as in the case of José Bouchet's *First Holy Mass at Buenos Aires*, a painting acquired in 1909 to commemorate the arrival of the Spaniards.[32] Yet this restless, almost hyperkinetic collection, production, and diffusion of historical imagery on behalf of the museum was underpinned by an anxiety of salvaging a memory always already verging on oblivion. The museum, in short, sought to construct a public refuge for a mnemonic material no longer shared by all: to build a home for history when it was threatening to move on.

The museum was particularly keen on attracting school pupils, following suggestions made by the National Education Council that children should be used as catalysts for the spread of national values among the populace and especially the immigrant population. As Carranza explained in a letter to the head of the council, Pedro Reyna, in 1895, "the museum was founded with a view to its usefulness, principally, for initiating children in the love of our Founding Fathers and in the knowledge of the past by way of portraits and objects." He offered to reserve opening times on certain days for school excursions, such that the youngsters could "visit and learn about the portraits and objects that guard so many lessons for them, when they study the Argentine past at an age when impressions engrave themselves so profoundly in the mind."[33] The still receptive child was the prototype of an ideal visitor figured as a blank mind into which the museum would perform its inscriptions, through the arrangement of objects that the eyes would translate into ideas. "The sensible objects such as statues, paintings, prints, weapons, instruments and other archaeological pieces," the teachers' journal *El Monitor* opined in 1890 on the occasion of the museum's inauguration, "due to their animation and liveliness, contribute admirably in providing [children] with clear and lasting impressions of historical facts and to associate their ideas with characteristics that can never be erased."[34]

To find a home for history, however, was a more daunting task than might have been expected. If the museum institution, in its natural science or anthropological version, had thus far served as an instrument of visual and epistemological possession of an object-world thus constructed as internal otherness, to found a museum dedicated to the historical origins of the nation-self meant to virtually reinvent the museum form, turning it into a space of singularity rather than of classification, a space in which to unfold the irreducible rather than the exemplary. This different material rhetoric called forth a gaze of nostalgic empathy rather than studious detachment; it invested the body of the spectator not so much as a progressive subject forging herself on the evolutionary path laid out for her by the museum apparatus, but rather as one that acquired her modernity as a gift bestowed by the past, whose remainders returned the visitors' gaze.

The attempt to put the past in a museum was also complicated by the political crisis that overshadowed its foundation almost from the outset. Created as a municipal institution by Francisco Seeber, the mayor of Buenos Aires, in the wake of the independence day of 1889, the museum's organization coincided with the stock exchange crash that provoked the frustrated Revolución del Parque of 1890, which overthrew Miguel Juárez Celman's federal government. Armed rebellions of dissident Radicals continued for much of the next decade. A commission invited by Seeber to draft some guidelines for the museum's organization reached no conclusions, despite (or because) it included among its members some of the main contenders of the political troubles of 1890, such as Julio Argentino Roca, Bartolomé Mitre, and Ramón J. Cárcano, Juárez Celman's favorite in the race for presidential succession. The institution was narrowly saved by Seeber who, shortly before resigning from his post on January 3, 1890, named the young diplomat, publicist, and collector Adolfo Pedro Carranza director and assigned provisional quarters to the museum on Calle Esmeralda 848.

Born in 1857, the son of a wealthy railway and mining entrepreneur with family ties to the northwestern regional oligarchies, Carranza had grown up in *porteño* high society and collected books and items of American history from an early age. A graduate in law from Córdoba University, he occupied minor diplomatic posts before founding, in 1886, the *Revista Nacional*, a journal dedicated specifically to historical themes—a history speaking itself through the centenaries and funerals of its aristocratic protagonists, remembered in the rubrics "Muertos Ilustres," "Grandes Ciudadanos," and, last but not least, "Próceres Olvidados" (Forgotten Founding Fathers). Carranza occupied the directorship of the museum from its foundation until his death in August 1914.

Despite the previous month's turmoil the museum was inaugurated on August 30, 1890, arranged over four rooms with a mere 191 objects on display. *La Prensa*, reviewing the ceremony, noted the "numerous and select" attendance, in particular of "many distinguished dames and young ladies of our society" who, in between the toasts, speeches, and lunch *de rigueur*, took a short object lesson observing the "interesting and very well-preserved manuscripts, weapons and trophies of our glorious tradition, standards from remote epochs, and some curiosities such as the collection of paintings representing the conquest of Mexico." However, the reviewer went on, "we must also observe that [the museum] is of poor birth, and that all of us need to contribute to enrich it. […] Private egotisms have to make way for public interest, and more so since the owners of important historical objects can have their names put next to each donation or even have their collections, if they are very numerous, installed in a special showroom carrying their name."[35]

The paper's call for patriotic generosity seems not to have gone entirely unheard since, only a year later, a collection already numbering 284 pieces would move into new quarters on Calle Moreno 330, occupying the ground floor of the city's Chemical Office (fig. 27). Despite Carranza's persistent attempts, intensified after the museum's nationalization in September 1891, to obtain a purpose-built location on the grounds of the old Retiro barracks, his complaints about the lack of exhibition space were only addressed in 1894, when the collection, now numbering 886 pieces, was moved north into a fourteen-room building inside the Botanical Garden on Avenida Santa Fe. In 1897, Carranza managed to secure, in exchange with the Department of Parks and Gardens, the old mansion of José Gregorio de Lezama on Calle Defensa, the hypothetical spot of the city's initial foundation by Pedro de Mendoza in 1536, where the collection of 1341 pieces moved in the same year (fig. 28). Even in 1915, however, a year after Carranza's death, his friend the historian and sociologist Ernesto Quesada still complained about the unsuitability of period buildings for collections of historical material; due to the architectural layout, he argued,

the visitor cannot move from one period to another in a suitable order; instead, if he follows the distribution of rooms, he suddenly moves from a latter epoch to a former one or, as in the case of San Martín, he will find part of the exhibits on one end of the building and the other part on the opposite end. […] A museum has to be installed in

FIGURE 27. Anonymous, Museo Histórico Nacional, showroom at Calle Moreno 330. Albumin print (ca. 1891). Biblioteca Nacional, Buenos Aires.

FIGURE 28. Anonymous, Museo Histórico Nacional, Quinta de Lezama. Albumin print (ca. 1900). Archivo General de la Nación (*Album de Fotógrafos Aficionados* no. 37), Buenos Aires.

a building constructed *ad hoc*, where everything is subordinated to the plan of organization and classification of the collections stored and exhibited there: such is the case of the La Plata Museum, which—among us and in the rubric of the natural sciences—is an absolutely recommendable model.[36]

History, Quesada claimed, makes itself at home only when it is removed from the spatial constraints of period architecture, when the present invites it into the room it has made for it. Exhibition space, says Quesada, is the equivalent of the written page of historiographic narrative, or rather its confirmation, as, having duly studied the historian's account, visitors "will already know how to appreciate correctly the diverse objects."[37] What exactly this "historical equivalent" of the La Plata museum's architectural simulation of natural evolution would have been was left open by Quesada, who nonetheless persistently criticized his friend Carranza's reluctance to select, classify, and distribute in museum space the objects of his collection. In short, Quesada urged the leftovers from the past to be elevated from the antiquarian singularity of the *souvenir* into the properly historical order of the *collection*. As Carranza himself admitted, "my mission has been to conceive and found the museum, dedicating all my efforts to the gathering of as many historical relics as I could get hold of, insistently and constantly pleading with their owners for donations; the material thus assembled is already considerable, but I will direct all my desire towards increasing it further, leaving to my successors the task of putting my work to use, of classifying what has been gathered, of selecting and exhibiting it according to the most adequate method."[38]

The amiable dispute between Carranza and Quesada on whether or not the accumulation of mnemonic material immediately "imposed the need to select,"[39] that is, to organize not only remembrance but also forgetting, resembled the discussion on the independence memorial or indeed on the Brazilian Historical Exhibition earlier in the decade in its concern with the present's responsibilities towards the past, and with the status of the historical object as an antique or as a document. For Quesada, following the lead of the natural sciences, historical museography had to distinguish from the very outset between pieces destined for display and others destined for archival storage and specialist research, so as "to educate the patriotism of the masses, reviving the different eras of our past, and at the same time offering to the erudite researcher a veritable treasure."[40] For Carranza, in contrast, the imminent danger of loss and thus the need to concentrate all efforts on salvaging the remnants of the past prevailed over the task of rendering them meaningful to the eyes of the present. The latter could be safely postponed, in any case, since the true meaning was supposedly immanent to the object itself, beyond change, independent of its place in the space-time of the museum. In the absence of a clearly defined principle of organization, rather than putting the past at the service of the collection, authenticating a discourse *on* history, the museum maintained an aesthetic of the souvenir that offered anecdotes and digressions rather than the complete, overarching historiographic narrative it nonetheless presupposed.

Thus, for instance, the inaugural exhibition of 1890 assembled in its first room a series of *militaria* from the campaigns of San Martín, Belgrano, and Güemes during the wars of independence, as well as a portrait of the civil war general Paz, dating from 1853. In the second, a chart of the battle of Maipú was placed next to the box in which President Rivadavia's mortal remains had been returned to Argentina. And if the fifth room was entirely dedicated to the Triple Alliance War of 1865–70, the seventh contained relics from different moments of the civil wars and the Rosas regime such as "the bullet that hit General Lucio Mansilla in the battle of the *Obligado*," "the *boleadoras* employed in the capture of general Paz in 1831," or "the door through which general Lavalle was shot in Jujuy," side by side with "the cart employed on the start of construction of the Southern Railway in 1864."[41] In subsequent years, entire rooms in memory of particular "heroes of independence" were organized around large donations made by their descendents, such as the uniforms, portraits, furniture, and personal items of independence warriors Escalada and Trelles donated by their widows in 1893. Foremost among these "heroes" were San Martín and Belgrano, the twin saints of the liberal pantheon. In 1897, Manuela Rosas de Terrero—daughter of Juan Manuel de Rosas, the federalist "tyrant"—had donated San Martín's saber, which the Libertador had given to her father as a token of appreciation. In 1897, the furniture and other objects from the bedroom where the

FIGURE 29. Sofia Posadas, *Last Days of the General San Martín*. Oil on canvas (1900). Museo Histórico Nacional, Buenos Aires.

exiled San Martín had died were shipped to Buenos Aires by his granddaughter and faithfully reconstructed at the museum using photographs of the original at Bologne-sur-Mer.

On personal request from Carranza, Quesada explained,

the families of the founders of independence have volunteered to give up these relics of honor, for the people to be able to admire them, reunited in this establishment, and to learn in this way how to venerate those who with their own blood gave them liberty and a Fatherland. [...] Certainly many are missing, but this is the fault of their respective families: we know more than one who continues to preserve faithfully these memories of their forefathers, as if they feared to profane them by allowing them to be seen, while their place is in [the museum], next to those that belonged to their companions in arms.[42]

The state's sites of memory, such as the historical museum, Quesada argued, superseded the social milieux of remembrance in which the objects had previously dwelled. State collecting spectrally reunited the armies of the dead, transferring the material leftovers of an ever-increasing pantheon of founding fathers from the family shrines of the Creole upper class onto the stage of the museum, exposing them to the eyes of a populace that had to be instructed in how to duly revere and venerate them. The state, in Quesada's view, had a rightful claim on these objects as a mediating instance between donors and viewers. The museum, for him, was a kind of debt collector that received the tribute the present owed to the past. On the one hand, "the people" had a duty to admire and revere the leftovers of their forefathers (not their fathers in a literal sense, for sure, but rather those who had bestowed on them the gift of nationality). On the other hand, the real descendants of the heroes of independence had a patriotic obligation to sacrifice private ownership of their family memorabilia in favor of the state. In making these public, they would help ensure the symbolic reproduction, in a ritual of vision, of the social hierarchy the museum prolonged into the future precisely by tracking it back into the past. "What a feeling of profound respect," the reviewer of *El Coleccionista Argentino* exclaimed on visiting the museum on Calle Esmeralda, "seizes the spirit on entering these galleries whose walls expose at first glance the trophies conquered in bloody contests, representative of a glorious page or witnesses of an act of heroism, placed there as a lesson and example for future generations!"[43]

To insist on the privacy of material memories, from this point of view, became an act of high treason not just against the national collective but against class solidarity, as the blanks in history's material record could only too easily be usurped by other memories and other histories, an intrusion to be avoided at any price. In fact, then, a peculiar kind of retention anxiety underlay the museum's practice of collecting. If watches, walking sticks, household items, and looking glasses touched by an epic history of foundational heroism commanded almost the same degree of devotion as the trophies conquered on the battlefield, the compulsion to collect and expose even the most spurious and insignificant leftovers of the heroic founders also bespoke, inversely, the fragility of the narrative they were supposed to authenticate and verify.

Indeed, precisely in attempting to reconstruct it as a public place, a temple of state worship, the museum testified to the crisis of a social hierarchy embodied in the Creole family home: a crisis of the symbolic, or better, metonymic, relation between the domestic space of the Creole elite (in its duality as urban mansion and as rural estancia) and the political sphere, both essentially obeying one and the same mode of patriarchal rule. Precisely around the time of the museum's foundation, the crisis of the speculative economy instituted in 1880 and the emergence of a new kind of self-made man on the urban stage had sparked a literature focused on the fear of social intrusion. Its most notable examples were Eugenio Cambaceres's xenophobic farce *En la sangre* (In the Blood, 1885) and Julián Martel's anti-Semitic conspiracy thriller *La bolsa* (The Stock Exchange, 1889). An incipient social mobility that was threatening to claim political expression was figured here as a diabolic assault by a class of neobarbarians, who cunningly disguised their inferior pedigree, on a virtuous Creole elite that had, until then, successfully avoided the degenerative effects of industrial mass society. Once again, in the trope of the violation of the patrician family home, already common to the Romantics' literary resistance against Rosas, the threat of an emergent public sphere not entirely confined to the values and practices of the ruling elite appeared as a sexual menace. A kind of barbarian horde attacking not from the far reaches of the desert but from overseas, the lustful gaze of ethnic others threatened the purity of Creole maidens and, thereby, of the blood bonds of the ruling elite itself (one largely descended, of course, from previous waves of French, Spanish, and Italian immigrants). Miguel Cané's appeal to his upperclass peers to close ranks in protection of their womenfolk emblematizes a social paranoia which takes the home and the female body as metonymic extensions of a social order that has come under threat from outside:

I would ask you for more sociability, more solidarity with the restricted world to which you belong, more respect for the women that are its ornament [...] to prevent the first democratic scoundrel who has made his fortune selling shoe soles on the street from thinking he has the right to use his little Don Juan's hand in a dining room he has entered bumping into the furniture. You have no idea of the sordid fury that invades me when I see a fine and delicate creature of caste, whose mother had been a friend of my own, attacked by some rude nobody, brushed over by a tailor, when I see his eyes brutishly clinging to her virginal body offering itself in all innocence. [...] Look, our first, sacred duty, above everything else, is to defend our women from the oafish invasion of the heterogeneous, cosmopolitan, hybrid world that is now the base of our country. [...] Honor and respect for the pure remnants of our national stock; since every day we Argentines diminish. Let us save our legitimate dominion, not just by nourishing and developing the spirit whenever possible, but by raising our women, through veneration, to a height the low aspirations of the crowd cannot reach. [...] Let us close the circle and veil over it.[44]

This "closure of the circle," spectrally reconstructing an imagined interior space of Creole sociability and purity—that is, an endogamous sexual economy designed to ward off the undesired effects of the speculative financial boom on which this same Creole oligarchy was thriving—was also the unwritten program of the National Historical Museum. Indeed, the exhibition at the Quinta de Lezama comprised a room entirely dedicated to the "Patrician Ladies of Independence." Yet to make the state the home of history and to make history homely by exposing it to the eyes of the public implied destroying the domestic spaces where history's remainders and reminders had previously dwelled. In other words, it implied deploying on the Creole family home the same symbolic violence that the museum apparatus had previously exercised on animals and plants, native villages, and subaltern bodies, albeit with the opposite intention.

Quesada's description of the rooms dedicated to San Martín provides an insight into the ways in which the museum forged a refuge, an *intérieur*, for a patriarchal domesticity under threat. His text dates from 1915, following the reforms of the display implemented by Carranza's successor Juan A. Pradère. On each wall of the first room, dedicated to the Chilean and Peruvian campaign, there was now a large showcase, the one on the left containing San Martín's uniform as "Protector of Peru," medals and decorations, firearms, and other uniforms, as well as a raincoat and the woolen poncho San Martín had worn in Peru. The one on the right, meanwhile, featured the famous saber donated by Manuela Rosas, an ink flask formerly belonging to the Inquisition of Lima, a daguerreotype portrait, tobacco box, walking stick, and other personal items, as well as letters and documents of San Martín's own handwriting. In the middle of the room, two further showcases displayed, among other things, fragments of a Spanish flag seized in Chile, commemorative coins, medals, and other items of homage, culminating in a first edition of Mitre's *Historia de San Martín*. On the walls above the showcase, Spanish flags seized at Chacabuco and Maipú

FIGURE 30. Anonymous, Museo Histórico Nacional, Sala de la Independencia. Albumin print (May 1918). Archivo General de la Nación, Buenos Aires.

hung alongside battle scenes and historical paintings of San Martín's encounter with Bolívar at Guayaquil or his crossing of the Andes, as well as further coins, medals, and plates commemorating ceremonies in homage to the Libertador. Period furniture—San Martín's field bed from the Andean campaign, his desk and dining table—and a miniature of the monument erected in his memory at Boulogne-sur-Mer completed the display. In the adjacent room, warded off from the surrounding exhibition space by a large glass panel, visitors could peer into the reconstructed death chamber. On the other side of this was the "Independence Room," displaying the portraits and belongings of San Martín's principal officers "as if they were still standing guard over the last dwelling of the Liberator of the three Republics" (fig. 30).[45]

This spectral reunion of heroic ancestors was simultaneously calling on the past to save the present and attempting to exorcise history and replace it with myth. As in Lamas's collection exhibited a decade earlier (parts of which effectively ended up in the Quinta de Lezama), public display was a means of domesticating history, warding off the return of the *unheimlich* (uncanny). The celebration of independence as the founding epic of a male Creole ruling class systematically cleansed history of its female, popular, mestizo—in sum, heterogeneous—elements, confirming the death of the past it was meant to resurrect.

Making history homely, by erasing the stain of hybridity from the origins of the nation, demanded an aesthetic of miniature precisely because it aspired to a totalizing and exclusive image. In order to assemble "all the relics, all the memories of our short past,"[46] the museum could not help but exhibit the founding fathers as tin soldiers in a dollhouse. As Didier Maleuvre puts it, the miniature, as the construction of a space fully under control of its beholder, necessarily implies the self-exclusion of the subject, the becoming uninhabitable, by experience, of the very space designed to shelter it. The aesthetic of miniature, common to the museum and the bourgeois home, tries to take hold of the interior and the homely in the exact moment of its historical demise. It gives "an image of the world without experience and therefore without the human element, as though the bourgeois subject has fantasized his or her own absence in gazing at the dollhouse: one can grasp its interior as a totality only because one could never fit inside."[47]

The design of a state-sponsored museum of the past, at once a theater to expose and a refuge to shelter the phallic substitutes of a besieged patriarchal order—sabers, flagstaffs, pistols—resulted in a toy space as impossible to inhabit as the Creole family home itself, whose crisis was driving the more adventurous members of the elite out into the street. Eduardo Wilde, for instance, in a chronicle from 1899 entitled, significantly enough, "Modern Life," expressed his "desire to escape from my home, where on every step I took I would break my neck against some piece of fine art. [...] The air could not circulate for all the Spanish walls, the statues, the urns, and the great bitch that delivered us into life [la grandísima madre que nos dió a luz]."[48]

Besieged from the outside by an increasingly heterogeneous and mobile urban context perceived as a threat to patriarchal power, on its inside the closed-circle domesticity of Creole elite society exposed its inhabitants to the suffocation of a space converted into a mausoleum. The male subject, in Wilde's ironic formulation, was threatened with castration by the omnipresence of the maternal: the cult of the Founding Fathers, as manifested in the antiquarian obsession with authenticity, marks, and signatures that inscribe the paternal trace into the place of lack, would thus be but a screen memory for a regressive longing to return to the maternal womb. As Jean Baudrillard suggests, collecting is a narcissistic solution to the loss of order, imaginarily reconstituted through back-projection into the time of childhood and the home—a spectral reconstruction of the home, in fact, marked by the absence of its constitutive elements (mother and father). The history museum thus becomes a fetishistic space where "everything that cannot be invested in human relationships is invested in objects."[49]

But what the collector avoids in his exclusive relation with things that cannot return the gaze is the interpellation by the other. It is the avoidance of inter-pellation that is at the base of the antiquarian attitude towards history. Antiques are substitutes of history as *voice*, the voice of the specter returning to claim the debt of an unredeemed past. Spectrality—that is, history as unhomeliness, as the uncanny—is contained in fetishization. The paranoid underside of this fetishism of the antique is the fear of the intrusion of the Other, the fear of a generative power located outside the home and capable of distorting the rigid-ity of the patriarchal order: a fear of *bastardization*. Indeed, in the late nineteenth century's fetishism of the antique, a politico-sexual figure of discourse begins to take shape that would return, fully fledged, in Lugones's Ayacucho speech ("The Hour of the Sword"), a true founding document of Creolist fascism pronounced only a few months before the military coup of 1930, which it provided with an ideological platform. The anniversary of this first, and therefore paradigmatic, assault on the incipient democratic order was celebrated in September 1931 with a cocktail reception in honor of the dictator José Evaristo Uriburu and his cabi-net at the National Historical Museum, following a parade of historical flags and weaponry from its collections through the streets of the capital. Finally, history had regained the streets, reimposing on the modern city the rigidity of its afterlife embodied in the orderly mass of the military parade. In the words of a contem-porary reviewer: "Today will see [the flags] waving through streets lined up with monumental buildings, imposing traffic, enormous progress, which they could not see but for the sake of which they had been waving for the last hundred years. They will parade in the hands of the cadets of 1931, whom they will certainly watch with a certain maternal pride, feeling, perhaps, the revival of the old winds of glory when knowing themselves to be so well, and so rightfully carried."[50]

If by 1930 anthropology and the natural sciences were no longer central to the images of national selves in Latin America, giving way to highly formalized rituals and performances of the nation's historical origins, in the nineteenth cen-tury history had been rather slow off the mark in the formation of an "exhibi-tionary complex." In my analysis of the first attempts in Argentina and Brazil to make national history into a museum object, I have argued that this belated arrival among the disciplines of exhibiting had to do with the difficulties in fash-ioning the past as a self-enclosed object, a thing to be looked at. For most of the century, the past had been either too alien and hostile to call it back to the scene, as an object of remembrance, or it was still all too present to be safely put at a distance. Reclaiming the colonial past as part of a national history, for instance, involved finding a way of rereading it as always already striving towards national emancipation: thus, Brazilian and Argentine historians would associate the re-sistance against the Dutch and British invasions, for instance, with the emergence of an embryonic (yet in a sense also already fully formed) sense of nationality. On the other hand, memories of internal conflict among different regional elites, not to speak of peasant and slave rebellions, for most of the century were far too fresh for their material remainders to be exhibited to the public gaze.

Yet when the "short nineteenth century" of post-independence could finally be entrusted to the displays of exhibitions and museums, the visibility of the past was the very sign of its crisis. The urge of gathering and exhibiting the traces of the national past stemmed from an anxiety that the latter was about to be forgotten even before it could be recorded, made redundant by the very forces of progress it had unleashed. Historical collecting, in comparison with the natural sciences, was defensive and nostalgic; yet it also anticipated a particularly modern kind of reactionary politics that would only take shape in the second and third decade of the twentieth century. All the same, however, the longing for the past invoked by the historical object not only represented a fear of present social unrest and mobility; it also exemplified a wider sense of anxiety vis-à-vis the loss of substance and solidity that things, social relations, and even the subject itself appeared to be suffering under the onslaught of "progress." Historical collecting, as a desire for sameness and an expression of its perpetual deferral, speaks to the crisis of objects and selves proper to a context of (dependent) capitalism; the crisis of *presence* that comes with the alienation of people from the conditions of their own existence. The history museum, then, is a spectral image of the real: it is the material expression not of what *has been*, but of what *is not*.

# MAPS

We have now not merely explored the territory of pure understanding, and carefully surveyed every part of it, but have also measured its extent, and assigned to everything its rightful place. This domain is an island, enclosed by nature itself within unalterable limits. It is the land of truth—enchanting name!—surrounded by a wide and stormy ocean, the native home of illusion, where many a fog bank and many a swiftly melting iceberg give the deceptive appearance of farther shores, deluding the adventurous seafarer ever anew with empty hopes, and engaging him in enterprises which he can never abandon and yet is unable to carry to completion.

—Immanuel Kant, *Critique of Pure Reason*

## Cartography's Narrative

An island of truth in a sea of illusion: Kant's heroic portrayal of philosophy as exploration, published scarcely eight years before the public exposure of the first national topography, Jean-Dominique Cassini's *Carte générale de la France* (1789), could perhaps also be claimed as a founding passage of political geography.[1] For in its metaphorization of the colonial globe—the island of presence, the logocenter, the domain of the spirit beyond whose limits nature looms in its primordial state of pure appearance—the passage in fact turns on the fundamental aporia of a discipline entrusted with the task of writing the historically contingent into nature, and of naturalizing the historical process. If, however, political geography presents the state as the locus of truth—the realization, in essence, of the merely apparent order of nature—then beyond those "unalterable limits" there can only be lack, not merely the negation of its insular cohesiveness by *another* state-island, but utter negativity, mere "illusions" of firm ground that

119

melt away as soon as one has set foot on them. If the state is the terrain of immanence, it can only be Manichean or imperial: there must not be another one beyond its borders. The island of truth must be unique.

This need to locate what can nonetheless only impose its power over place in terms of the abstract universal— the need, in other words, to remain out of the place it assigns—inscribes the shadow of a doubt within the geographical rhetoric of presence. In Derek Gregory's intriguing phrase, a "cartographic anxiety" haunts the seafarer/truth-seeker in his attempt to clearly distinguish the island of truth from the icebergs of delusion.[2] Political geography is a border science, which has to constantly renegotiate its own foundational aporias in scenes of demarcation. In these, true space is divided from false space, so as to set the property and propriety of the self against a difference thus expunged from its own terrain into that of the other. It is just such a scene, taking place in southern Patagonia on a rainy day in late 1883, in which Captain Carlos María Moyano of the Argentine Navy will lay eyes on a landscape never seen before, and indeed, never again:

Thus, having reached the shores of the channel on the eastern end of the Gallegos valley, we needed only to follow its course to reach the Pacific *with no other obstacles ahead than woods and swamps instead of the high mountains old prejudice had made us imagine*. With a prospect so gratifying to our patriotism—to traverse, for the first time, the Continent from Ocean to Ocean without ever crossing the Cordillera—we began our preparations for the next day. [...] Rarely had we found ourselves possessed by a similar curiosity, for, even though what we were going to confirm was theoretically a reality, I nonetheless considered it necessary to personally witness the existence and conditions of this geographical accident which, strictly according to the present border treaty with Chile, puts the Argentine Republic in possession of doorways onto the Pacific.[3]

The challenge here consists in transforming "theoretical reality" into political fact purely through the intervention of vision. If the preparations are reminiscent of an army preparing for the final onslaught, it is because effectively what is at stake is a conquest, the annexation of a key portion of territory through a visualization that will replace "old prejudice" by the immediacy of firsthand observation. And in effect, when nature is eventually found to coincide with the presumptions made upon it, the language of description will give way to that of the sublime. Moyano's rhetoric is one of discovery, yet rather than to add new territories to the map, it reencounters an already familiar one from a new point of view and thus wrests it away from the false representations in which, until then, it had supposedly been caught:

As soon as we had crossed the last swamp and the last strip of woodland defending the passage of a torrentous stream, we anxiously climbed up to a height from where we could easily dominate the entire ensemble. There, a few steps away, in all its impressive grandeur, was the vast Worsley canal or sound, parallel to which lay the two large arms into which it breaches out, the Sound of Last Hope running directly towards the Northwest, and the other, Obstruction Sound, towards the South, as if searching for the waters of the Skiring, a Mediterranean sea in miniature, close to which it is stopped short by a narrow stretch of land. […] I feel incapable of giving a complete description, pale as it were, of this hydrographic marvel, hidden on this side of the Cordillera. […] To those approaching it by sea, this enchanting picture will certainly not reveal itself as it does to the one who sees it from this side, dominating the ensemble from above, because their spirit will have had time to adjust to these spectacles ever since they entered the straits.[4]

In this passage of geographical *réécriture*, the rhetoric of presence typically associated with scenes of first encounter in the tradition of European travel is ritually, even mechanically, deployed to forge an original vision where, quite evidently, a prior instance of mapping has already left its trace. The image is already saturated with language, replete with names (not Argentine or Chilean names, certainly, but those of an imperial power for which, rather than a "doorway," the straits are but a series of rather tedious obstacles and "obstructions"). By 1880, the Strait of Magellan had become not merely a major imperial trade route but also practically a part of the U.S. network of internal waterways, with a crucial role in the settlement of California. Yet nonetheless, this scene of visual revisiting is rendered here in the full splendor of an originary encounter, even including towards the end the conventional shift of register from the distributive language of the surveyor to the sublime rhetoric of artistic landscape, once the cartographic picture has been completed. It is only through this production of aesthetic surplus, of course, that the space-object can be symbolically appropriated, not merely on behalf of the viewing subject (which, on its own, cannot possibly take in the full marvelousness of the real) but also on that of the nation-state of which it serves as an emissary. Indeed, nature is being appropriated and possessed here, first and foremost, as a sublime image of the state. In the visual capture of border space, a new kind of state power can be enacted, one that recognizes itself as already written into the text of nature: "we are favored by the topographical position we occupy," Moyano insists, "so as to dominate the entire ensemble."[5]

Unsurprisingly, Moyano's claim was immediately (and, in the end, successfully) refuted by his Chilean counterpart Ramón Serrano Montaner in *La*

*Época* of Santiago, who accused him of having let himself be "carried away by his enthusiasm and patriotism [...] to claim facts that, although convenient for the interests of his country [...] do not conform to what either [he himself] has seen or what other explorers have observed."[6] In response, Moyano returned the blame and declared "that our investigations are devoid of any enthusiasm or patriotism, because we are fully aware that these sentimental grounds are poor guides for scientific investigations."[7]

The disavowal by both contenders of a "sentimental" dimension to their exploits, which, at the same time, is emphatically invoked at crucial moments of their travel accounts to turn the scene of arrival into one of visual conquest, points to a central aspect of late nineteenth-century productions of space in Argentina (as well as Brazil). If, as Mary Louise Pratt has claimed, Creole cultural self-fashioning began as a critique of naturalist explorers and of the capitalist vanguard of early nineteenth-century European travellers, a critique which, "in contrast with the visual appropriation of European science and aesthetics [...] projected moral and civic dramas onto the landscape,"[8] then Moyano's Pacific panorama posits a national viewing subject that both reclaims a quantifying and distributive perspective from the European explorer *and* a gift for spiritual empathy with the American scenery from the Romantic writers of the midcentury. Yet this scenery is now significantly devoid of historical drama, in the first place because it is, just like that of European travel, an empty landscape, a purely natural scene entirely at the disposal of its new beholder and master: the state.

Visual recapture in the final decades of the nineteenth century not only became a key form of representing territorial expansion, but it also, and perhaps even more importantly, imposed on the nation-state's margins a novel conception of spatial power that reverberated towards the center itself. In 1880, some three years before Moyano's Patagonian journey, Augusto Fausto de Souza, a military officer with academic training in mathematics and physics, submitted a "Study of the Territorial Division of Brazil" to the journal of the Brazilian Historical-Geographical Institute, in which he proposed to redraw the political space of the nation-state according to the principles of physical geography. The institute, one of the oldest learned societies in Latin America, had been founded in 1838 to forge a sense of national identity by saturating the national map with edifying memories of epic foundations. By compiling colonial legends, documents of the struggle against the French and Dutch, or accounts of the war against Argentina in 1825–28, the institute was chiefly concerned with the construction of an archive capable of turning cartographic into affective space, a "realm of memories," to paraphrase Pierre Nora, in which the nation-state could be situated and legitimized.[9] Unsurprisingly, as Lilia Moritz Schwarcz has shown, historical contributions to the *Revista do Instituto Historico e Geographico Brasileiro* far outnumbered those dedicated to geographical subjects, which only covered about a fifth of the total contents.[10]

Rather significantly, then, for a piece to be published in a journal so crucially concerned with linking geography and history, De Souza's study dismissed history as a mere distortion to the transparency and harmonious order of natural space, which physical geography, by contrast, was qualified to record. Anticipating the anti-Lusitanianism of the first years of the Republic, De Souza denounced the Empire's subdivision into provinces of vastly dissimilar size, population, and resources as the flawed legacy of Portuguese colonialism, which had deliberately chained the Brazilian land body to a political grid that rendered its emancipation and self-organization impossible. The Portuguese Court, he complained, "considered the Portuguese as subjects and the Brazilians as slaves."[11] That this was, effectively, still the legal status of vast numbers of "Brazilians" did not overtly concern De Souza (whose text was published, we should remember, eight years before the official abolition of slavery). Instead, he argues from the point of view of a nation of citizen-settlers, projected into the past as an "imagined community." Remarkably, then, if slavery had been a colonial misrepresentation of Brazilians similar to that of Brazilian natural space as tributary to the Luso-colonial core, the Brazilian Empire could in turn be imaginarily equated with the cause of abolition. De Souza's text—which was dedicated to the Emperor in his role as patron of the institute—promoted physical geography as the natural language of this attempted reinvention of the Imperial state as an agent of modernization. History's capricious cartography, he announced, was finally going to be rectified by a gaze guided exclusively by nature's empirical evidence and by a common sense of geometry and proportion. It is useful to quote De Souza's opening paragraphs at some length in order to illustrate this new epistemological status of vision:

You open a map of Brazil. Even on brief examination, you will notice that this immense region, whose surface represents four fifths of Europe's, is split into two almost perfectly equal parts along the line of the Pará River; but whilst on one side you count seventeen provinces, on the other there are only three!

In all twenty of these, what an amount of irregularity in both size and form! Some are enormous, bordering on others which are but tiny fractions of them; some have their widest extension on the Atlantic coast, others are entirely enclosed in the center, or open themselves a narrow gauge between their neighbors to reach the sea. You will also notice the variety of their outer limits, some advancing on, and eating into, those next to them, retreating here whilst extraordinarily stretching out over there, so as to compose, on the whole, a most complicated mosaic.

If you still wanted more detail, you would see that they are separated by small streams of water or minor mountain ranges, or even by entirely imaginary lines, although in close proximity there are mighty rivers and towering peaks. And by the end of this examination, it is only natural that your spirit should nurture the following question: What ideas have governed such an incongruous and capricious demarcation?[12]

The old political map, which recorded the complex arrangements and struggles between regional elites, was now an almost incomprehensible hieroglyph to the rational and unprejudiced beholder, a relic from the muddled prehistory of statecraft. It was, in short, an image that made no sense to a new geographical reason. As Michel Roncayolo points out, geography achieved true self-sufficiency only towards the end of the nineteenth century, not accidentally at precisely the moment when the representations of space and time were internationally standardized. (Only in 1884 would an international conference at Washington adopt Greenwich Mean Time, measured at the British Royal Observatory, as the universal standard according to which a range of time zones was established around the globe.) In France, Roncayolo explains, geographical research was boosted in response to the traumatic defeat by Prussia in 1870, foregrounding, for the first time, the geological gradations and partitions of the terrain rather than its administrative, demographic, or infrastructural organization. With the emergence of geology, space had attained its own natural language, one that was largely indifferent to human interaction with the environment. "Geology not only provides a 'scientific reading' of landscape, but the reading as such. Topography and administrative divisions are now considered arbitrary and are substituted by the idea of natural regions as principles for the analysis of geographical reality."[13]

Geology provides the terrain with a natural language that turns it, under the trained eye of the surveyor, into a transparent system of layers, connections, and divisions. This results in an apparent depoliticization of geography, whose task is now merely to arrange administrative units according to the boundaries already indicated by nature itself. The supposedly immediate accessibility of De Souza's map even to the untrained viewer recalls Foucault's description of the Panopticon as a viewing platform that enables each and every one of its contingent occupiers to perform the tasks of surveillance and control over that which is thus put fully at their disposal.[14] Panoptic seeing removes the subject of the gaze from the process of historical becoming, such that her task can now be conceived as an *architectonic* or *geometrical* ordering of, rather than *political* intervention into, the field of vision. De Souza continues:

As Mr. Varnhagen has rightly put it, it is not only in order to follow the rules of symmetry that the architect uses staves of the same size for the construction of a vault, but in order to obtain through them the same degree of resistance at all points, and thus a maximum solidity for his work. Convinced of the truth of this principle, we have tried to divide Brazil into parts which (without losing sight of the conditions imposed by natural divisions) would convey to every single one of these a number of variables (area, population, rent, etc.), such that there would be equilibrium between its products, or *moments*, if we may use this term from the language of mathematics.[15]

If colonial history has left the state edifice with a flawed architectural design, the task is now to reorganize it according to the principles of (geopolitical) statics—that is, to accommodate political space within the natural volumes of geological space. This redrafting of the national map not only increases the efficiency of administration but it also produces a new metapicture of state order as the political image of nature, a reasoned transcription of the real itself.

As in Moyano, seeing in De Souza is simultaneously a form of rewriting. The visual image is called upon to challenge and eventually replace previous notions of national space, which must now be considered false to the extent to which they are not able to be summarized and verified in visual forms. As the Argentine Geographical Institute's chairman Carlos Corra Luna would put it in 1896 in the *Boletín del Instituto Geográfico Argentino*, looking back on the institute's first fifteen years of activities, "there was ahead of us an immense task of research, not in old libraries but in the terrain itself. In all directions, the territory of the Republic had to be turned into the object of exploration and study, so as to implement, among other factors, the rapid development which its privileged position and climate forespelled."[16] The call here is for the replacement of the library by the cartographic archive (*mapoteca*) as the storage medium of the nation's territorial substance, which is now to be gathered, moreover, through firsthand observation in "the field" rather than through the perusal of written documents.

Not necessarily, then, are the new spatial images of the nation-state always radically different from previous ones. What varies, instead, is the epistemological status attached to visual representations (maps, landscape sketches, photographs), which are now seen as superior to written ones in terms of their truth-value, their immediate access to the real. At the same time, I will argue in the following chapters, these new visual languages of national space informed an emerging "progressive" discourse of intervention into the social, modelled on the distributive, panoramic gaze of the geographer-engineer. If in the previous representation, forged around midcentury by Romantic literature's narratives of foundation, national space had only been one of the faces of the transhistorical forces clashing with one another at the convulsive origins of the nation-self, now society itself would be perceived as something in need of being mapped, such that each and every one of its elements came to rest in the place assigned to it by nature.

### Liminality and State Capture

A key aspect of the emergent Argentine and Brazilian state orders of the final quarter of the century was the material and symbolic expansion into areas that had remained outside the space of colonial rule, or which had been only marginally integrated into colonial and postindependence society. The capture of frontier spaces was the critical challenge the state had to master in order to impose itself as the sole instance of interpellation of its subjects as citizens. Yet this movement of capture, which intruded into social and affective as much as into territorial spaces, was preferably represented in images of nature. This natural iconography consisted of two complementary aspects, which individual images often combined in an endless number of variations. On the one hand, nature was represented as the mythical enemy at the origin of the state. Nature was the plane of exteriority that had to be removed beyond the state's frontiers for national society to become one with itself. Yet in a second strand of representations, nature was precisely the image of what society still aspired to become: an atemporal, sublime image of the fatherland already written into the soil—a monumental vision of state power.

In this double invocation of nature—as enemy of the state and as the state's primordial and eternal substance—the dialectic of the state's capture of the social is elliptically made present (and thus "naturalized"). The emergence of the state as the transcendental subject of national society is mirrored in mythical images of struggle with, and recognition in, nature, because political power is precisely the return of nature within the fabric of the social, as an external force that disrupts the reciprocity of social exchange. Hence, nature, in this iconographic tradition, is both the force in whose name the state takes power over society and the image of society in its raw, primitive state prior to the imposition of the state-form. The frequent association of marginal populations with the natural environment, and their depiction as a type of society still living "in a state of nature," therefore also puts them at the center of debates about nationality.[17]

Frontier space and its appropriation, then, are crucial to the representation of an emergent state power because it is on the border between culture and nature that a whole new relation between political power and social exchange can be visualized. As the space where a new relation between the state and society is emerging, the frontier is simultaneously a spatial trope of capitalist accumulation. Its pure exteriority as a natural space at the same time makes it absolutely available: space becomes place through an act of appropriation, of taking possession, an act of violence that simultaneously inscribes the law and turns nature into objects to be possessed and exchanged. The violent extraction of "primary resources" on the colonial and imperial frontiers is, in Marx's striking image, the dawn of the capitalist era, the "principal moment of primitive accumulation."[18] The expanding frontier is the site and image of capital's "annihilation of space with time," in Marx's phrase: its incorporation depends on the previous elimination of obstacles in order to minimize the turnover time of capital (the time that elapses before surplus value can be realized). Thus the frontier presupposes state capture as much as it entails and intensifies it. Its appropriation relies on a previous construction of networks of transport and communication as well as on the transformation of social relations on its inside, all of which must be put at the service of accelerating the movement of things from the site of primitive accumulation to the site of consumption. Nature turns into a frontier once it is reached by a technological and symbolic apparatus that has removed the obstacles posited in and by space. Railway networks, for example, not only accelerated the transport of humans and goods to and from the frontier, their construction also created or intensified capitalist relations by transforming local produce into commodities and drafting local workforces into the wage contract.[19]

Frontier expansion, then, created new forms of central and marginal space and relations between them, tearing down spatial barriers to accelerate and intensify flows of merchandise and labor power, but also of discourses, symbols, and images. This construction of networks relentlessly advancing on a receding horizon turns the frontier into the spatial site of a relation between the state and capital that could be conceived under the general notion of "credit." It is through credit that nature is turned into a frontier, as its exteriority is always already in a relation of indebtedness towards the interior space of capital. This is why the taking of the land is represented not as an original act but as the collection of a debt. A space of the constitution of sovereignty, the frontier is simultaneously a place where property becomes the original form of social exchange.[20]

In the following chapters, I discuss the visual productions of space in late nineteenth-century frontier expansion in Argentina and Brazil. As I attempt to show, the very notion of frontier, and the relation between an inside and an outside it posits, is used in different ways in the process of Argentina's territorial expansion following the military occupation of the Río Negro in 1879, on the one hand, and on the other the subsequent civil and military campaigns to measure out, "pacify," and "sanitize" the rural interior, which ensued on the Republican overthrow of the Brazilian Empire ten years later. Yet in both contexts a marginal space figured as still in a state of nature would be turned into a stage on which to enact the drama of (re)founding state sovereignty: a space of national initiation. Indeed, the movement by which men and images travel through a national space taking shape precisely on account of these movements—from center to margin and back to the center—resembles a ritual journey, a rite of passage. The expeditions of geographers, engineers, medical hygienists, and others to the confines of national space acted out a script of national initiation that had already been written before their departure. The frontier, in this script, figured as a liminal space of revelation, holding the answers to the nation's existential questions.

Very likely, the names used by Argentine and Brazilian lettered culture of the nineteenth century to invoke these critical spaces refer back to the same colonial etymology: the Portuguese *sertão* appears to be a corrupted form of *desertão* (desert), not so much a particular geographical area ("the interior" as opposed to "the coast") as the radical other of colonial space. Before it became identified, towards the end of the century, with the semiarid plains of the northeastern interior and its cattle-raising "civilization of leather," *sertão* was used in a wider sense to refer to an anomic space beyond colonial control, the domain of savagery and the devil, but also (and precisely therefore) a space awaiting redemption through its eventual passage into the colonial order.[21] *El desierto* was also how Argentina's lettered elite, ever since the famous opening stanzas of Echeverría's poem *La cautiva* (1837), had referred to what remained beyond the control of the cultured city, a space devoid of physical as well as moral limits, dragging the native countrymen down a bottomless, infernal spiral of degradations, from the primitive, roaming life of the "barbarian" to the almost infrahuman cruelty of the "savage." If late nineteenth-century notions of frontier space in Argentina and Brazil shared a common origin in colonial demonologies of uncultured space, they subsequently underwent similar processes of geographical—or geological—objectification that turned them into "scientifically exact" representations. *Desierto* and *sertão* became particular areas within the new spaces of expansion of state sovereignty: the Patagonian *meseta* (plateau), for example, or the *caatingas* (bushlands) of Western Bahia, Sergipe, and Ceará. Yet at the same time, the wider moral and political implications these terms had once carried remained available to be mobilized in new contexts, more powerful than ever now that they could be "objectively" found in nature itself.

This, however, is where similarities end. Whereas, in Argentina, the consolidation of the national state was the direct outcome of the violent military conquest of the larger part of its present-day territory, in Brazil, frontier expansion was synonymous with an attempt to readjust the power balance between local patriarchates and a still feeble central authority. This does not necessarily mean that the spatial advance of state capture in Brazil was a less violent process than in Argentina, as the Brazilian army's retaliation against rural penitents in the Canudos War of 1897 made only too obvious. Rather, I am concerned with the differences between the spatial iconographies of the nation-state, many of which remain powerful even today. The Argentine state, I shall argue, forged representations of spatial capture that imaginarily aligned it with the concert of imperial powers, as a local expression of the European *bourgeoisie conquérante*. It thus maintained with its new territorial possessions a colonial relation of subordination and exteriority. At the same time, however, the tabula rasa of mapped space during the military conquest of the south also provided the visual template for a novel conception of the relations between state and society, in which the latter became an empty surface to be inscribed. In Brazil, meanwhile, the interior would be depicted as in need of state intervention, often in the image of the medical reformer administering the cure to a sick land-body. Yet here it was precisely the colonial imbalance between interior and coast, the fraught heritage of the Imperial state, which the reformism of the Old Republic's early years would feel compelled to submit to its therapies. Once again the *sertão* would be redeemed, in a secular version of the colonial narrative of the spread of faith, to fulfil its "manifest destiny" of civilization and progress. In the process, the spatial setup of the Brazilian nation-state would be made to coincide with nature's indications:*sertão* would turn not into the sea but into Planalto Central, the symbolic center of a new Brazil.

As Nísia Trindade Lima has pointed out, this new centrality of the *sertão* as a composite image combining a complex set of assertions about national society and the role of the state dominated Brazilian social discourse for more than half a century, from the "third generation" of Romanticism (Alencar, Taunay, Bernardo Guimarães) to the construction of Brasília. Its discursive foundations, she argues, were laid down during the Republic's early years, with the first great wave of expeditions and engineering projects such as the construction of the Mato Grosso telegraph by Cândido Rondon, the surveys of the Commissão Geológica of São Paulo and the Planalto Central expedition under Luiz Cruls in 1892, the inspections of the new Drought Prevention Agency, or the medical expeditions of Oswaldo Cruz, Carlos Chagas, and other members of Rio's Manguinhos Institute to the "sanitary frontiers" of tropical railroad and telegraph construction sites and the rubber boomtowns of the Amazon. Often serving more than one purpose, these journeys of inquiry reconfigured the relations between coastal metropole and tropical backlands in terms of a secular form of missionary discourse. In these writings a new theory of Brazilian nature as a medium of contagion and debilitating force emerged, inverting the trope of tropical abundance inherited from Romanticism. Brazil, in the words of medical hygienist Miguel Pereira, was one large hospital, the victim not merely of its natural environment but of centuries of abandon.[22] Visual forms—exhibitions, topographic maps, and especially photographs—were of key importance in bringing the *sertão* into the public gaze. Yet the distance posited by the perspective implied in these forms was now used as a shock technique, urging viewers to take action in order to save the nation from imminent disaster. The viewer's eye, Nancy Leys Stepan argues,

is not passive here: many of the photographs can be interpreted as overtures to social intervention—pictures of dilapidated mud houses, puddles of water in unpaved streets and chickens scratching the earth, or of people in the northeast grinding sugar-cane with equipment no more advanced than that which had been used by the Dutch in their seventeenth-century tropical colony here. These images can be said to fit the genre of documentary photography popular in Europe and the U.S. at the time. The same might be said of the many pictures of police barracks—they represent the forces of order necessary for the country's development.[23]

Hygienism, then, was a cure against history almost as much as against nature. Yet to civilize the *sertão*—*desbravar* (to tame or break) is a term often found in texts of the period—for engineer-explorers such as Cândido Rondon also meant virtually to refound the state on the basis of the interior's mestizo population in which, like Euclides da Cunha, he would find "the bedrock of our race." Like Euclides, too, Rondon would find mirrored in the vigorous space of the *sertão*, his own self-image as a "new *bandeirante*," a descendent of São Paulo's legendary mestizo backwoodsmen and slave hunters, credited with opening the western interior to the advance of colonization. Two kinds of knowledge—the discourse of the geographer-engineer and that of the medical hygienist—thus vied for the representation of the interior and called the state to intervene into its spatial entrails. While mostly interwoven with one another (expeditions would usually be staffed with engineers and medical doctors alike), there is nonetheless a dominance of engineering in the early years of the republic, in parallel with a first wave of infrastructural projects of communication and drought prevention, whereas medical hygienism gained the upper hand after the turn of the century. Here I will mostly focus on the visual representations belonging to the first type of discourse, asking for the ways in which they made sovereignty visible on the very surface of the earth.

Rather than from previous colonial and national representations, the Argentine state in its expansion southward had to reclaim Patagonia from the imperial discourses in which it had figured as a global frontier from as early on as

Magellan's discovery of a southern passage connecting the oceans.[24] Its role in the expansion of a Eurocentric world order, as a last obstacle as well as a threshold, had produced images of an archetypal space of liminality and passage, of beginning and end of the world, revisited in the nineteenth century by FitzRoy, Darwin, and others. Their descriptions forged visions of a barren, inhospitable ur-space of evolution, a kind of geographical fossil from the origins of the earth. To reclaim such a non-site as a theater of national sovereignty meant, as Gabriela Nouzeilles has shown, "to reinvent Patagonia and question the imperial fictions that represented it as unconquerable space."[25] This struggle against previous imperial representations—the traces of which are visible on maps of the region to this day, where a dystopian and a triumphant nationalist toponymy vie with one another—reimagined Patagonia within a narrative of the natural history of the nation-state. As we have already observed in our guided tour of the Museum of La Plata, Patagonian space was made to represent simultaneously the past and the future of Argentina. It was both a place of the mythological origins of nationality and, as a source of wealth yet to be exploited, the spatial image of a glorious future. Two types of natural images corresponded to these apparently contradictory locations on opposite ends of the temporal axis; in turn-of-the-century travelogues, these would often appear in the sequential order of a rite of passage, a trial laid out for the traveller by nature itself. At one end of this symbolic itinerary would be the arid and empty landscape of the desert *meseta*, at the other, rewarding the traveller for his or her previous endurance, the lush forests and lakes of the *precordillera*. Thus the geographical explorer who mastered the hardships of the desert and was rewarded with the beauty of an Edenic landscape already anticipated experimentally the experience of the pioneer-settler, who would effectively turn the barren space of the desert into fertile and prosperous lands. Nature itself had already written out the script of its own conquest and transformation, waiting for those with eyes to see.

Hence Patagonia supplied sublime landscapes in which (as we have seen above in Moyano's travelogue) the state's power could be almost tangibly experienced in the relation between nature and its beholder. Conversely, the region also provided, in its arid version, natural images of emptiness, of pure unshaped availability, a primal mass still awaiting the Word of its Demiurge. As Nouzeilles suggests, Patagonian space in between these two archetypal representations is saturated with violent resonances, not only because of the harsh opposition between them, but because it is a "natural" stage of the state's violent imposition of its power over society. The natural sublime of the Patagonian landscape, in other words, is also the fetishized image of the violence of the state against its enemies (the Indians, the rural poor, the workers), a natural image heavy with the histories it disavows. It is only logical, then, that apart from quixotic attempts (from Orllie-Antoine de Tounens's short-lived Araucanian empire to Raúl Alfonsín's project of a national capital at Viedma), Patagonia would never turn into an interior space in the way of the Planalto Central, but on the contrary into a space of expulsion and banishment of the undesirable. The creation of prison colonies at Ushuaia, Neuquén, and Trelew not only turned Patagonia into a space of confinement, an Argentine Siberia, or "Australia," in Payró's surprisingly unironic phrase; it also renewed its status as a marginal space, a constitutive outside of the state where the protection of the law ended.

In the following chapters I want to investigate the origins of these different notions of margin in the spatial iconographies of state power in Argentina and Brazil. I want to find out why Patagonia has remained to this day a space connoted not only with utopian images of the nation (and the world) but also with associations of violence and war, and with the frustration or betrayal of the national project. By contrast, I will look at why Brazil's República Velha (Old Republic), which so often failed to make a lasting impact, nonetheless succeeded in forging a powerful new representation of national territory. Indeed, the late nineteenth-century image of the *sertão* as abandoned space, suffering because of the lack of attention from a vain, Europe-focused coast, has in many ways survived even its most spectacular consequence: the construction, from 1956 onward, of the new national capital, Brasília. For, even if the modernist utopia of reform from above has long since entered history's scrap yard of failed ideas, the figure of a spatial abandon continues in its various guises to be a powerful representation of Brazil's unresolved conflicts.

# CHAPTER 4

# Into the Heart of the State

## THE PLANALTO EXPEDITION

> The power of a country road is different when one is walking along it from when one is flying over it by airplane.... The airplane passenger sees only how the road pushes through the landscape, how it unfolds according to the same law as the terrain surrounding it. Only he who walks the road on foot learns of the power it commands, and, of how, from the very scenery that for the flier is only the unfurled plain, it calls forth distances, belvederes, clearings, prospects at each of its turns like a commander deploying soldiers at the front.
>
> —Walter Benjamin, *One-Way Street*

### Enframing Brasília

The foundation of Brasília inverts the biblical myth of the Tower of Babel: rather than employing the science of the architect to elevate human vision to the divine height of all-encompassing knowledge, the creators of Brazil's modernist capital simply presupposed the view from above as the starting point of urbanist creation. The airplane-shaped axial cross onto which Lúcio Costa, the winner of the 1956 contest for a general outline of the new capital, mapped the modernist cityscape allegorically compresses the notion of a perspectivist utopia made possible by technological progress, as well as referring it back to its religious and colonial origins. Brasília was a city conceived by the ideal gaze from above, which Angel Rama characterizes as the mode in which the city form had been implemented in Latin America since the beginnings of colonization. City power, he sustains in *The Lettered City*, appears as always already overcoded in terms of state power, entirely preconceived in the symbolic orders of writing and the map.[1] In this chapter I propose a critique of the modernist myth of origin put forth in Costa's pilot plan and in the gesture of autogenesis it proclaims, by referring it back to the historical beginnings of its foundational rhetoric.[2] More specifically, I will analyze the visual and discursive production, at the end of the nineteenth century, of the "Planalto Central" (central plateau) as the predestined heart of Brazil and future site of the national capital. This project symbolically refounded the state by means of a return to the source, the lost center, the Natal. In the exploration of this mythically invested place and its representation as a geographical mission, a territorial ritual of state-worship was invented, which subsequent projects to study, prepare, and eventually realize the relocation of the federal capital continued to reenact.

In 1892 the Republican government had commissioned Luiz Cruls, the Belgian-born director of Rio's National Observatory and professor of geodesy and astronomy at the *Escola Superior de Guerra* (where Euclides da Cunha was among his disciples), with "the exploration of the plateau at the center of the Republic, and demarcation of the area that is to be occupied by the future capital of the United States of Brazil."[3] Two years earlier, the Constituent Assembly had passed a proposal to include under article 3 of the new constitution the relocation of the federal capital to the Planalto Central. (Another project suggesting Cidade Tiradentes as a name for the future capital, in honour of the "martyr" of the Mineiro insurgency of 1789, was rejected.) In 1891, Deodoro da Fonseca's military government allocated 250,000 reis to the expedition, which was to consist, apart from Cruls himself, of two astronomers, two medical doctors, five assistant secretaries, one pharmacist, one botanist, two mechanics, four mule drivers, a commanding officer, and two adjutants. The total equipment, including theodolites, sextants, chronometers, barometers, and a photographic camera and laboratory, occupied 206 boxes and weighed almost 10,000 kilograms.[4] On June 6, 1892, the explorers departed from Rio by railroad to Uberaba, Minas Gerais, from where they would travel by mule and on foot to the old towns of Goiás, Catalão, and Pyrenopolis and onward into the western interior, eventually covering during their exploits a total distance of 4,373 kilometers. Upon their return to Rio, having completed "the tasks of the study,"[5] the commission issued two luxurious folio volumes, published jointly by the observatory's printing press and the prestigious publishing house of Lombaerts, in a bilingual Portuguese and French edition. The first tome contained the commission's report, with special sections on the geology, botany, and climatology of the region, lavishly illustrated with photographic plates.[6] The second, entitled *Atlas of the Itineraries, Longitudinal Profiles, and of the Demarcated Area*, contained sixty-nine plates of itineraries (*caminhamentos*, literally "walks") with the corresponding profiles of altitude, topographical plans of towns and villages of the region, preceded by two maps indicating the position of the proposed federal district and its relation

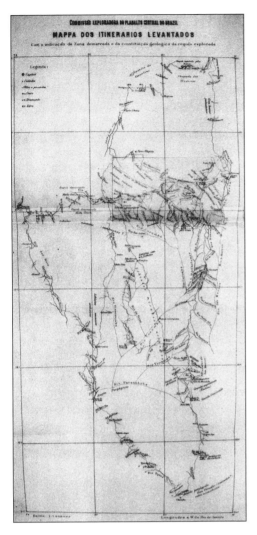

FIGURE 31. Exploring Commission of the Brazilian Central Plateau, "Map of the Itineraries Covered." In *Atlas dos Itinerários, Perfis longitudinais e da zona demarcada* (1894). Ibero-Amerikanisches Institut, Berlin.

to the expedition's trajectory.[7] On these introductory maps, a rectangular-shaped grey shadow, crisscrossed by blue lines indicating waterways and red ones indicating the expedition's itineraries, appears superimposed on the white surface, singling out the area that had been chosen to become the new center of the Brazilian Republic (fig. 31).

Studies of Brasília's planning and construction tend to gloss over this prehistory of the modernist city in a paragraph or two, duly registering previous ideas of relocating the federal capital in Pombaline colonial reformism, the proto-republicanism of the Minas Conspiracy (Inconfidência Mineira) and in the diplomatic and historical thought of the First and Second Regency. Yet, once a previous discursive tradition is thus acknowledged, the greater part of the critical corpus on Brasília then moves on from the anecdotal to the analytical, in a gesture that is not altogether unlike the way in which its critical object itself disavows history with its claim to a creation ex nihilio.[8] I will argue, instead, that the visual utopianism that materialized in the construction of Brasília constitutively depended on a previous production of the void into which an inscription that paraded as foundational could be performed. If, in other words, Juscelino Kubitschek's answer to the economic and political challenges posed to his presidency in 1956 was a symbolic "flight into space" as a way of eluding the contradictions classical populism could no longer articulate, such a move only became feasible through reference to a spatial archive whose decisive formalization had occurred under the Florianist state of the early 1890s. The unfulfilled promise of this historical precedent would now finally be met by the Kubitschek administration. Both in 1892 and in 1956, the symbolic reorganization of national space was intended to neutralize the influence exercised on central government by regional pressure groups, in moving forth into a truly national space beyond the grip of regional elites. The Planalto expedition, rather than merely a picturesque forerunner to Lúcio Costa's and Oscar Niemeyer's modernist city, was in fact its constituent moment: the construction of a visual and discursive frame within which their radical architectural statements became possible. It is of no minor importance that this act of enframing occurred precisely at the time when a particular kind of "new city" was being created—Belo Horizonte, the artificial capital of Minas Gerais, construction of which began in 1894—and another, Canudos, was destroyed.

Enframing, Timothy Mitchell explains in his acute analysis of the colonial capture of Egypt, was a production of order by way of constructing an invisible grid laid out across the entire fabric of society. In spite of its immateriality, this "frame" rendered itself transparent to an observer skilled in the art of arranging the material world as always already destined to the gaze: as a picture. The material world, Mitchell argues, drawing on Heidegger's notion of the world-picture, "appears to the observer as a relationship between picture and reality, the one present but secondary, the other only represented, but prior, more original, more real."[9] Enframing, then, is a way of presenting space as the neutral, inert canvas on which a production of order can take its place, intervening into social practices in the name of the superior harmony of the picture.

What I want to discuss in this chapter is the construction of a spatial frame that resignifies not only the interior it circumscribes but the entire space of the nation-state. For if a frame, an empty rectangle drawn into the national map, was indeed the only tangible outcome of the Planalto expedition, this inconspicuous addition nevertheless changed the meaning of the entire image. On the surface of the map itself, a window was opened onto another, more ideal space that lay at once beneath and in the future of the cartographic image. The indication of a future capital district infused national space—and in particular the space of the interior, the backlands—with a teleological temporality: space became the medium of Brazil's transformation into a modern nation, the dimension in which its historical destiny lay already inscribed. At the same time, this remapping of the nation made it possible to bypass social practices and imagine the state as the demiurgic creator of society. As I will show, this form of cartography, in which the map appears as constituent of social space, relied on a systematic emptying out of actually existing marks of human habitation and interaction with the environment. Instead, it called on "nature" in a twofold way—both as a telluric mandate in which state sovereignty is already encoded, and as a permanent excess of this very order that has to be confined through measures of geographical engineering. The principal (and most basic) visual tropes of this cartographic enframing of space are the line and the rectangle.

Luiz Cruls, unlike Lúcio Costa some sixty years later in his pilot proposal for Brasília, begins his report on the Planalto expedition not by inscribing a timeless and blank surface, in a self-consciously mythical rite of foundation, but on the contrary by a *historical review* of previous proposals to relocate the capital. "The authors," he writes, "who have busied themselves with this project unanimously point to the area containing the sources of the rivers Araguaia, Tocantins, São Francisco, and Paraná, in other words, the Planalto Central."[10] Cruls's own mapping of the center of the state is a historical as much as a geographical exercise: not merely to locate the sources of rivers but also those in the archive, to return to the origins of national discourse—a journey upstream through time, to be eventually repeated in space. In this way, we learn that the name "Brasília" had already been proposed by José Bonifácio de Andrada e Silva, Brazil's first prime minister, in a note from 1823. A year earlier, it had been suggested for the first time in an anonymous constitutional proposal, which also indicated a spot near the sources of the two great river systems as the location best suited for the project. Cruls also quotes extensively from an even earlier piece by José da Costa Furtado de Mendonça, published in 1808 in the London-based pro-independence paper *Corréio Brasiliense*, in which he already finds all the main strands of argument for the capital's removal from Rio de Janeiro to an inland location, including, first and foremost, a discourse of national security, insisting on the defensive advantages of an inland over a coastal capital (a point certainly made under the impact of the French invasion of Portugal, but which, in 1893, must have struck a chord in the ears of military engineers who had only recently participated in the defence of Rio against the insurgent navy). More importantly, it demonstrates a cultural and political discourse that distributes an intensity of national belonging across geographical space:

Rio de Janeiro has none of the qualities that are required from the city destined to become the capital of the Brazilian Empire: and if the courtesans arriving from Lisbon had any patriotism and gratefulness at all towards the country which has welcomed them, they would generously sacrifice the comfort and luxury they enjoy at Rio de Janeiro, and establish themselves somewhere in the heart of the interior, in the immediacy of the sources of our great rivers, to build a new city there and begin to open up roads to all the seaports, remove the natural barriers from the navigable rivers, and thus lay the cornerstone for the largest, the best-connected and best-defended Empire yet existing in this part of the world.[11]

Finally, Medonça's essay displays a providential discourse of nature as impregnated with a promise of plenty: "In its vicinity are the banks of mighty rivers, running to the North, the South, the Northwest and the Southwest, vast grasslands on which to raise cattle, an abundance of stone for all kinds of construction, woods for all the carpentry work necessary, and rich mines of every range of metal; in short, a situation which can be compared with the descriptions we know of earthly Paradise."[12]

In a nutshell, then, Mendonça's text from 1808 already contains all the principal ingredients of the modernizing discourses of the late nineteenth and even the mid-twentieth century: geographical organicism—the nation-state as an a priori spatial entity whose integrity has to be defended against a hostile exterior, and whose internal cohesion is imagined as an anthropomorphic system of vital fluids; a discourse of nature as simultaneously providential and potential; and, thirdly, a dream of autochthony, of inverting the flows of material and symbolic value from the inside to the outside. The coincidence of political and geographical center in the inland capital is the core figure of this geopolitical imagination of the nation—a term chosen in 1946 by the General Poli Coelho, head of yet another Planalto expedition:

The majority of our state capitals lack a convenient location in the center of the territory. It has been difficult to correct this defect. It seems as if we were in no hurry to tear our administrative activity, taking place in the capitals, away from the unhealthy influences that conspire for the failure of all our governments. *We lack a heroic sense of nationality.* The solution proposed by the Commission for the Demarcation of the Planalto, presided over by Dr. L. Cruls, was the only one to this day to have resolved the problem from the geopolitical point of view, which is the one the problem really requires. The balance between geographical conditions and political advantages [...] plainly justifies that Cruls's solution be called *geopolitical*.[13]

The echoes of Furtado de Mendonça in this piece of military prose are evident in its contempt for the civilian governments' "unhealthy" proximity to the coast (that is, to commerce and foreign capital), as opposed to the "heroic" self-conquest of military (or, "geopolitical") reason, for which a fortified, inland-centered national space becomes a means of controlling the flows of influence. If it is possible, indeed, to organize a history of the Brazilian state along the variations and reappearances of the idea of relocating the national capital, the Cruls mission as the moment in which this discourse becomes, in Poli Coelho's words, genuinely geopolitical, marked a key point of disjuncture between nineteenth- and twentieth-century conceptions of space and sovereignty. We must therefore first insert it into the spatial tradition invoked by Cruls himself, in order to fully understand its pictorial and verbal representations.

## The Continental Island

The production of an imaginary of the nation-state, in Brazil, relied more heavily on geographical representations than in other parts of Latin America, due to the particularities of its independence process. The fact that its separation from the Portuguese motherland had occurred as a reform from above, in dynastic continuity between the colonial and the national order, conspired against any historical emphasis on the heroic beginnings of national *time*. The persistence of slavery as the dominant mode of production, furthermore, deprived such a history of its collective subject—the people-nation. Territorial cohesion, on the other hand, was of prime importance for the defense of a slavery-based mode of production, both internally and externally. The preservation of a territorial unity already indicated by nature, therefore, became a cardinal virtue the Imperial state attributed to itself. What distinguished the Brazilian Empire among its neighbors, Demétrio Magnoli suggests, was the production, from very early on, "of a specific geographical imaginary, designed to project into the future, as a reality, the myth of a pre-existing territory."[14]

Colonial cartography had developed as a way of legitimizing the continuous Portuguese violations of the Tordesillas meridian, the pictorial tradition of the Ilha Brasil (Brazilian Island). The Brazilian Island, it was suggested, was surrounded by the waters of the Amazon, the Paraná, and their tributaries, which were supposed to spring from a great lagoon at the heart of the continent. Over the nineteenth century, Brazilian cartography would insistently maintain this fiction of aquatic enclosure by having at least some minor tributary of the Paraná and the Guaporé meet in the little explored western interior. Brazilian space was thus shown to have preceded, and conditioned, Brazilian history, which had unfolded precisely as a realization of the spatial destiny already assigned to it by "nature." The doctrine of natural borders was tenaciously defended by Imperial diplomacy to sustain Brazilian claims to the northern shore of the River Plate (eventually resulting in the independence of the Banda Oriental, through British arbitration), as well as in a number of other border disputes, in which Brazil proved exceptionally successful, thanks in great part to the sophistication attained by the discipline of historical geography.

The importance of the picturesque for Brazilian national discourse in the first half of the nineteenth century stems precisely from this defining role assigned to nature. Picturesque landscape, as closely interwoven with naturalist inquiry, displayed an attitude towards nature capable at the same time of deploying scientific surveys and aesthetic empathy. Picturesque landscape was the site of convergence between natural, political, and aesthetic space, the mirror image of a state that, while receiving from nature one of its principles of legitimacy (the other being the dynastic continuity of the House of Bragança), also exercised on it a benign, civilizing authority. We could, perhaps, speak of a Habsburgian version of U.S. frontier mythology: not so much the mutual transformation of a violent, primordial wilderness and a libertarian, free-floating population, but the mild, even sensual, convergence between two imperial orders. On the other hand, the rising importance of the myth of the *bandeirante*—the *paulista* slave hunter and backwoodsman—towards the end of the century not only reflected the increasing influence on a national scale of the thriving immigrant state of São Paulo. It also expressed a discursive shift starting in the 1870s in which the genteel and contemplative attitude of the picturesque gave way to a more boldly utilitarian stance towards a nature now more and more openly conceived as a reservoir of marketable resources.

Cartography was deployed now not just to define, for diplomatic purposes, the Empire's "natural borders," but as a key to unlock the vast wilderness sheltered by the coastal mountains, in response to increased land demands of an expanding coffee economy, as well as a general increase and diversification of overseas demand for crops and primary materials. A first *Atlas do Império* was published by Cândido Mendes in 1868; in 1875, on occasion of that year's National Exhibition, a more detailed *Carta do Império do Brasil*, drawn under the supervision of the Barão da Ponte Riveiro, was revealed to the public. In 1879 the British engineer James H. Wells published a general map of the railway network spanning the provinces of Rio de Janeiro, São Paulo, and Minas Gerais; in 1883, the Ministry of Agriculture issued a map of the Empire "with the designation of the railroads, colonies, telegraph lines and steam navigation." Two years earlier, Honório Bicalho had already published a *Plano Geral de Viação*, which, in spite of contrary evidence depicted the Guaporé and Madeira rivers as navigable throughout, and proposed to link them by inland railroad tracks, the same as, farther south, the Guaporé, Paraná, and Paraguay rivers. Effectively, while cartographic publishing was on the rise, inland railways such as the infamous Ferrovia do Diabo from Madeira to Mamoré in Bolivia—a disastrous project claiming the lives of up to six thousand workers—were now being built not merely for the purpose of linking the coffee plantations to the nearest seaport, but also responding to a strategic rationale of infrastructural integration.

At a time when medical hygienism began to submit the cities' popular quarters to large-scale sanitary campaigns, a new discourse of geographical engineering reimagined the state as a territorial organism ridden with colonial inertia and therefore in need of technical intervention. Luiz Cruls himself, in an article published in 1901 in the journal *Federação*, argued that technical intervention into natural conditions might improve even the seemingly inhospitable environment of the Amazonian jungle:

A region's climate does not, alas, constitute an element beyond change; little by little it can be modified, for better or worse, depending essentially on the nature of human intervention. Certainly it is not in razing the forest, or in removing the soil, that one will succeed in improving these, but the local conditions, considered from the point of view of the constitution of the terrain and the natural distribution of water and attending to the lessons of public hygiene, will indicate the means to improve a region's salubrious conditions. It is wrong to attribute solely to Nature a state of things for which Man is largely responsible.[15]

In this passage from "Nature" to "the nature of human intervention," emphasis has shifted from romantic providentialism to the active and transforming agency of the engineer-geographer. Yet the trace of picturesque natural history with its game of mirrors between nature's and the monarchy's essential harmony and equilibrium has not completely vanished. In fact, if improvement and progress now depend on the distributive reason of the engineer, his method consists in a kind of ecological hermeneutics, in deciphering the immanent intention that is already codified in the natural environment itself.

## Engineering Nature

The paradoxical character of this notion of nature is also evident in Cruls's introduction to his report on the Planalto expedition. The objective, he writes, is "to indicate the region of Brazil assigned, as it were, by nature, to become one day the seat of a new capital." Nature has already pronounced its verdict, now it takes the intervention of the engineer to intercept this signal and make it resonate in the political geography of the state. The voice of the state has to be made to interpret the voice of nature. The operator of this transmission, or translation between natural and political language, is the engineer-geographer: "Let us look, in the first place," Cruls invites his readers, "at the sense of the words in article 3 of the Constitution, where we find the expression Brazilian Central Plateau [*planalto central do Brasil*]."[16]

The struggle is, then, first and foremost with the elusive character of reference itself, and the objective to endow an expression that is defined as constitutive with self-revealing presence. The challenge, in other words, is to translate political will into natural evidence. As Gilles Deleuze and Félix Guattari have suggested, an engineer is a technician who mediates between smooth and striated space, between national space and that which it excludes and at the same time presupposes, an organizer and neutralizer of the flows of energy that fuel, yet also potentially threaten, the reproduction of state power.[17] It is in this way, too, that the geography of the Planalto Commission conjures the rival yet complementary powers of national and natural space, whose tension is reflected (and increased) by that between different forms of verbal and visual imagery in the commission's report.

As we have seen, Cruls locates the spatial meaning of the constitutional mandate on the crossroads of historiography and hydrography, in the space where the geometrical center of the map comes closest to the providential origin and point of arrival in the nation's quest for the self, amid the sources of its great waterways. In fact, as both the Amazonian and the Platine river systems are composed of tributaries springing from sources far distant from one another, the choice of relatively minor ones as origins on the grounds of their mutual proximity represents a reading of the map very much informed by the territorial legends it supposedly confirms. As Cruls himself admits, moreover, the nomenclature of *planalto*—just like that of *sertão* that it is in many ways supposed to overwrite and replace—could be applied almost indiscriminately to the entire backland region beyond the coastal mountain range. "This plateau," Cruls writes, "occupies most of the states of Rio de Janeiro and Minas Gerais, the lesser part of Goiás, and reaches out, in the form of long stretches, towards Bahia, on the eastern bank of the São Francisco River, as well as, on the western bank, towards the border of the state of Goiás with those of Maranhão and Piauí, and finally, southward along the coastline until it reaches Rio Grande do Sul. Hence, in great strokes, the general configuration of the Brazilian plateau which interests us here."[18]

In this monumental geological synthesis, a territorial organism is made present through the invocation of its constituent parts. The central plateau is a geopolitical necessity, it *has to* spread from the southernmost to the northernmost states because it is conceived as the spatial articulator that binds the individual members of national space into a single territorial body. Hence, it is at its geometrical zero point, rather than in any of the space units into which it branches out, that the capital city as the spatial embodiment of the national bond has to be located.

Once this abstract, mathematical-historical emplacement has been realized, however, the discourse of landscape returns, as if in a cinematographic zoom shot, to bestow on the chosen spot a different kind of presence. It is a different "nature" that is now called to the scene, facing the beholder on a horizontal plane and confirming in its picturesque plenty the geographer's election. Himself a rather limited prose writer, Cruls calls on a fellow expatriate and member of the commission, the French botanist and chief inspector of parks and gardens at Rio de Janeiro, Auguste Glaziou, to describe the marvels of the designated area. The letter carrying Glaziou's response to Cruls's assignment, dated "Planalto central do Brasil, 16 de novembro de 1894," duly lays out a verbal picturesque of softly undulating hills, gentle valleys, and clear springs, observed from the vantage point of the wandering tourist. Unsurprisingly, the association of French and English park landscapes, the archetypal homesteads of picturesque nature, is never far away, as Glaziou artfully arranges foregrounds and horizons without, at the same time, losing sight of the potential usages of its primary resources:

The aspect of the area [...] is that of a softly undulating country, which reminds me of the Anjou, of Normandy, or even more of Britanny, except towards the West, where the mountains of the Pyrenees tower picturesquely. Towards the East, a beautiful and grandiose valley stretches out towards the little shrublands surrounding the Parnauá River, at times branching out into multiple directions. This immense plain, of a softly inclined surface, is tremendously rich in clean and delicious streams of water, which spring from even the smallest depressions of the terrain. These sources, like the great rivers that irrigate the region, are protected by giant trees, which Man's axe must never fell but with the greatest prudence. The pastures are of a lush green, and certainly better than any I have seen in Brazil. All these elements, the arrangement of which could be attributed to the inspiration of a sublime artist, confer on the scene a most delightful aspect, comparable only to, on a smaller scale, the old English parks designed by Le Notre or Paxton. So profoundly has the benign quality of the climate impressed me that it continuously comes to my mind.[19]

As in many other accounts of scientific travel in turn-of-the-century Brazil, "what is being represented is not so much the landscape per se as the landscape as an impediment or invitation to progress."[20] Picturesque nature provides the visual grammar for domesticating space and thus reassuringly introduces into the traveller's narrative a metonymical reference to home and homecoming. However, its deployment in Cruls's report in order to promote the Planalto landscape as the best choice for a future capital was at the very least contradictory. For, if the parklike plateau faced the traveller as homely and inviting, this was, of course, because it had effectively been colonized and settled for centuries. The empty center was, in fact, a colonial backwater that had lapsed into oblivion after an ephemeral gold rush in the early eighteenth century.[21] The image of parklike, picturesque nature was thus at the same time an active erasure of the material, historical practices that had produced it. The "mythical production of the Garden-Country," in Marilena Chaui's words, "throws us into Nature's bosom at the same time as it throws us outside the historical world."[22]

Several of the commission's members commented favorably on the neatness and tranquil pace of the towns and villages of Goiás, Formosa, Pyrenopolis, and Catalão. Antônio Pimentel, the expedition's medical officer, highlighted the near absence of tuberculosis and other contagious diseases, which had become the scourge of many cities on the coast. Eugênio Hussak, the commission's geologist, personally inspected some of the diamond and gold mining sites around Catalão and Agua Suja and diagnosed widespread reserves of coal, metals, and minerals throughout the region, "a truly opulent state of wealth," concluded Cruls, "which has to this very day remained virtually unknown."[23]

Yet if the region's insular tranquility made it possible for Cruls and his fellow commissioners to counterpose a picturesque idyll to the unfavorable images of the Brazilian interior as insalubrious and desertlike, fashioned earlier in the century by European travellers such as Castelnau and Saint-Hilaire, it also contradicted the geopolitical axiom of a place of pure potentiality, awaiting the state's foundational inscription. The commission's report thus had to refer at one and the same time to the picturesque present of the region as proof of its inhabitability, and to immediately disavow this very image to recreate a space still unmediated by history and therefore available for the staging of an original encounter between nature and the state. Already in Glaziou's introductory sketch, the "parklike" character of the region appears, rather than as the imprint of a human landscape, as a feat of nature itself, which turns it into an indicator of *future* settlement. In their final reports, several of the commission's members tackled the problem even more explicitly, asking how a landscape that had revealed itself as promising could at the same time be home to a backward population. The answer was, of course, that is had been misused by its present inhabitants, descendants, Cruls explained, of *paulista* gold diggers whose greed and lack of foresight had made them neglect the development of industry and agriculture that would have made the region flourish. Pimentel, on his part, described the colonization of Goiás in the language of contemporary psychiatry as a case of mass pathology, in which the stimulus of "ephemeral opulence" exercised a corrupting influence on the local population, eventually returning it to a state "dominated purely by the instincts of animal pleasures."[24] Precisely because the region suffered from the aftereffects of a dysfunctional colonial order, however, it could be reclaimed by a discourse of improvement brought about by geographical engineering. What was more, its past and present misuse made Goiás into an emblem of the problems shared by the entire Brazilian interior, and as such, its redemption, which would turn it into the center of a new spatial order, also redeemed national space as a whole. Planalto space was, then, the result of a constant refocusing, an oscillation between visions of fullness and emptiness. It is this paradoxical simultaneity of presence and absence, this game of *fort/da*, which also organizes the visual accounts of the Cruls expedition.

## Natural Geometry

When deciding on the contours of the future federal district, Cruls was responding to the Republican constitution's contradictory assignment, on the one hand, to reconcile political and "natural" space and, on the other, to impose on it an abstract, utilitarian rationality, which expressed itself in the rather arbitrary figure of 14,400 square kilometers as the prescribed size of the new center. If the entire project of capital relocation implied a notion of the naturalness of national space, the determination of the area's size prior to its localization referred to the opposite idea of the priority of abstract political over natural space. The natural center, in short, had to be outlined within artificial borders. If the question of locality had been conveniently resolved with recourse to the tradition of the Brazilian Island, Cruls simply pretended to ignore the conceptual contradiction into which strict adherence to the constitutional mandate would invariably have brought him. Although, he claimed, a demarcation of the prescribed area within the natural borders of the terrain would have been possible, time had been too short for a careful inspection of the region's orography and hydrography. He had therefore opted for the rectilinear divisions already adopted in other areas of frontier expansion, such as Australia or the United States, which, he argued, carried the additional benefit of precluding objections from the local governments affected: "the rectangle best fulfilled the purpose we had proposed ourselves and, thanks to its regular geometrical shape, provided the additional advantage of avoiding future border disputes."[25]

Rectilinear subdivision of lands, Paul Carter has shown, enabled governments to accelerate territorial capture and taxable settlement without having to incur costly explorations.[26] Land, in much the same way as labor, was thus turned into an abstract and quantifiable commodity, regardless of its concrete physiognomy. Rectilinear demarcation was imperial capitalism's visual means of submitting places to the logic of universal equivalence. In the case of the Planalto expedition, moreover, and despite Cruls's reluctance to acknowledge the iconic properties of his rectangular frame, its elementary geometry conveyed with striking efficiency a notion of national space as at once rooted in nature and transforming it through state intervention.

However, when Cruls dispatched subcommissions to each of the four sides of the rectangle with the assignment to walk in a straight line from center to margin and, once there, to march along one of its angles before returning to the central meeting point, the concrete conditions on the ground forced each of them into enormous detours. As the opening map of the commission's *Atlas* shows, the rectangle's borders and the actual trajectories of the expedition hardly ever coincided, so much so that the itineraries' purpose of "confirming" the rectangle *en lieu* becomes almost unrecognizable (fig. 31). Insofar as they invariably went astray, the itineraries left on the very surface of the map a trace of the tensions and conflicts between the cartographic space of the state and the spaces of practice onto which it sought to impose itself.

The expedition's most distinctive visual testimonies, however, were the sixty-nine plans of walks (*caminhamentos*) that followed on the national map, thus making up almost the entire documentation of the *Atlas*. The length of each walk was calculated on the base of readings from the pedometer, an instrument recording the number of steps taken during the period of measurement by the mule with the most regular pace. Geodesic measurements and views from or onto prominent features of the landscape served, in addition, to indicate the direction of the walks and the altitude levels that they reached. Yet rather than to combine these data into a single cartographic image, Cruls displayed them separately, so that each table contained representations operating on different levels and according to different visual logics.

At their most basic, these plans only consist of two jagged lines running across the blank page alongside their axis of orientation, while other more elaborate ones include particular features such as rivers and hills that are mapped out, from a vertical top-down perspective, as far as they would have been observable from the itinerary itself. Occasionally, too, little insets feature landscape views as well as the indication of the vantage point and angle from which they had been drawn.

Different types of writing also figure prominently on all the plates, at times

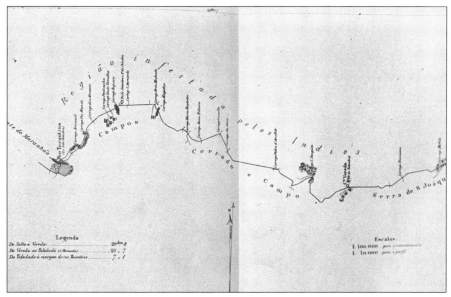

FIGURE 32. Exploring Commission of the Brazilian Central Plateau, "Walk from Chapadão dos Viadeiros to Pyrenopolis via S. José de Tocantins." In *Atlas dos Itinerários, Perfis longitudinais e da zona demarcada* (1894). Ibero-Amerikanisches Institut, Berlin.

recording particular incidents during the march (camps, river crossings), at times adding information about the characteristics of the white space bordering the expedition's track. Plate 38, for instance, records an itinerary syncopated by regular crossings of rivers and creeks. The itinerary appears to have followed the fault line of a frontier bordered on one side, by plains, steppes, and mountains— an alternation of landscapes—and to the other by "a region infested by Indians," where the view of nature remains literally obstructed by the malign presence of the colonial other (fig. 32).

Although in their almost abstract minimalism, the walks recall premodern cartographic forms such as medieval road maps, unlike these they are not organized in an exclusively temporal sequence, even if in both cases it is the traveller's own body that serves as the measure of distance. Or rather, the traveller's mule's body, in the case of the Cruls expedition, which points us to the difference between the two forms of cartography. For, while the medieval traveller would have recorded distance in terms of the time it took him to get from A to B—not the empty, universally equivalent time imposed in the late nineteenth century, but a complex narrative entanglement of local space-times held together only by the body of the narrator—here the travelling body turns into a mechanical extension of the apparatus attached to it. The body is but an (imperfect) machine whose movement eventually allows calculating the "objective," disembodied distance between both points. Paraphrasing Foucault, we could say that the body is submitted to an "instrumental coding" that transforms it into an extension of the spatial discipline that is imposed onto the terrain.[27] As such, the travelling body can be separated from the abstract, all-encompassing perspective, which translates the *space* opened up by the action of travel into a cartographic *place*, a selfsame object excised from the journey's performative rhythms.

As a *caminhamento*, the journey becomes a line that, stripped of temporality, represents by means of scale, extension, and direction the *objective* distance between, and respective position of, two points. The traveller's engagement in and with space is reduced to an abstract, biunivocal relation between points. The time of journeying is erased from a page that remains, significantly, almost blank. Journeying, of course, is one of the "spatial practices" that, Michel de Certeau has suggested, constitute space as a domain of human experience, as a form of engagement between a body and its environment.[28] The *caminhamento* marks the exact limit between this notion of space as social practice and its reification by cartography as an "objective" relation between places. In its inaugural gesture, the tracing of a line, cartography overwrites the social relations of its own making and classifies the void left behind by their absence as nature.

The Planalto Commission's cartography, like its writings, cleared space of social relations, first and foremost those the explorers themselves maintained with the environment and its inhabitants. Yet while the written depiction of space, the travelogue, as a work of language, can never entirely erase social space from its space of representation, the map as a visual image has more powerful means of disavowal at its disposal. The white background and the solitary line do not merely transcribe material space, they also forge a powerful visual rhetoric of foundation. The minimalism of the *caminhamento* maps is a trope in which the foundational character of the Planalto Commission's task finds a performative expression.

Yet why was it necessary to travel across remote backlands in the midst of winter, carrying heavy equipment across thousands of kilometers, only to produce a heap of almost abstract drawings indicating the location of an empty rectangle that was self-consciously a cartographic fiction? What exactly had to be confirmed on the ground, if what the expedition had been asked to define—the future center of a new Brazil—was by definition absent from physical reality? If, in fact, the rectangle's borders had been consciously drawn in utter disregard of any existing physical or cultural units and obstacles, why the need to physically experience what was, by definition, an imposition of *nomos* over *physis*? What was the purpose of the Planalto expedition?

There are two ways of answering these questions. As we have seen, the cartography produced by the commission disavowed the process of its own making. As a result, the empty, objective space constituted by quantitative distances between points, appears to forego its own capture: space is always already "out there," ready to be measured and recorded, rather than being produced in the interaction between traveller and environment. This convention of disavowal that is constitutive of mapmaking in the West also dictates the order of tables in the Planalto Commission's *Atlas*. The general map of the nation-state, followed by a close-up on the region with the indication of the rectangle and an overview of the commission's itineraries (fig. 31), precedes the individual plates of the *caminhamentos*, when actually the former was only the final result, the summary, of the latter. Thus the impression of tautology is produced here by a sequential order in which the practice of travel appears merely to have confirmed, rather than produced, a cartographic image already fully composed even before the expedition's departure. By simply inverting the order of tables, then, the expedition's real task becomes clear again: not to verify the rectangle but to produce the cartographic surface onto which it could be inscribed. This production of (cartographic) space implied a double relation with local practices of space: on the one hand, to collect and classify local knowledge, observe the uses of space, and follow local guides through the unknown; on the other hand, to actively erase these engagements in the production of the map, which is but the composite image of all these data.

However, we have still not fully grasped the performative, indeed ritual, dimension of the Planalto expedition as a form of symbolic pilgrimage, a journey into the heart of the state. Indeed, I suggest, the commission's hikes across plains and valleys call for a reading as a ritual voyage to the liminal core of Brazilian territory and society. For, indeed, the expedition's itinerary not merely to but along the margins of the space singled out to become the federal district, the home of the state, was to produce not only a visual knowledge in the form of the map but also a visionary state of liminal *communitas*, in Victor Turner's expression.[29] That is, the visualization of Planalto space also had to produce a visionary form of seeing, one that already glimpsed, beyond the appearances of the present, the future Brazil. I will now turn to the photographs and narratives contained in the first volume of the commission's report to study how this transparency of a space that was simultaneously a window through time was manufactured.

### Double Exposure

Like a frontispiece, a verbal prologue, the first image of the volume, "Pessoal da commissão" ("Members of the Commission," fig. 33), presents us with the dramatis personae posing in gentlemanly attire, names displayed on the bottom of

FIGURE 33. Henrique Morize, "Members of the Commission." Photographic plate, in *Relatório apresentado a S. Ex. o Sr. Ministro da Indústria, Viação e Obras Públicas, por L. Cruls, Chefe da Commissão* (1894). Ibero-Amerikanisches Institut, Berlin.

the page (Cruls himself is third from left in the back row, physically larger than the others).

The image, taken by Henrique Morize, who also served the expedition as astronomer, is noteworthy for its careful and subtle composition: the expedition members are gathered under a semicircular treetop and along the axis of a stone wall that splits the frame in half. This horizontal axis is crossed in a right angle by the vertical line of a garden path that continues, above the men's heads, in the tree's crown, itself split into two almost identical halves resembling a set of antlers. Rather than merely presenting us with the group of travellers, this complex photographic stagecraft seems actually to do much more, virtually setting the scene of the expedition. For, in fact, the axial cross on which the commission takes its place measures out the photograph's rectangular frame in exactly the way in which, on the first map of the expedition's *Atlas*, the itineraries seek to cover the surface of the future federal district with an X-shaped grid departing from the center towards the four points of the compass (fig. 31). The photograph also seems to make a comment about the contiguity between human geometry and the forms of nature, in the way the trees in the background oppose yet also complement the garden in the foreground. The place of encounter between the upper and lower half of the picture (between natural and engineered space) is precisely the one occupied by the bodies of the explorers.

The point here is, of course, not merely about the intentions of an authorial subject, about what may or may not have driven Morize to correct his colleagues' posture and choose his camera angle. It is, rather, about a certain form of order, which seems to impose itself more or less automatically in certain ways of rendering space. This spatial reason, I have argued above, is at the core of a Western cartographic tradition that emerged simultaneously with the earliest forms of centralized state and of mercantile capital at the end of the Reconquista and the beginnings of Iberian colonial expansion. Its visual expressions, indeed, seem to be especially prone to geometrical forms, which inscribe the human body's elementary axes of orientation (up/down, left/right) into the space in which the body moves, thus dominating this space and rendering it inhabitable. Yet this elementary articulation of space and the body is immediately seized here to possess place as an external, self-contained object. It is just this active disavowal of the mutually constitutive relation between space and the body (a relation that is simultaneously exhibited and hidden from view) that is at work in the Planalto expedition's maps and photographs. In a wider sense it is also constitutive of the particular relation between territory and the people in the imaginary of the Brazilian Republic.

The theme of the contiguity between natural space and spaces of human intervention is present throughout the expedition's photographic record. The vast majority of images show the explorers swarming out into the wilderness, reassembling, and setting up camp. It is not so much the Planalto landscape, which is the subject of these photographs, but rather the different forms in which the explorers engage with and inhabit the land. River crossings and campsites are among Morize's favorite subjects, as they comprise the alternation of movement and rest that make up the journey's rhythm. "Camp on the Margins of Paranahyba River" (fig. 34) is, in this sense, one of the volume's most iconic images: in the foreground, a native canoe steered, apparently, by a dark-skinned *candongo*, or native of the region, carries two explorers in gentlemanly outdoor gear across the river; one of them (Cruls?) is standing defiantly erect and seems to be studying a map. In the background, another group of explorers stand watching on the shore, while behind them several neatly arranged white tents contrast with the dark foliage of the adjacent forest.

The conventions of picturesque landscape, laid down in the late eighteenth century by art critics such as William Gilpin and popularized by British and French colonial photographers, provide the terms of visual organization: a division of the image into several planes by the play of light and shadow, or the use of foliage and rocks to indicate foregrounds and thus the implicit place of the viewing subject. As James R. Ryan argues with regard to British imperial photogra-

FIGURE 34. Henrique Morize, "Camp on the Margins of Paranahyba River." Photographic plate, in *Relatório apresentado a S. Ex. o Sr. Ministro da Indústria, Viação e Obras Públicas, por L. Cruls, Chefe da Commissão* (1894). Ibero-Amerikanisches Institut, Berlin.

phy, picturesque landscape as "an instrument of visual colonization" organized remote nature according to the aesthetic canon of the English landscape, with which it was thus brought into a metonymic relation.[30] Once domesticated by the frame of the picturesque, foreign places could be safely made exotic again by the use of native people (preferably women) both as a means of emphasizing the image's planar structure and of suggesting the availability to Western eyes and wills of human subject and surrounding space alike.

Yet while Morize duly follows picturesque convention in the distribution of natural planes and human figures, local *candongos* are conspicuously absent. They only appear on the few occasions when, as coolies and boatmen, they assist the explorers who instead populate most of the frames. The landscape is thus emphatically possessed by the geographers, as, for instance, in "Group of the Commission on the Summit" (fig. 35), where the said summit is literally blocked from view by the exploring party. There is in these images something like a stereoscopic effect, a duplication of capture: not only is the landscape made into an object of visual purchase by the camera-eye, but it is also, in the very moment of its visual capture, physically occupied by the operators of the optical apparatus. A particular rhetoric of self-reference thus pervades these images: not only do they render the landscape available to the viewers' gaze—the gaze of "civilization"—as a natural space that gives itself immediately to the eye; they

FIGURE 35. Henrique Morize, "Group of the Commission on the Summit." Photographic plate, in *Relatório apresentado a S. Ex. o Sr. Ministro da Indústria, Viação e Obras Públicas, por L. Cruls, Chefe da Commissão* (1894). Ibero-Amerikanisches Institut, Berlin.

also depict the explorers as the first inhabitants of this virgin nature. Hence the photographs also provide a kind of visual commentary to the cartographic language of the *caminhamentos*, presenting the exploring journey as an original spatial practice—not an interaction with space as a human environment, but a foundational occupation of places that clears a visual field.

Only two types of places are pictured without this supplementary presence of the explorers, thus distinguishing them as part of the spatial frame itself. One is the vantage point, as in "Highest Point of the Pyrenees," although we have seen that vantage points are also depicted in the moment of their physical occupation by the commission. Postcolonial critics of travel have drawn attention to the importance of the viewing platform, whose attainment on behalf of the traveller is celebrated in many texts as a dramatic climax. At the same time, it can be read as a self-referential account of how questions of intelligibility and representation are negotiated and resolved in terms of the construction of a distance that is at the same time an elevation. The mountaintop anchors these negotiations once again in nature: it is not by accident that mountaineering, during the nineteenth century, became a favorite activity in colonial leisure, and a prime subject for colonial photography. The mountaintop, as a natural obstacle that, once mastered, offers privileged visual purchase on reality, is a powerful symbol of the colonial enterprise itself, as well as a monument to the truth claims of mimetic representation.

It is interesting to notice that this representational autonomy is only shared in Morize's photographic narrative by the images of old towns and settlements such as Goiás or Formosa. These are generally depicted without the presence of posing explorers, an element all the more interesting as it was certainly here that the different subcommissions dispatched to the cardinal points of the rectangle would have gathered before and after marches. Mountaintops and settlements seem to provide the vantage points between which a field of vision is opened up and organized. However, like the mountaintop views, towns and villages are also at times framed according to the overall pattern of a double exposure. A particularly intriguing image is "Campsite near Sta. Lúzia" (fig. 36), similarly split into two horizontal halves as the commission's group portrait by a path that indicates the limit of the small town, iconically represented by its white colonial church. In the foreground, the expedition has set up camp in a depression of the terrain, a second settlement neatly distinguishable from the first, not only by the difference in altitude and the dark fringe of trees and shrubs that literally functions as a borderline between town and camp, but also because the latter seems to be

FIGURE 36. Henrique Morize, "Campsite near Sta. Lúzia." Photographic plate, in *Relatório apresentado a S. Ex. o Sr. Ministro da Indústria, Viação e Obras Públicas, por L. Cruls, Chefe da Commissão* (1894). Ibero-Amerikanisches Institut, Berlin.

buzzing with activity, while the town consists merely of silent façades. There is an odd sense of anachronism, of noncoevalness, in this photograph, half elegiac heritage postcard and half safari adventure. Yet this contrast seems to be precisely the point, a spatial coincidence of two different moments in national history, the old and the new, a legacy and a new departure.

The mission of the Planalto expedition, it seems, was an exercise in seeing double: on the one hand to record locations, and on the other hand to anticipate in their distribution a spatial order as yet still absent but already invisibly "written in space." "Campsite near Santa Lúzia" manifests this double vision in the division of the image into opposite planes. In the textual narrative in which this visuality of double exposures is embedded, one of the most frequently recurring figures is precisely the double allusion to localities, first by their present names and then by their geodesic characteristics. Yet the relation between the two orders of reference is not a complementary one but rather a partial invalidation of the former on behalf of the latter, exposing the arbitrary and hence provisional character of the name as opposed to the objective data provided by geography:

[W]e crossed [Paranahiba River] at the place known as Pôrto Velho, where there is a boating service for the crossing of travellers, animals and cargo. The measurements carried out by the Commission established a medium width of 155 meters, maximum depth 12 meters and an average velocity of 0,80 meters per second on the surface. [...] On July 13, on the eve of our arrival at Catalão, we set camp at the *fazenda* of Mariano dos Casados, whose barometrical altitude we fixed at 490 meters.[31]

Many of the toponyms featuring in the commission's report would effectively disappear in favor of more "modern" and programmatic ones (Planaltina, Brasiliana) in the run-up to Brasília's construction. In the Cruls report, the inherent mysticism of geodesic measurements as virtual repossessions through the inscription of the true name (a numeric code) becomes fully explicit in the baptism ceremonies held on reaching the lateral borders of the rectangle. Cruls himself devised the proceedings of the rite in the form of a symbolic burial of the geographical scriptures, which thus become one with their referent:

On the site of each border, an excavation of 1 x 1 meter and 1,30 m in depth is to be opened in the soil. It is to be filled up with rocks piled to the height of 1 m, which will then be covered with earth, so that vegetation will overgrow the spot in a couple of days. On the ground of the excavation a document will be deposited, in a properly sealed box, signed by the head and members of the unit, on which the coordinates of the border will be written, *having been established through observation*. Immediately afterwards, the position of the border will be confirmed by means of views taken of nearby mountains, hills or buildings, and through topographical triangulation with any other natural accidents of the terrain such as rivers, sources, etc. etc., such that it will be possible at any moment and in any era to discover the spot where the borders of the demarcated area have been established.[32]

The practical function of the artificial mound as a means of orientation *en lieu* for future users of the map coincides with its ritual function, the inscription of the map into nature, as a secret signature that is buried under the soil. The regime of visibility at work in this operation is of no minor significance. While remaining hidden from the view of local inhabitants (from whose profaning gazes it has to be doubly protected) the truth-bearing scripture is revealed (recited) to the urban, lettered public on the pages of Cruls's report. The state, in this openly colonial gesture, secretly takes possession of what is already its own. In a rite of foundation, the margin is secretly (and magically) turned into a place, a "first place," so to speak, as it is here that a cartographic abstraction becomes an affectively invested landscape (on a par with mountains, rivers, springs, etc.). This seems to be the demiurgic logic of this rite of foundation: to bury a set of numbers is to provide them with a tangible form, a spatial body, and conversely to transport material space into another time (the time of the state). It is in the light of this place-founding ritual that we should look at Morize's and Cruls's photographs picturing the commission on the borders of the rectangle (fig. 37).

FIGURE 37. Luiz Cruls, "Camp on the Southwestern Border." Photographic plate, in *Relatório apresentado a S. Ex. o Sr. Ministro da Indústria, Viação e Obras Públicas, por L. Cruls, Chefe da Commissão* (1894). Ibero-Amerikanisches Institut, Berlin.

For, actually, these photographs still belong to the rite of possession I have just described; like the buried writings, they make visible a new spatial order. The explorers' itinerant performance of inhabiting the border and its photographic recordings transform this border into a natural place rather than merely a cartographic abstraction: a place ready to be inhabited. The margin of the rectangle becomes a home to the geographers because, in fact, geography is the only spatial practice that can inhabit it, as a place, at the same time as it hijacks it from local practices of space. The white space of cartography in the photographs of the Planalto expedition turns into a landscape of reification, where territory becomes one with nature and the state a form of life. In what is perhaps its most stunning version, this foundational moment of inhabiting the map as a landscape is captured on "Camp on the Southeastern Border" (fig. 38), where only the explorers' campsite (and a solitary tree) interrupt the borderless monotony of the plain. Again, too, the iconic power with which this image immediately assaults us may be due, in part, to the geometrical composition along a horizontal and a vertical axis crossing at the center of the scene.

Lúcio Costa, it seems, was only partly right in claiming, in the famous opening sentences to his master plan for Brasília, that this composition unconsciously underlies every act of placement—"that initial gesture which anyone would make when pointing to a given place, or taking possession of it: the drawing of

FIGURE 38. Henrique Morize, "Camp on the Southeastern Border." Photographic plate, in *Relatório apresentado a S. Ex. o Sr. Ministro da Indústria, Viação e Obras Públicas, por L. Cruls, Chefe da Commissão* (1894). Ibero-Amerikanisches Institut, Berlin.

two axes crossing each other at right angles, in the sign of the Cross."[33] For, in order for the inscription of the cross to become a place-founding act, space first needed to be transformed from a social relation into a visual form. As such, it became a "natural given"—a gift received from a metaphysical instance situated outside and before society. The addressee of this divine gift of a nature laden with a providential mandate, moreover, was not Brazilian society in its present shape but rather the state as the historical agent of its transformation into the nation it had always been destined to become. Costa's cross reproduced Cruls's inscription of geometry into nature because it reproduced its founding myth, according to which "God and Nature are the founding agents of the Brazilian land and its people. Ideologically, then, the state institutes the nation on the base of the creating acts of God and Nature."[34]

The iconic form of the cross is thus a performative sign of this simultaneously divine (transcendental, vertical) and natural (earthly, horizontal) origin and its historical realization in the form of the state. It is a performative sign because, in 1892 as much as in 1956, it relied on complex ritual practices articulating profane, material space to the sacred, providential space of the founding myth. The task of the Planalto expedition was to ritually perform a way of seeing that hijacked space from the "existing relations between human beings and the material conditions of their lives," turning it over to the detached gaze of a spectator.[35]

In this chapter, I have been arguing that the Planalto expedition was characteristic of the way in which the incipient Republican state turned its gaze inward and thus transformed the interior into an object of the gaze. Nísia Trindade Lima claims that "The first years of the Republic staged an expressive movement of re-evaluating the *sertão*, as a space to be incorporated through the civilizing effort of the country's elite, or as a referent of national authenticity."[36] This visualization of the interior sought to render space transparent: exposing the decay and abandon into which it had fallen was at the same time a way of seeing through its present state into a bright future that was already inscribed, as a silent promise, in the natural conditions themselves. This production of space as a visual object, then, was simultaneously a way of constructing a mythical history of the Republic as a foundational moment of national emancipation. In rectifying the misreadings and misuses of national space and taking the interior into their care, the geographers, hygienists, and *sertanistas* of the Old Republic claimed to have eliminated the flawed legacies of colonial submission and brought about the true independence that the Empire had failed to deliver. Yet at the same time, this discourse of reform, whose cause and object was "nature," made it possible to reinscribe the disavowal of popular agency that had already been at the core of Romanticism's natural picturesque half a century earlier. Space, then, became a trope and a point of view associated with a discourse of reform from above that would result in a modernized society. This is not to say, of course, that this rediscovery of and intervention into the internal margins of national space did not actually make a difference in terms of the material expansion of state power and capitalist forms of production. As Marilena Chaui argues, the notion of a "natural fullness and harmony," whether as always already realized in tropical nature's picturesque abundance or as still awaiting the state's action, really represents "the country historically articulated to the colonial system of mercantile capitalism."[37] Visual forms, then, express historically specific modes of seizure and incorporation of local practices of space into neocolonial networks of capitalist exchange. In the following chapter, I will attempt a closer look at this interplay between visual forms and the capitalist production of space in images of the Argentine "conquest of the desert."

# An Essay in Segmentarity

## THE DESERT CAMPAIGN

This soil calls for a hard-hearted man, indomitable and restless: nothing to receive
and so much to give; to impose if necessary, and to divide by force. And nowhere a
place in this perfect space. It is but one vast open field for the deployment of vigor.
—Roger Caillois, *Patagonie*

### A War of Images

The military expedition that occupied the new line of frontiers on the northern
shore of the Río Negro on May 25, 1879, under the command of the minister
of war Julio Argentino Roca instantly became a powerful and lasting political
myth. Its power did not stem solely from the sheer scale of operations, although
size mattered, too: five army divisions of between 400 and 2,000 soldiers each,
deployed across the entire width of the southern provinces, as well as a naval
squad, several commissions of naturalists and engineers, and various groups
of *indios amigos*, "clearing" a strip of 15,000 square leagues between the old and
new line of frontiers. In fact, the troops' advance between April 26 and May 25,
the Argentine Day of Independence and occasion for some triumphant flag-
raising on the shores of the Río Negro, owed its smooth and efficient appearance
to the almost complete absence of violent hostilities. Most of the fighting had
already taken place between 1876 and 1878 in a strategy of relentless surprise
attacks (*malones blancos*) adopted under Roca's predecessor Adolfo Alsina, which
had forced the Pampa Indians farther and farther away from their natural water

supplies and shelters. Exhaustion and malnutrition had subsequently caused tremendous smallpox and measles epidemics. Farther south, fighting was still to occur. In the infamous Patagonian and Andean campaigns of 1881–85 entire communities were massacred or deported to the sugar plantations of Tucumán and Entre Ríos. Towards the end of the century, the incipient local sheep barons of Tierra del Fuego would destroy the complex cultural universe of the archipelago's Selk'nam, Haush, Alacaluf, and Yahgan population in a matter of one or two decades.

I can give only the briefest of overviews here of this deliberate and concerted ethnocide, which must nonetheless be on our minds if we want to say anything meaningful about the symbolic productions of state power in the same period. Military and geographical preparations for the advance of the southern frontier, which had receded since Rosas's Expedición al Desierto of 1832–33, had intensified again after 1870. In 1875, Minister of War Adolfo Alsina decreed the construction of a 56,000-kilometer trench from Carhué to the Andes, a line well in advance of the frontier garrisons. An uprising later the same year by the supposedly friendly Pehuenches led by Juan José Catriel, who were facing forced resettlement under Alsina's plans, was quashed in a series of counterinvasions under the colonels Vintter and Levalle. In April 1876, armed forces occupied Carhué, the main residence of the Mapuche *tóqui* (chief), Manuel Namuncurá. In November 1877, the colonel Villegas attacked the dwellings of Pincén, while Catriel was attacked by the colonel García at Treycó, killing 150 men and taking a further 300 prisoners. Farther west, the Ranqueles of Ramón Platero were permanently settled and their warriors recruited into the new Escuadrón Ranqueles. Unable to continue offering protection of trade routes, water supplies, and cattle shelters, Namuncurá's authority over the neighboring groups rapidly waned. In May 1877, the remaining tribe of Catriel surrendered (Catriel himself would do so only in November 1878), in July those of Manuel Grande and Tripailao. In December, Alsina died of a stomach ulcer, to be succeeded by Roca, who, on taking office, immediately intensified attacks in order to further debilitate indigenous resistance and explore the local topography. In November 1878, Pincén was captured by forces under Villegas; at the same time Roca marched on the Ranqueles of Epumer and Baigorrita, in open violation of the peace treaty his secretary Olascoaga had signed only four months earlier. After Roca's return from the Río Negro in 1879, Villegas as the new head of command carried out a series of "beatings" (*batidas*) in the southwestern pampa and *precordillera* before "sweeping" the valley of the River Neuquén in a high-speed operation that reached Lake Nahuel Huapí in April 1881, taking advantage of an extremely cruel winter with temperatures around minus 15 degrees Celsius. From 1882 to 1885

Villegas and his successor Vintter chased dispersed indigenous bands through the Cordillera in a series of massacres euphemistically known as Campaña de Patagonia y los Andes, which Vintter declared officially terminated on February 20, 1885, following the surrender of the Manzanero chief Saihueque.[1]

As David Viñas has observed, rather than to disavow the violence implied in this virtual refoundation of the Argentine state through expansion beyond its former frontiers, Roca's expedition of 1879 had in fact taken great pains to ensure the public representation, indeed exhibition, of bold, unforgiving force when such force had hardly been used at all. Roca's major success, in fact, lay in his ability to cast his own "aggressive" strategy in stark contrast to the "defensive" one of his deceased predecessor, to whose military and technological preparations for the final coup his own expedition nonetheless owed almost everything. The march to the Río Negro, in short, was indeed a "campaign," but in the advertising rather than the military sense: a concerted, carefully plotted media effort, a piece of political theater that deployed a characteristically modern apparatus of specularity.

Over the three months Roca spent with the troops in the south, a multimedia archive of texts and images was assembled: military instructions telegraphed across the front line, many of which found their way into newspapers and books; photographs (reproduction of which had become easier since the introduction of albumin prints); maps and scientific memoirs, drafted in record time to be exhibited at world's fairs and circulated among geographical societies. If Argentine political discourse instantly manufactured a personal myth of "Roca the Fox" as a supreme strategist, this was due not so much to his military feats as to his uncanny ability to take advantage of the same long-range technologies that had allowed for the relentless velocity of conquest, to bombard an emergent public sphere with representations. His use of telegraph lines, another of Alsina's infrastructural innovations, to maintain constant contact with all bodies of troops and thus suggest the presence of his invisible hand in each and every decision, is instructive in this regard. As military historian María Aurora Sánchez tells us,

Roca gave the orders, yet he did so not merely as Minister of War but also for his prestige, the direct knowledge of the terrain received through the telegraph wire. This turned his actions into an idealization of his person, since in alerting them to the proximity of lagoons, sand dunes, quicksands and swamps where their existence was unknown to them, he would imbue the soldiers with absolute confidence in their itinerary, for they knew that Roca was invisibly assisting and watching over them.[2]

This magic presence of an idealized person (that is, of an image, a representation), who, as the center of monopolistic appropriation of knowledge

(knowledge of the terrain even before it is reached), watches over the bodies at his disposal, is of course also the way in which panoptic power is experienced by those subjected to it. Yet this disembodied charisma is not only the effect of Roca's strategy of deploying long-range technology (telegraphs, railways, rifles) in the conquest of a spatial exterior (the desert), which is precisely the reservoir of this "knowledge." Its magic spell also reaches out to the space inside the frontier, in a movement that inverts the outward advance of the troops. This inward movement essentially relies on the same technological means as the conquest of the desert: the occupation of a space of representation, turning it into a carrier medium for the simultaneous presence of images of power and knowledge at the most diverse points.

In this chapter I will discuss the novelty of this representation of state power (or, power by representation), by analyzing what are arguably the two most iconic visual renderings of the Desert Campaign, Juan Manuel Blanes's monumental painting *Ocupación militar del Río Negro*, and Manuel José Olascoaga's *Plano topográfico de La Pampa y Río Negro*. The first was commissioned by the National Historical Museum in 1889 to commemorate the tenth anniversary of Roca's expedition; the second had been drawn up immediately after his return to the capital in June 1879 and published the year after with a description of the operation and a compilation of military reports, also edited by Olascoaga who, before directing the Armed Forces' Office of Topographers (established in December 1879 to coordinate the survey of the annexed territories), had served as Roca's personal secretary in the field. In comparing a painterly image and a military map of conquest, I continue to develop some ideas from the previous chapter on the relations between cartography's apparently detached and self-sufficient visual space and that of a landscape invested with, and redefined by, a particular human agency. On the basis of these images that emphatically bring to the fore the violence involved in state capture, which had been silenced in the Planalto expedition's visual record, I shall also introduce an argument on the interplay between order and excess. How are the impressions of orderliness associated with visual genres such as historical painting and topographic mapping reinforced or crossed out by the violence of a late colonial war of extermination?

## The Desert and the City

If violent struggle did take place in General Roca's ascent to political power, it was not on the frontier but in the center. Roca's election in 1880 to succeed Nicolás Avellaneda as president sparked the rebellion of the defeated candidate and governor of the province of Buenos Aires, Carlos Tejedor, in May of the same year, followed by an uprising in the northern province of Corrientes. Tejedor's rebellion in particular, whose forces were concentrated in the city of Buenos Aires, pushed the federal state to the brink of collapse. Avellaneda's government during its final months was forced into exile on the far outskirts of the capital. The insurgency only came to an end after several months of street fighting, during which heavy artillery was used on both sides and large contingents of troops shipped in from the southern frontier.

The significance of the episode, in addition to its being the last of the traditional wars of election, lay in the political profile of both contenders. While Roca had the support not only of a new generation of army officers and technocrats but also of an interprovincial coalition of oligarchies with strongholds in his native Tucumán and Córdoba, Tejedor, a traditional champion of *porteño* politics, had stepped into the gap left vacant by the death of Alsina. The main exponent of Buenos Aires autonomism, Alsina had been almost unanimously regarded as the natural candidate to succeed Avellaneda, precisely on account of his record as minister of war. Roca's bold use of this same position thus appears as not merely a brilliant example of political opportunism, but also as the breakthrough in a larger movement of readjustment that we could conceive as the imposition of state power over city power. Indeed, the nominal case of dissent between both factions was the legal status of the city of Buenos Aires, which Roca had committed himself to separate from the province and turn into a federal district directly controlled by central government. What I am referring to, however, is also a more general refocusing of the entire space of the nation-state, similar to and yet fundamentally different from the Brazilian case discussed in the previous chapter. Both the Desert Campaign and the federalization of Buenos Aires, which Roca immediately decreed upon taking office in December 1880, could be seen as complementary aspects of this wider refocusing of national space.

A new kind of state power thus emerged in Argentina in the moment of seizure on behalf of Roca's interprovincial coalition (loosely held together in the Partido Autonomista Nacional), of the legal and political apparatuses constructed by the port city in order to deactivate and incorporate the war machines of the provincial caudillos. The civilizing project of the Generation of 1837 had been an imposition of city power over tributary rural spaces, a segmentarization of the exterior. Alsina's strategy of a gradual, fortified advance of the frontier, paralleled by a radial movement of government-engineered settlement of native and immigrant populations, represented a last attempt to realize the project laid out in Alberdi's famous slogan "to govern is to populate."

A singular piece of military engineering, the Zanja de Alsina (fig. 39) consisted of a ditch three meters wide and two meters deep, followed by a bank or wall between one and two meters high, depending on the conditions of the soil.

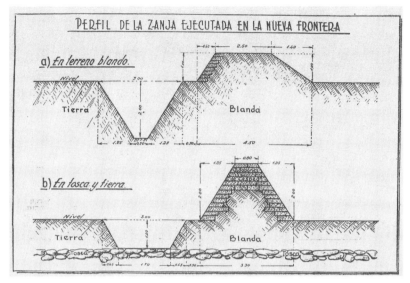

FIGURE 39. "Profile of the trench dug along the new line of frontiers (a: in soft terrain; b: in clay and earth)." Illustration taken from Juan Carlos Walther, *La conquista del desierto* (Buenos Aires: Eudeba, 1970).

Its total extension was to be 56,000 kilometers, from the lagoon of Carhué to the foothills of the Cordillera south of Mendoza. If its design is reminiscent of flood protection and drainage systems, it is because the threat it was supposed to contain (the Indian raids on the pampean cattle stock) was imagined in the figure of a wave whose force had to be broken. Sarmiento's and Echeverría's topography of a terrestrial sea threatening to burst over the urban island on its shore is still at work here. Yet the novelty of Alsina's project was the belief—akin to that of the Brazilian reformers who started to think, around the same time, about sanitizing the interior—that it was possible to drain this sea through technical intervention. Military engineering was able to secure and protect a terrain that could then be "consolidated" through the construction of model towns and agrarian colonies on the inner side of the Zanja.

Incidentally, the technicians employed to design and build the border ditch were mostly European exiles, military geographers and engineers who had abandoned or fled their countries in the aftermath of the Franco-Prussian War and the defeat of nationalist uprisings in the Austro-Hungarian empire. Alfred Ébélot, the chief engineer, and Friedrich Melchert, a former Prussian official and head of the Office of Military Engineers, who prior to the beginning of works had carried out geodesic studies of the area, had both closely witnessed the defeat of the Paris Commune and the Prussian occupation of 1871. Jordán Czeslaw

Wisocki and Juan Fernando Czetz, military engineers trained in Polish and Austrian academies, had emigrated to Argentina as political refugees and went on to work as geographers and military technicians on the southern frontier. A whole science of counterinsurgency was imported from Europe and deployed to expand the terrain of primitive accumulation. In the rear of the Zanja, the Ferrocarril Sud (Southern Railway) was extended by 85 percent between 1874 and 1877, strategically focusing on the areas most affected by Indian invasions; in 1876 telegraphic cabling was established between Buenos Aires and the new military outposts on the frontier line. Between the inauguration of the service in April 1876 and July 1877, the ten stations of the military telegraph processed 52,218 telegrams with a total word count of 1,554,086.

Yet, before 1879, the "machinic assemblage" put in place by these engineering measures had still been subjected to a rationale of containment, that is, of progressive land gain in concentric circles laid around the urban center. It was only when the vertical line of advance inscribed by Alsina and his engineers was seized by Roca to unleash a movement devoid of horizontal lines of containment that the possibilities of speed implied in the new long-range technologies (telegraphs, railways, rifles) were fully realized. These technologies would deploy a centrifugal movement rather than contain a centripetal wave, releasing technically enhanced velocities onto the exterior rather than improving fortifications. The desert, as Roca's chief pamphleteer Estanislao Zeballos put it in *The Conquest of Fifteen Thousand Leagues* in 1878, rather than being contained had to be understood as the perfect medium of expansion:

Alsina lacked the convictions based on study and practice to proceed to a pure and simple offensive, without trenches and fortified positions. [...] Dr. Alsina gave more importance to the Indian and feared the desert more than was really reasonable, thus his obstinate negative to a march on the Río Negro, as the first and main objective; and instead his resolution to spend torrents of money on the preparation of parallel and successive lines, in the manner of the Spanish conquistador.[3]

This presentation of Roca's politics of acceleration as a radical new beginning rather than as the logical conclusion of Alsina's politics of fortification, was of course already part of the communicational offensive in which, I have argued above, the same technological assemblage that expanded towards the frontier also "overcoded the center." Martínez Estrada may be right, as he so often is, when he claims that in conquering the desert, Roca brought the desert to the city: not merely because he reconquered the city a year later with the divisions from the southern frontier, but because the Desert Campaign was really the monumental expression of a general overcoding which, rather than on the urban logic of spreading and fortifying settlements (*"gobernar es poblar"*), was primed on a rationale of abstraction and quantification (*"gobernar es capitalizar"*) for which the emptiness of the desert provided an ideal medium.[4]

## Apparatus of Capture

Let us now turn to the visual archive, the compiling and exhibition of which started immediately after Roca's departure from the south on June 24, 1879. Ten years after the event, the recently inaugurated National Historical Museum commissioned the Uruguayan painter Juan Manuel Blanes to produce a large commemorative painting of the campaign, which Blanes delivered in 1894, a giant canvas of 3.55 x 7.10 meters depicting the *Military Occupation of the Rio Negro under the Orders of General Julio A. Roca* (fig. 40).

His compatriot, the social columnist Angel Floro Costa, visited the painter's workshop in 1893 and filed this report with his editors at the Montevidean newspaper *El Siglo*:

The artist has interpreted with profound philosophical zeal the synthesis of the great historical episode that he was asked to deliver. [...] According to Mr Blanes's explanations, the scene takes place on a 25th of May opposite Choele-Choel, the spot singled out in General Roca's plans to serve as headquarters and to which all the divisions of the army had to report. [...] Beyond any doubt, it is this central situation of all forces converging on the line of the Rio Negro, which provides the argument for the artist's grandiose allegory, concentrating on this stage the major part of chiefs and commanders of the different divisions operating in the North, the South, the East and the West.[5]

FIGURE 40. Juan Manuel Blanes, *Ocupación militar del Río Negro bajo el mando del General Julio A. Roca, 1879*. Oil on canvas (1894). Museo Histórico Nacional, Buenos Aires.

Rather than select a particular image from the campaign's visual archive, Blanes chose to compose a synthetic historical allegory, the genre in which he had already excelled in works such as *La Revista de Rancagua* and *Los Treinta y Tres Orientales*.[6] This allegorical synthesis takes the celebrations of Independence Day on the shores of the Rio Negro as a theatrical frame in which to display, on a plane of simultaneity, the principal actors and iconic elements of the conquest of the desert. As Floro Costa notices, the allegorical composition relies on the fiction of an encounter of all five divisions and their commanders and principal officers at the island of Choele Choel, whereas actually only the three brigades of the first division and the crew of the steamer *Triunfo* had met on the eve of Independence Day. As Julio Vezub explains, Blanes not only frequently met with eyewitnesses of the event—including Roca himself, who discussed the distribution of figures and even details of uniforms, weaponry, and saddles with the painter—but he also almost certainly knew the photographic albums of Antonio Pozzo and of Carlos Encina and Edgardo Moreno, some of whose images obtained after the campaign of 1879 (and thus devoid of the presence of both Roca and his General Command) display remarkable similarities to Blanes's *Ocupación militar*.[7]

In the background of the image, moreover, troops representing the three branches of the military (artillery, cavalry, and infantry) can be seen, the infantry occupying the center, the cavalry the left, and the artillery the right of the canvas. In fact, in the 1879 expedition Roca had made do without any heavy artillery in order to quicken his troops' pace. Yet these historical liberties, Floro Costa contends, were necessary to reveal the higher allegorical truth, that of the culmination of a secular struggle and of a national self-encounter in the promised land, embodied in the armed forces in their totality.

Let us take a closer look at these allegorical purposes of the painting's composition. In the foreground, two human groups frame the central ensemble of officers on horseback, all of them aligned at the same time in a great serpentine that connects the groups in the front with the soldiers forming in the background. This serpentine lends a dynamic sense of movement to the painting's otherwise static choreography, a dynamic whose apex is located precisely in the group of riders advancing towards the space of the beholder. In the lower left-hand corner, almost being pushed out of the frame by the momentum of the horsemen's advance, a small band of Indians watches in consternation, some shamefully burying their faces in their ponchos, as a stern-faced missionary (the chief vicar Espinosa, the representative of the Archbishop of Buenos Aires) reads them the gospels. "Their physiognomies," Floro Costa explains, "suggest the natural stupefaction these uncultivated minds must have felt in the face of the mighty spectacle of triumphant civilization, which would expel them forever from their dominions, and which makes them serve, humiliated and sub-jugated, as a symbolic trophy in the artist's great allegory."[8] In its vision of the defeated, the painting skillfully combines the discursive tradition of a "merciful civilization" and its notion of the Indian as a victim of his own ignorance, with the demonic image of the abductor of white women, embodied by the captive who, sheltering her dark-skinned baby, advances towards her redeemers with an expression of intense relief.

On the opposite end of the canvas, and completing the symbolic portal through which the central group is about to pass, several marines of the steamer *Triunfo* surrounding their captain, Martín Guerrico, salute Roca, the commander in chief. Slightly towards the rear, the naturalists Lorentz, Doering, Niederlein, and Schultz of the Scientific Commission of Exploration, identified by their civilian clothes and the "Hildebrandt" theodolite in their midst, watch the scene with a somewhat distant expression, as if eager to return to their studies. On one side, then, we have the pole of savagery and evangelization, the image's colonial pole, so to speak, which already retreats into the shades of history, pushed aside by civilization's great serpentining movement, with the exception of the white-clad captive who, placed to the right of the priest who is also a barrier to the Indians, is returning towards the light. On the opposite side, the nexus between science and the navy points towards the future and the exploration of rivers, coastlines, and "open spaces" that is yet to occur, beyond the painting's horizon. It is in the portal, the space of tension opened up by these two groups, that the occupation referred to in the title takes place, personified by the commanders of the invading army who surround Roca, flashing their sabers. In the twenty-two figures on horse-back, an entire military pantheon of the frontier wars is assembled: the commanders of the four divisions—Levalle, Villegas, Racedo, and Uriburu—pose slightly behind Roca, followed by a great number of commanders of divisions and squadrons: Campos, Gramajo, Fotheringham, Vintter, Leyría, Ortega, Villegas, and others. Olascoaga, author of the map we shall analyze in the final section of this chapter, is in the back row, slightly to the left of Roca. The only subaltern figure in this group of gentlemen-officers is the dark-skinned trumpeter on the far left, next to the group of Indians, perhaps indicating the place to be occupied by "the people" in this allegory of the nation-state's triumphant refoundation.

Roca himself, in the exact center of the painting, under the aureole of light rushing through an opening in the clouds, is pictured in reflexive mood, having brought his dark stallion to a halt. "What visions," Floro Costa wonders, "might be unravelling, in such a moment, before the sharp-sighted inner eye of the illustrious conqueror? His work is finished; almost all the divisions of the expeditionary army have accomplished their tasks, fulfilling with mathematical precision the indications of his vast plan, conceived less from the scarce knowledge of the enormous theater of operations than from the pure intuitions of modern warfare."[9] Being the point of convergence of gazes and salutes, as well as the figure that first captures the beholder's eye, however, Roca's own gaze—almost leading ours astray, away from the monumental spectacle that unfolds behind him—is absorbed by that of a dog, looking back at the general while it crosses the riders' path. In compositional terms, the dog provides a first plane or foreground, a device frequently used in hunting paintings, that leads out of the illusionist space of the canvas into that of the beholder, signalling the place of this gaze within the painting's fictitious space. This function is accentuated here by the contrapuntal line of the dog's movement, which returns our gaze to the army's great serpentine and thus leads it around the ensemble in an almost perfect visual circle. Yet beyond its formal properties, the dog, and the place it assigns to the gaze of the beholder, is ambivalent.[10] To begin with, who does this dog belong to? The exchange of looks with the commander in chief seems to betray a certain familiarity, even intimacy. Yet the fact that the dog has, as it were, only just entered the space of the painting from beyond its frame would suggest the opposite: namely, that it is a stray dog, a dog of the desert, an emissary from what is still outside and subject to future capture. Thus the look it exchanges with Roca would indeed be one of recognition, but between the conqueror and the desert. More importantly, the desert would also be the place the painting assigns to our own gaze, a perspective that is not without logic. In fact, the desert is the only place from which it is possible to observe the state in its entirety. The place of the beholder in *Ocupación militar*, in fact, must still be a nonplace: the desert in the instant immediately preceding its capture. Historically, it is the nonplace of genocide (a scene that must remain outside: before the law, out of sight).[11]

Indeed, then, we are seeing the scene of the frontier's military occupation from the position of what precedes as well as succeeds it in space and time: the erasure of spaces of autonomy and their inhabitants, the state's foundational violence that prepared, as well as succeeded, Roca's expedition of 1879. What does it mean, however, to see from such a position of exteriority? And what is it we see from there? What, as Blanes seems to suggest, cannot be seen from anywhere but the nonplace of violence and exteriority that must itself remain invisible? If these are the questions at which we have arrived on carrying out what Panofsky would have called a formal and iconographic description of Blanes's painting, to answer them it is necessary to find a different point of view, a plane of exteriority different from the one *Ocupación militar* urges us to occupy. What I am looking for is a position from which to observe the "event of seeing" propelled by the painting's composition, the event of the gaze, which, as Norman

Bryson has pointed out, in the Western tradition is entrusted with reinstating the painter's own "founding perception" in which the painting claims to have its origin. The gaze, Bryson argues, reactualizes the mythical atemporality of the founding perception: the eye addressed by Western painting is not that of any particular beholder but a disembodied vision that simultaneously takes in all the elements and their mutual relations, just as the painter had once arrested the flow of things and contemplated the entire visual field from an ideal vantage point outside the mobility of duration.[12] What interests me, then, is the way in which Blanes, in *Ocupación militar del Río Negro*, draws on this constitutive element of Western painting's visual rhetoric to construct a founding scene of the state: how the sovereign gaze deployed by visual convention is made to behold the very scene of sovereignty's foundation. Yet this event of seeing, which takes place simultaneously in the physical space of the National Historical Museum (the painting's institutional frame of reception) and in the imaginary space of the desert (the space beyond the frame from which it demands to be seen), is actually a highly complex one. Not only is the scene of the foundation of sovereignty a mirror image of the viewing subject's self-empowerment, but it also commands it (precisely in order to become a viewing subject) into a performative position of absolute subjection. The gaze, we might say, is compelled by the painting's peculiar mirror structure, to occupy all of its viewing positions, to become not only Roca but also the dog.

One way of reading this convergence of artistic and political forms in the visual space of Blanes's painting is by relating it to Deleuze and Guattari's concept of state capture. For them, primitive accumulation is the work of an apparatus deploying "that particular kind of violence that creates or contributes to the creation of that which it is directed against, and thus presupposes itself." The violence of the state always presents itself as preaccomplished, in the same way as it is the state that constitutes the exteriority of the outside onto which it deploys its repressive action. This moment of self-presupposing, indeed magic capture functions on the three levels of *land* (capture of territory), *work* (capture of activity), and *money* (capture of exchange). Land, work, and money are the three simultaneous aspects of the formation of the stock: "Land is stockpiled territory, the tool is stockpiled activity, and money is stockpiled exchange."[13]

The formation of the stock is also at the root of the process of capture, whose culmination Blanes's painting takes as its allegorical object. The spread of wild cattle (*ganado cimarrón*), an ecological side effect of the Spanish conquest in the pampean basin, was to become a main catalyst of capitalist expansion and state formation in the nineteenth century. A Creole landholding elite constituted itself thanks to the conversion of stray animals into cattle stock, with the consequent illegalization of alternative economies based on the use and trade of meat and leather among the mestizo and Amerindian populations of the South. Recent ethno- and eco-historical research has definitely rebuked the traditional claim that the indigenous societies of the southern pampas did not breed cattle and horses themselves. Rather, the military and legal means of state consolidation need to be seen as an attempt to enforce a concept of landed ownership of the stock that unilaterally favored an emergent *latifundista* oligarchy. The construction of fortified settlements starting in the seventeenth century coincided with subsequent law enforcements to suppress *vaquería*, the use of wild cattle to supply food, clothing, and housing materials, which was the Creole rural population's principal subsistence activity. In the nineteenth century, the southward advance of the cattle economy due to expanding agriculture and sheep farming put further pressure on the Amerindian groups, eventually transforming a semi-sedentary agricultural economy into nomadic societies of warriors and traders.

It is, I would argue, precisely the threefold apparatus of formation of the stock, which we see deployed across Blanes's almost cinematographic screen ("almost" in a temporal rather than conceptual sense: only five years separate Blanes's painting from Argentina's first moving images, Alejandro Py's short film of another raising of the national flag). If the group of scientists and marines on the right, as I have suggested, stands for the capture of land (exploration, mapping), the group of Indians on the left, exposed to the twinned vigilance of the military and the church, represents the capture of labor. Effectively, the capture of indigenous communities as a cheap workforce (often in the sugar and yerba maté plantations of the North, where they would be deported en masse) proceeded in a joint operation of army and church, in which the latter was entrusted with the task of producing civil subjects (subjects with a proper name and a "soul"). One can hardly think of a more eloquent document of this simultaneity of spiritual conquest and the subsumption of living labor (stockpiled bodies for production and reproduction) than the report of field chaplain Pío Bentivoglio, accompanying the Desert Campaign's third army division, about his missionary efforts. These included the distribution of native women among soldiers so as to "eradicate the pestilence of polygamy," at the slightest indication of which "the woman would be instantly returned to the deposit of prisoners." The report was accompanied by lists of baptisms performed on adults and children, displaying, in alphabetical order, the "Indian name," "Christian name," and "date of baptism." These lists do not so much represent as constitute the stock of exploitable bodies: their newly acquired "soul," as expressed in the new name, is synonymous with their exchangeability as living labor.[14]

What passes through the portal of captured land and captured labor is the apparatus's third component: money. Or rather, state power as the agent of production of territory appears in Blanes's synoptic vision of the apparatus of capture as, first and foremost, the carrier of the money form. In fact, this is a surprisingly exact depiction of the military's role as a vehicle of the spatial expansion of capital. The army was the virtual embodiment of a capital pressing to expand into its exterior in order to absorb the surplus generated by the technological revolution in the industrial centers of northern Europe. This expansion of the radius of capital flows into a spatial exterior implied a particular use of the nomadic space of the desert, in which capital was expressed in the first instance as military violence. I will return in more detail to this appropriation of nomadic spaces in my discussion of Olascoaga's map; here I want to draw attention to the fact that the permanent mobility of troops across the entire zone of operations was made possible by a massive infusion of international speculative capital. Railroad and telegraph expansion and the improvement of armaments had already begun to absorb considerable capital flows under Alsina. Roca, in addition, raised enormous funds for maintaining mobile divisions on a permanent basis, necessary in order to move beyond a politics of fortification, by mortgaging the territories yet to be conquered to national and foreign trustees. Prior to the advance of the frontier to the Río Negro, four thousand government titles of four hundred *pesos fuertes* each were emitted, on which the government guaranteed a minimum interest rate of 6 percent, which could either be cashed in at an established date or amortized against land slots of ten thousand hectares (four square leagues), at a base price of one title per square league. Tellingly, only four of the twenty-one articles of the Law 947 of October 1878, which regulated the annexation of the southern territories, were dedicated to military operations and the demarcation of frontiers, while fourteen referred to the capitalization of lands.[15]

Thus the curved line on Blanes's painting, on whose most advanced point we see Roca himself, is no other than the line of speculative capital in its military embodiment. This line of militarized capital is a machine fuelled and sustained by the polarities of population and territory (labor and land), which it posits at its opposite ends. It is important to keep in mind, however, that both are represented in the painting in fundamentally different ways: the former is "incarnated" in captive bodies commanded into submission, the latter "projected" through the presence of the actors and instruments of its penetration and measurement (marines, scientists, optical instruments). In the movement from left to right of Roca and his staff, moreover, labor is associated with the past, the land with the future; it is towards the land that Roca and his officers advance.

Commodification of nature clearly takes primacy over that of labor power in the emergent rentier capitalism of the Patagonian south. It is land, not labor, which will absorb the vector of capital launched by Roca and his troops.

### Theater of Operations

Blanes's painting makes us face, quite literally, the state as an apparatus of capture. Contrary to Blanes, who attempts to picture this apparatus at work in the genre of historical allegory, Manuel José Olascoaga in his *Plano del Territorio de La Pampa y Río Negro* of 1880 ("the graphic culmination of the Desert Campaign," in the words of one military historian[16])– focuses exclusively on the functions that define the apparatus's components. In other words, that which Blanes's painting omits (or only presents allegorically, by way of the distribution of emblematic figures on the canvas) is Olascoaga's central concern: the machinery of conquest, so to speak, the micro- and macropolitics of de- and reterritorialization.

Olascoaga's work as a cartographer and military commander on the southern frontier had begun in 1864, when he submitted a report on the state of frontiers to the government, earning him the post of frontier commander in the Cuyo region. In 1866 he produced a map of Paraguay to be used by the invading armies of the Triple Alliance and also authored a study of the southern frontier of his native Mendoza. Between 1867 and 1873, he lived exiled in Chile, where he became a close friend of General Cornelio Saavedra, the future "conqueror of Araucania." Returning to Argentina in 1878, Olascoaga was immediately employed as secretary by Roca on his Chilean credentials and took an important part in preparing the Desert Campaign, drafting reports and plans of operations. In 1888 he was appointed governor of the new National Territory of Neuquén, of which he subsequently produced a topographical study (*Topografía Andina*).

Olascoaga's map, a register in the scale of 1:200,000 of geographical data and of military bases and itineraries between latitudes 33° and 43° south, was the key piece of his nearly homonymous compilation of the campaign's official accounts, *Estudio Topográfico de La Pampa y Río Negro* (figs. 41–42). Lavishly printed in a state-funded edition by the publishing house of Ostwald & Martínez, *Estudio Topográfico* received a medal at the International Geographical Exhibition of Venice in 1881 and was also displayed at the Continental Exhibition of Buenos Aires the year after. In the words of Ramiro Martínez Sierra,

in the history of mapping the Pampas, it is a cartographic expression of exceptional value, not so much for its execution, which is far from outstanding, but because it reflects a moment of transition between two eras. For, effectively, whereas on one side it shows the direction in which the blows were struck that brought down the empire of the Indian, on the other side it makes us see the time of colonization, which seemed about to begin, full of great expectations.[7]

Martínez Sierra is correct in observing the complex juxtaposition of various cartographic idioms on Olascoaga's map: spatial barriers are juxtaposed onto temporal divides, both of them being crossed, moreover, by vectors indicating different kinds of movement.

To put it simply, we could distinguish between "horizontal" lines of demarcation (state and provincial borders, military frontiers, etc.) and "vertical" ones indicating routes and itineraries—the same distinction we have already made when comparing Alsina's and Roca's strategies of territorialization at the beginning of this chapter. Beneath this intricate net of lines, a semitransparent, yellow frame open at the base contains the lower portion of territory, including two strings of bright yellow patches alongside the Colorado and Negro rivers. Indeed, in its combination of lines indicating movement and fields representing a demarcated terrain, the image immediately reminds us of Cruls's rectangle drawn into the white space of the Planalto Central. Here, however, the web of itineraries and spatial segments presents a much more complex and conflictive constellation. This may be due, in the first place, to the fact that Olascoaga's is a map of conquest: rather than the picture of an empty territory, it narrates the story of how lands have been wrested from an internal other.

To understand the dynamic of zones and movements at work in Olascoaga's image, we need to refer once more to Deleuze and Guattari, in particular their notion of "segmentarity." Rather than distinguish between the segmentarity in which primitive societies organize space and the Western logic of centralization, they propose a distinction between "supple" and "rigid" forms of segmentarity. Rigid segmentarity is characterized by biunivocal oppositions, arborescent organization of lines, and geometrical distribution of volumes in space. Supple segmentarity, by contrast, avoids binary choices and inhibits the development of nodes of power into apparatuses of resonance, which is precisely the aim of rigid segmentarity. Yet every social or natural unit, Deleuze and Guattari suggest, is simultaneously folded by rigid and supple forms of segmentarity alike. They therefore introduce a further distinction between the levels of the molar (or macropolitical) and the molecular (or micropolitical). While lines and segments are molar forms of organization, the molecular is composed by quantum flows, which are the prolongations of lines into a different domain, or the impulses that precede and induce their inscription. At work here, in short, is a model of energy flows and releases, according to which power is forged at the points of translation of quanta into segments, in the border areas between flows and lines.

FIGURE 41. Manuel José Olascoaga, *Plano del Territorio de La Pampa y Río Negro.* Upper half of map (1880). Archivo General de la Nación, Buenos Aires.

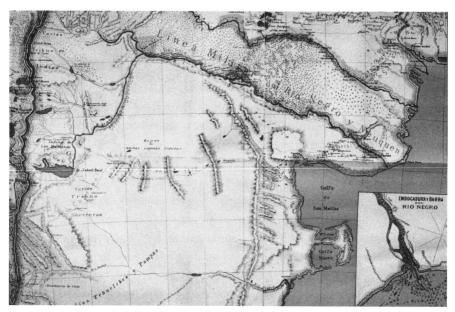

FIGURE 42. Manuel José Olascoaga, *Plano del Territorio de La Pampa y Río Negro.* Lower half of map (1880). Archivo General de la Nación, Buenos Aires.

This translation can never entirely succeed but must always release a remainder of mutant quanta opening "lines of flight." On the Deleuze-Guattarian map, then, we have three different orders of lines: first, the supple lines of interlaced segments and territories; second, the rigid lines, which construct a system of places that is biunivocal, arborescent, and geometrical. Finally, there are the lines of flight opened up by quanta, which are continuously released anew through the loopholes left, or rather opened up, by processes of capture.[18]

If we now return our attention to the legend of Olascoaga's *Plano*, we see that it distinguishes between at least four classes of lines, most of which are further divided into subclasses (fig. 43). First, there are the broken red lines representing, in different sequences of hyphens and points, the trajectories of the campaign's five divisions, as well as that of other relevant military expeditions. Second, we have two different orders of limits or demarcations: the previous military frontiers, identified by a thick red strip, and the projected outlines of "terrains reserved by the Government for Colonies and Villages," colored in yellow. In fact, though, yellow coloring is used on the map both as a line and as a field (the colored patches along the Colorado and Negro rivers). Not just the spots indicated for future settlement, but in fact the entire area, the contours of which correspond almost exactly to the northern borders of today's provinces of La Pampa and Neuquén, is "reserved by the Government." Like Cruls's Distrito Federal, the yellow frame on Olascoaga's map singles out a space of the state within the territory of the nation: a terrain of direct intervention, and thus a spatial model for a new type of state power exercised as direct intervention into "nature." As I have suggested above, this intervention was actually not one of settlement (*"gobernar es poblar"*) but the inscription of an abstract sovereignty, to be materially realized in the leasing-out of space as landed value (*"gobernar es capitalizar"*). This explains the rather peculiar way in which, in the space into which

FIGURE 43. Manuel José Olascoaga, *Plano del Territorio de La Pampa y Río Negro.* Legend (1880). Archivo General de la Nación, Buenos Aires.

the Argentine nation is supposedly about to expand, small portions of terrain are being "reserved" for settlement (for "colonies and villages"). It is state capture itself that produces, rather than eradicates, empty space (that is, land as pure value), whereas the reserve army of labor power necessary to perpetuate value extraction is confined to "reservations" limited to an indispensable minimum.

Third, we have the straight black lines of railways and telegraphs, which prolong the red lines of the expedition's routes on the rear of the old frontier and towards the port city. Conversely, the expedition's itineraries could be seen as hypothetical future railway extensions, which are themselves based on the flight lines of the retreating Indians. These escape routes (which are actually old trans-Andean trade routes) are immediately seized to accelerate capture, using the trajectories and velocity of the prey as the very means to unlock its spaces of refuge. Substantial extensions of the railway network would effectively be built over the second half of the 1880s, always in keeping with the double imperative of accelerating the transport of merchandise and the movement of troops (not merely to the frontier, but across the entire national territory, which is thus consolidated, as Colin Lewis rightly suggests, parallel to the railway network's consolidation as a gridded space of organized and policed flows). The first trans-Patagonian lines would open around the turn of the century.[19]

This politics of seizure of the other's movement becomes clear once we observe the final two subclasses of lines on Olascoaga's map, which are related to one another in exactly the same way as railway tracks and military routes (one black versus one red line). In fact, the meandering black line of "Caminos Generales y de Indios" (general and Indian tracks) could also be understood as still pertaining, as its lowest echelon, to the nomenclature of telegraphs and railways, channels leading from the satellite-shaped "Comandancias" and "Fortines" (commanding posts and fortresses) to the triangular icons of "Toldos habitados" and "Toldos abandonados" (inhabited and abandoned indigenous settlements). Yet such a reading would already take for granted the movement of seizure, which is, on the contrary, only the effect of the map. In fact, the lines depicted by Olascoaga as general and Indian tracks and as tracks from Chile to the Pampas compose a different regime of flows. They point to an economic, cultural, and political network of traffic that altogether escapes the logic of linear advances and retreats in a deserted environment that underlies state capture: who, for one, is the collective subject alluded to in the nomenclature of "general and Indian"? Is it everybody including the Indians? And how does the alterity of "Indios" fit in with the inclusiveness, the generality, of "general"? What the Caminos Generales inscribe into the cartographic space of the state is a vector of indifferentiation, a line of flight that exposes the inconclusive character of the spatial closure the state seeks to implement. The Caminos Generales do not merely point to a past of trans-Andean trade and social exchange beyond the grasp of the Argentine or Chilean states, and to a present of genocidal violence and forced migrations; they also look towards the future of Patagonia as a border space that will defy, time and time again, the "national" boundaries imposed upon it. These will remain routes of clandestine symbolic and material flows even after the state has formally imposed its sovereignty on both sides of the Andean Cordillera: as in the "illegal" crossings of migrant workers, political fugitives, smugglers of contraband, and so forth. In highlighting these problematic openings and gaps in the state's spatial envelope, Olascoaga (who knew both sides of the Cordillera and was familiar with the strategies and obstacles of state conquest in the south) shows that state capture is not the production of space from anomic emptiness, but the appropriation and subjugation of alternative spatial orders. The great merit of *Plano topográfico* is to expose this struggle between different productions of space, to have found a cartographic language to expose their clashes in the space of the map (if only to collaborate with the violent imposition of one mode of production over the other).

In the textual narrative accompanying the map, Olascoaga expounds further on the hierarchy of lines and their relation to past and future scenarios (the "simultaneous presence of several times" noticed by Martínez Sierra). In his account, the campaign is a modern epic, the culmination and closure of national history brought about by Roca who, as an Argentine Oedipus, deciphers the enigma of the desert. Conquering the south is therefore also a conquering of the self, turning ignorance into knowledge: "The operation recently carried out against the Indians and other foreign bandits who have dominated our great and unknown lands of the south, has made its principal triumph in the topographical knowledge of the vast region it has subjugated (*batido*) and explored. This triumph of Geography seals the results obtained as definite and enduring."[20]

The geographer turns into a historical analyst who cures the national self of its territorial delusions. To become a subject of civilization and master of its actions, the Argentine nation must expel from its own interior the foreign bodies, which have stimulated its own atavistic impulses. The map, it soon becomes evident, has to be read here immediately (not just figuratively) as an image of the national self, a psychogram or medical chart of the state's organism. Like the map, the text's main interest lies with the capture of flows that, once deciphered, cease to undermine the productivity of the organism:

This entire zone of territory which, until recently, had not only been unknown to us but surrounded by mystifications and irresolvable problems, is now made manifest, having been studied in all its topographical detail, in all its possible applications to the growth of national wealth, the absolute domination over the indigenous tribes and the infinite spread of civilized populations. [...] Perhaps new *Caciques* would have emerged, as dextrous in warfare and as brave as Epumer, Pincen and the Catriels, and the Indians would, in time, have returned to their invasions and depredations, had the Pampa remained what it had been for us until a year ago—a territory unknown in its topography and its uses for banditry and for the immoral contraband with the neighbouring Chilean provinces. [...] Yet today everything is different. [...] Today all the itineraries are recorded by which to reach all points of the desert; the water reservoirs, the soils of good and bad quality, the shelters of Indians and Christian smugglers are all known to us, and the day and hour in which a Division will attack a village can be established beforehand. Such is, purely from the perspective of Geography, the importance of this operation.[21]

To map means to impose panoptic visibility on a spatial exterior, exterior not so much for its location outside fortified borders (rather, Olascoaga insists, such fortification had been an illusion constantly disproved by the permeability of all lines of demarcation) but for its propensity to generate movements of superior speed, which had escaped the optic of the state. Only once the possibilities of acceleration provided by long-range technology have reversed this advantage does it become possible to impose panoptic knowledge power on movements and flows that can now be transparently mapped out. It is important to realize that the *Plano topográfico* is essentially dependent on this point of view in continuous, rapid displacement, rather than on a stable perspective: its point of view is primed on the mobility of the glance rather than the fixity of the gaze, as on Blanes's painting. Only superiority of speed makes visible the movements of the other and the space they open up; this mobile perspective, in which cartography appears inextricably bound up with the operation of conquest, also likens mapping to another genre of indexical conjecture, namely, the detective's inquiry. And indeed, Olascoaga's narrative of the expedition casts history as a whodunit. The desert turns into a crime scene, a surface of traces and indices that, under the skilled eye of the investigator, reveal the real course of history:

At every instant, the notion that we were marching across lands only recently discovered by civilization fled our minds, and instead we seemed to find ourselves right on the road from Buenos Aires to Luján or from Córdoba to Rosario. The earth, trampled solid, deep tracks running two feet away from one another, occupying an extension of two miles, bones in different states of decomposition, everything indicated the constant traffic, for centuries, of millions of animals and men. [...] What, then, has happened in the Pampas? Here's the dark and unknown story of our country.[22]

This, then, is what has been going on, "for centuries," on the Caminos Generales: a "traffic" of animals and goods that, rather than leading towards the port city as the single outlet of commodities onto the capitalist world market and as radiating center of state power, opens up a trans-Andean circuit between areas still beyond state control. Until far into the nineteenth century, the archipelago of towns composing the former Viceroyalty of the River Plate had been spanned by three major networks of traffic: to the north, the silver and metal trade route from Alto Perú to Buenos Aires, with its turnoffs into Chile and the Cuyo provinces; to the south, the salt route from Buenos Aires and the littoral to the great salt lakes of the southern pampas (salt being a crucial substance for food preservation, and thus for the food supply of towns and cities); and finally, the indigenous network of tracks connecting the pampas and eastern Patagonia with what is today the south of Chile. The illegalization of this economic and cultural space as a "zone of theft"[23] was an essential moment of the state's "taking control over the public ways" (which, as Paul Virilio reminds us, is precisely the original sense of *polis*, political or police power).[24] The terms in which national space was eventually circumscribed in the Argentine-Chilean treaty of 1881, which established the border between both countries on the Andean watershed, reified this moment of seizure by attributing to nature the regime of flows monopolized by the state (fig. 44).

It is this vast process of de- and reterritorialization, or literally of overcoding of space, that we can see at work on Olascoaga's map. As if swallowing up the silent lines of the indigenous tracks—lines that, from the state's point of view, are nothing but pure movement—the expedition's itineraries advance as a naming machine, leaving in their wake a trail of inscriptions (fig. 45). Observations of landscape features, locations of settlements and campsites, of orchards and ponds, begin to striate the nomadic exterior. Yet most of these names are in Mapudungun (or "Araucanian"), as if the Indians had left behind, in their flight, a linguistic echo, a voice that continues to speak its own absence. Indian names are useful, Olascoaga comments in a note to the legend, because "they are always descriptive of the topography or other features of the places to which they are applied." Precisely because they are the trace of an experience, a practice of space, they can now be brought to use in its appropriation, as places, on behalf of the state. Just as the Caminos Generales will provide the grid for the infrastructural integration of marginal spaces into the space of the state, the virtual space of the Mapudungun language, as the archive of spatial practices and their articulation with the time of social memory, is grasped and translated by the state into a language of pure description, into topography.

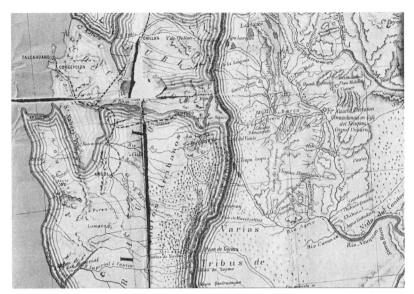

FIGURE 44. Manuel José Olascoaga, *Plano del Territorio de La Pampa y Río Negro.* Detail (1880). Archivo General de la Nación, Buenos Aires. Note the interplay between the itineraries of military vanguards (Coronel Urquiza, Coronel Guerrico) with the continuous lines of the indigenous trans-Andean tracks, and the highlighting, by lines of altitude, of the Argentine-Chilean border as a natural limit.

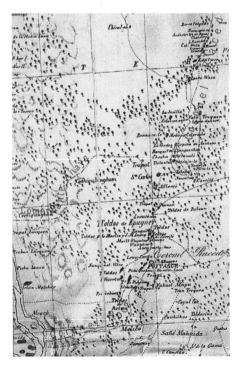

FIGURE 45. Manuel José Olascoaga, *Plano del Territorio de La Pampa y Río Negro.* Detail (1880). Archivo General de la Nación, Buenos Aires. Indigenous toponyms cluster along both sides of the expedition's track.

Significantly, the density of indigenous toponyms does not increase but actually decreases in the still unconquered regions of the far south (fig. 42). Instead, cartographic capture proceeds here by means of quantification: "Region of many salt lagoons," "Several belligerent tribes," "Pampa and Tehuelche Indians," and so on. The southern part of the map still displays a state of unsecured quanta, which can only be approached through approximations and estimates, from the point of view of the engineer-geographer. Yet it is precisely this lack of previous encodings that turns the desert into the most advanced place of state consolidation, more so, even, than the telegraph- and railway-spanned areas on the rear of the frontier, for it is only here, in the desert, that a new mode of power can be inscribed directly and without interference on the part of social agencies.

## Internal Imperialism

A map of conquest, Olascoaga's *Plano* is a battle chart, a production of space that highlights rather than disavows its own provisional character. A balance of military operations, it also suggests strategic options for the future and warns of possible risks. Unlike a "plain" scientific map, it represents space as a social relation, a struggle in and over "nature," its meanings and short- and long-term uses. Territory, for the battle plan, is important only to the extent to which it interferes (actually or potentially) with tactical operations, as part of the action, as practiced space.[25] In effect, in this and the previous chapter I have been reading the visual forms of state capture in and of space as battle plans—sketches made by particular agents in moments of struggle. I have thus been trying to unhook the state's productions of space from their place in the archive, as preliminary and imperfect representations of a nonetheless already existing national space, and reinsert them into the process of struggle over its nature and meaning. Following Henri Lefebvre's suggestion, I have been attempting to reconnect the representations of space to the spaces of representation in which they became meaningful, and to the spatial practices (the field of social relations in and with the environment) which these representations had to engage with, insofar as they themselves represented a new spatial practice that sought to impose itself over all others.[26]

W. J. T. Mitchell has pointed out the affinities of this visual production of space with the discourse of imperialism. Imperialism, he argues, "conceives itself [...] as an expansion of landscape understood as an inevitable, progressive development in history, an expansion of 'culture' and 'civilization' into a 'natural' space in a progress that is itself narrated as 'natural.' Empires move outward in space as a way of moving forward in time; the 'prospect' that opens up is not just a spatial scene but a projected future of 'development' and exploitation."

Mitchell's characterization of landscape as an imperial genre allows us, in turn, to grasp a dimension of internal imperialism in the visual forms of the Argentine and Brazilian state in the late nineteenth century. Yet unlike in the spatial discourses of European imperial expansion, here the movement of capture of marginal or frontier spaces, figured as an expansion into nature, is not accompanied "by a new interest in the representation of the home landscape, the 'nature' of the imperial center,"[27] as it had been, for example, in English and French gardening and park design in the nineteenth century. Rather, the nature of the frontier becomes the space where the nation-state is finally, for the first time, at one with itself: an initiatic space of identity, a natural stage where history can recommence, a founding scene. However, we have also seen nuances and differences between the two processes of capture of marginal environments. In Brazil, turn-of-the-century discourses of infrastructural or medical intervention into the *sertão* often implied a narrative of the reencounter with the nation-state's true self, providentially encrypted in the natural conditions. Southward expansion in Argentina, on the contrary, provided the spatial figure for a linear conception of historical progress at the same time as it introduced a new idea of state power as a nomadic force imposing itself on flows of capital that decentered the previous regime dominated by the port province (if only to reinforce the dominance of the port *city*, now cut loose from any ties with the surrounding region). The state's production of space in Argentina and Brazil, we might summarize, sought to generate regimes of symbolic and material flows that ran in opposite directions: from coast to interior, in the case of Brazil, and from the frontier to the coastal metropolis, in Argentina, and on into the space of transatlantic capital transfers. It would be interesting to speculate further about the nature of interrelations between geography and history, the ways in which each appears to be determined by the other (a theme that, having made its first appearances in the final decades of the nineteenth century, would become a common obsession among classical modern essayists such as Euclides da Cunha, Gilberto Freyre, Raúl Scalabrini Ortiz, and Ezequiel Martínez Estrada). What I will be looking for in the next chapter, however, is rather their moment of separation: the elusive moment of violence that is constantly implied in the visual productions we have looked at in this and the previous chapter, but which has thus far remained outside the frame of representation, out of sight.

# Disappearing Acts

## PHOTOGRAPHY AND
## PRIMITIVE ACCUMULATION

> Thanks to the camera's power to expose, the photographer also has something of an explorer; insatiable curiosity driving him to advance into areas as yet unknown, and to capture their curious forms.
>
> —Siegfried Kracauer, *Theory of Film*

> If colonialism takes power in the name of history, it repeatedly exercises its authority through the figures of farce.
>
> —Homi K. Bhabha, *The Location of Culture*

### Visual Primitive Accumulation

Among the technologies of the state's capture of space, photography by the end of the nineteenth century had attained a key importance. Even before their inscription into the abstract space of cartography, the camera collected places as sights. As a serialized collection of sights, photographic travel albums combined elements of the map and the museum: like the map, they put space at a distance through the work of an apparatus; like the museum, they employed the art of excision and the fragment to carry away samples of the real that they made stand in for the whole. Photography had become involved with imperial expansion almost immediately after its inception: within months of its presentation by Daguerre in 1839, the camera had already become a regular travel companion, taken along to record "exotic" nature and culture as sights, transforming them into discrete objects to be safely consumed at home in the Western urban centers. Thus the camera's relation with imperial conquest and capitalist accumulation was an intimate one from the very beginning. As Susan Sontag has noted, photography as "a device [...] to record what is disappearing," emerged at precisely the historical moment in which the natural and social world fell prey to the destruction wrought upon them by capitalist primitive accumulation.[1]

In this chapter, I will study the relations between photography, violence, and forms of narrative and rhetoric in two photographic albums depicting the imposition of the state form on marginal regions and populations in Argentina and Brazil. The first of these series of images records the beginnings of the colonization of Tierra del Fuego at the hands of freelance adventurers between 1887 and 1893; the second the siege and destruction in 1897 of the penitential community of Canudos in the backlands of Bahia, an event that was to achieve literary fame years later through Euclides da Cunha's monumental geohistorical essay *Os sertões* (*Rebellion in the Backlands*, 1902). My intention in looking at these series of images is a self-confessedly paradoxical one: while I will try to reconstruct the purposes and intentions invested into these pictures and thus to unmake their illusory promise of immediate purchase on the real; at the same time, I nonetheless draw upon their indexical capacity to capture a particular moment in the expansion of state power and of capitalist relations. To put it another way, what I am interested in is the way in which photographs were at one and the same time representations and means of a moment of capture that I call "visual primitive accumulation."

### Receding Horizons

Photography, over the second half of the nineteenth century, became available to a rising number of practitioners and consumers in Latin America thanks to the introduction of dry plates, albumin paper, and, after 1888, flexible film, processed in positive-negative technique and thus allowing for multiple copies. Despite its almost immediate introduction into all the principal Latin American cities, the daguerreotype, available only to a small elite, had effectively remained limited in its scope of themes to the late colonial traditions of genteel portraiture and (to a minor degree) exotic landscape. With the emergence of paper prints, however, not only did these become accessible to the new urban middle sectors, but, moreover, studio photography and new formats such as the album and the *carte de visite* also revived and transformed low colonial forms such as the *album de vistas y costumbres* (album of vistas and customs) or the *pintura de castas* (caste paintings), representing in picturesque fashion the socially and ethnically "inferior." Visiting cards and prints of Indian, black, and mestizo types, sold and circulated as visual collectibles, reorganized the spatiotemporal "outside" against which the new social subjectivity of an urban bourgeoisie could be mapped out. Photographers such as Christiano Júnior, a native Portuguese working in Brazil and Argentina in the 1860s and 1870s, advertised "a plentiful collection of

FIGURE 46. José Christiano de Freitas Henriques Júnior (Christiano Júnior), Picture from series *Types of Slaves from Rio de Janeiro*. Carte de visite (ca. 1860). Museu Histórico Nacional, Rio de Janeiro.

customs and types of blacks, particularly useful for those about to travel to Europe" (fig. 46).[2] Nature and the body of the other, in this emergent visual economy, provided the contrasting backgrounds against which the agency and visual citizenship of the subject of portraiture could be established. In a very similar way, I will argue, the transcendental subject of the state was an effect of the capture and exposure, in an emergent documentary photography, of a spatial and a socioethnic exterior, over which sovereignty was imposed, first and foremost, through panoramic seeing. As in Blanes's painting, the capture of land and of the other's body, when made to converge in a single image, produced a scene of foundation: the violent origin of the state's visual economy.

Photography really came into its own wherever it was recruited to document the advances of long-range technology into the frontier areas of capital. Writing on the pictures taken by Antonio Pozzo in 1879 on accompanying Roca's divisions to the margins of the Río Negro, Héctor Alimonda and Juan Ferguson stress the importance of the photographic record for the military narrative of crossing and occupying a "desert" already "cleansed" of native inhabitants.[3] Pozzo's visual record of the expedition, they point out, is organized by the complementary tropes of the disavowal of violence and the suggestion of vast, empty spaces in large panoramic shots of soldiers posing in the half-distance between the lens and the horizon. In the few images where Indians appear at all, they do so as already exposed to the state's sovereign decision. In an arrangement that mimics the advance of the troops from already pacified areas into the heart of the desert, the photographic gaze departs from a vision of indigenous huts clutched against the outskirts of Carhué, now a military colony, followed by images of Indians rounded up and uniformed, awaiting baptism, or crouching (still in their native costume) while they receive their first catechism, under the vigil

FIGURE 47. Antonio Pozzo, "Choele Choel, Indian Prisoners, Catechism." Albumin print (1879). Archivo General de la Nación, Buenos Aires.

of military officers standing behind them. The final image of the series (the one spatially and temporally most removed from "civilization" and therefore closest to the initial moment of capture), entitled "Choele Choel, Indian Prisoners, Catechism" (fig. 47), shows three priests circulating among crouching women and children, some of whom anxiously cover their faces or embrace each other, absolutely exposed to the gaze and will of the beholder, while a group of officers stand watching them from behind, completing their encirclement by foreign gazes.

The violence in which these photographs have their origin is simultaneously denied and invoked. Pozzo's series seems to be moving towards a moment of origin that organizes its meaning, yet which must in itself remain in the future of the image, beyond the desert's empty horizon, precisely because it is already its past. The violence of the origin is absent from the image because it has to have already occurred for there to be an image. Yet the album's sequential organization, moving towards its absent original scene, also converts this absence into a potential future.

It is precisely this paradoxical temporality of a past perpetually deferred, as a threat, into the future, that is also proper to Marx's concept of *ursprüngliche Akkumulation* ("original" rather than "primitive" accumulation, as the English translation suggests). We should recall here that the famous chapter of *Das Kapital* on the mystery of primitive (original) accumulation approaches its object on two levels: (a) the analysis of violence as an "economic potency" that operates the simultaneous subjectification and subjection (*Befreiung* and *Freisetzung*) of living labor into labor power and the parallel emergence of capital and the state as the ends and means of accumulation; and (b) the rhetorical, poetic invocation of the arcana of violence in which the "mystery of primitive accumulation" has its murky origin.[4] Violence, and the enigma of its production of consciousness through the spectacle of physical pain, remains the irreducible supplement, the excess that spills over, in an array of poetic figures and images, into the analysis of its economic function as the original object of exchange. What we will be looking for in the images of the other's violated body on the margins of the state is a foundational moment of representation itself, one however that can only be grasped in deferral. Like the mimicry of colonial discourse, I will argue, the snapshots of state capture can only generate a partial presence, both constituted and undermined in metonymic displacement. Its visibility is therefore "always produced at the site of interdiction."[5]

## Epic Farce

If indeed the state's capture of the outside, the expansion of state power into frontier space, is represented in a permanent deferral of its origin in violence, I suggest we begin by looking towards the end rather than the beginning of state expansion, for a clear vision of this violent origin. The first series of images I wish to discuss at some length is from the photographic album of Julius Popper's "scientific expedition" to Tierra del Fuego in 1887, first exhibited on occasion of a talk Popper gave at the Argentine Geographical Institute immediately after his return to Buenos Aires. They show a naked man, presumably a Selk'nam warrior, lying dead beside a rudimentary structure of branches and grass, while several uniformed men are kneeling close by, rifles pressed against their shoulders, firing (as does the camera) at different angles into the distance. We know the dead Indian is a man not because we can see his face (his head, sunk into the grass, is cut off by the low camera angle), but because his genitals are directly exposed to us, almost as a macabre trophy.[6] On the second of these images, Popper himself appears standing virtually on top of the corpse, commanding his firing squad. All three images have captions scratched directly onto the plate: "Killed in the Field of Honor" (*Muerto en el terreno del honor*) (fig. 48), "Aim Low" (*Bajad la mira*) (fig. 49), and "Shower of Arrows" (*Lluvia de flechas*) (fig. 50).

The pictures, then, depict a fight that would have eluded our gaze if not for its invocation through language and, most importantly, for the dead man lying in the foreground, framing the scene, making it "real." "It was a strange combat," Popper would describe the incident in his presentation at the Geographical Institute:

FIGURE 48. (*above*) Julio Popper, "Killed in the Field of Honor." Albumin print (1887). Royal Geographical Society, London.

FIGURE 49. (*left*) Julio Popper, "Aim Low." Albumin print (1887). Royal Geographical Society, London.

FIGURE 50. (*below, left*) Julio Popper, "Shower of Arrows." Albumin print (1887). Royal Geographical Society, London.

We were pursuing a guanaco, when we suddenly fell in with eighty Indians, with their faces painted red and in a state of compete nakedness, scattered about behind some short bushes. We had scarcely seen them when a shower of arrows fell upon us and stuck fast in the ground close to our horses, happily without causing us any loss. We were soon alighted and returned the complement with our Winchester rifles. [...] While we were firing the Indians lay with their faces to the ground and left off shooting their arrows; but the moment our shots ceased we again heard the whistling of the missiles. Gradually we managed to get to windward, which obliged the Indians to withdraw, for the arrow cannot do much harm when shot against the wind. On this occasion two Indians were left dead on the field.[7]

To make us hear the invisible arrows is indeed the purpose of the compositional arrangement of corpse and "firing squad" on the three photographs, and also of the captions, which, quite literally, inscribe Popper's narrative into the albumin surface. Yet this narrative legend is not merely a verbal reconstruction of the event. Rather, verbal inscription takes on the function of stage directions here, describing a scene that the image imitates. For, of course, these are images not of an event in real time but of the dramatic representation of one: the homicidal slapstick of late colonialism, an epic farce of civilization's victory over savagery. At closer look the mise-en-scène remains strangely incoherent, allowing us not so much a glimpse of real-time heroism but of a macabre ritual, a piece of borderline Dadaism, a scene of the obscene. To begin with, why is the dead man lying in the foreground of the image, a few feet away from the firing "soldiers," when supposedly the Indians are attacking from afar, so distant we cannot see them? (Only the whistling of their arrows, likewise invisible to both the eye and the camera, is heard when the shooting stops.) And from where exactly are they attacking, if in each image the soldiers are firing in different directions, judging from their position towards the dead body (or is the body moving as well)? Where is the other dead man mentioned in the narrative? (Is the same Indian used in different photographs to represent several casualties?) And why, finally, does the corpse lie immediately next to what are clearly the remains of a wind shelter, the kind used by the Selk'nam when travelling in search of game, when the combat has supposedly taken place on the open plain, with Indians appearing out of nowhere to attack Popper and his men?

As Timothy Sweet notes, the rearrangement of corpses on the battlefield to obtain more formally satisfying or ideologically explicit images was already a common practice among U.S. Civil War photographers such as Alexander Gardner, Timothy O'Sullivan, or George Barnard.[8] To make violent death meaningful, to reinsert it into narrative, the cadaver had to be brought back to life, to be reanimated by the magic of the camera. The lifeless body was in many ways the ideal customer for photography's art of arrested movement, but only if he could be made to act. He had to represent his own death—to become a ghost, a spectre—so as not to disturb the living with his unmediated indexicality. But if Popper's "combat photographs" are really scenic compositions arranged around the stage requisite of a lifeless body, the questions they raise also return us to the problems of violence and deferral in the relation between photographic and military capture, and of the partial presence of a power that has to be constantly supplemented by mimicry. In fact, just as his writings on Tierra del Fuego that he would publish in the Buenos Aires press over the following years, Popper's Fuegian photographs represented, first and foremost, an offering to the authority of the state on behalf of an emergent frontier capital that was still more fantasized than real. His album, incidentally, following the presentation at the institute, was given as a gift to President Juárez Celman, Roca's successor and brother-in-law.

Popper's presentation at the Geographical Institute on March 5, 1887—surrounded by displays of maps and indigenous weapons decoratively arranged in heraldic patterns as colonial trophies (fig. 51)—was crucial for his attempt to rally the support of national speculative capital for his Fuegian adventure. A

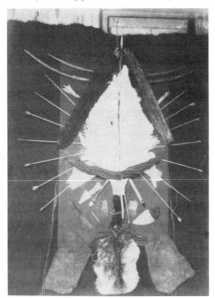

FIGURE 51. Julio Popper, Coat of arms made of Selk'nam garments and weaponry, exposed on occasion of Popper's talk at the Instituto Geográfico Argentino, March 5, 1887. Albumin print. Museo del Fin del Mundo, Ushuaia.

Romanian engineer and adventurer trained at the École Polytechnique in Paris, Popper had only been in Argentina for little more than a year, after having received news of the gold discoveries in southern Patagonia when travelling through Brazil. Upon arriving in Buenos Aires, he had quickly made contact with the upper echelons of *porteño* society, setting up his own Compañía Anónima Lavadero de Oro del Sud (Southern Gold-Washing Company) little more than a year later. Between March and May 1886 he explored the northern shores of the Strait of Magellan and, upon returning to the capital, received a mining concession for the province of Santa

Cruz from none other than President Roca himself. Not satisfied with his findings, however, in August of the same year Popper announced a "scientific expedition" to Tierra del Fuego, whose Eastern half Argentina had formally annexed in 1884, requesting special permission to take along fifteen armed men, "in anticipation of attacks by hostile Indians."[9] Again, permission was granted by the highest levels of government, despite the fact that another expedition under Ramón Lista, founder of the Sociedad Geográfica and governor of the territory of Santa Cruz, was also on its way to the island. In October 1886 Popper's little platoon disembarked at Punta Arenas, Chile, not only armed with Winchester rifles but also impeccably dressed in uniforms mimicking those of the Austro-Hungarian army. Much to the excitement of the locals, they set up camp in large white tents reminiscent of the Crimean and Abyssinian wars. It being the day of President Balmaceda's ascension, Popper and his men gracefully agreed to parade up and down the muddy main street of the remote frontier town.

Across the Strait, Popper entered into a tight race with Lista to be the first to name rivers, mountains, and lakes, a writing of state geography that was closely tied to the imminent rush for Fuegian gold and Fuegian lands. Where Lista wrote "Río Pellegrini," in honor of the vice president, Popper would write "Río Juárez Celman," in honor of the president (posterity settled for a simple "Grande"). At Bahía San Sebastián, Popper eventually found gold washed up on the beach, samples of which he would display at the Geographical Institute, and he immediately established a mining site at the northern edge of the bay. Legal confirmation of his mining rights immediately followed on Popper's talk at the Institute. Yet even though Popper quickly mounted a massive industrial operation—his mines, between 1887 and 1893, the year of his death, employed as many as 750 workers, largely drawn from the Serbian-Croat colony around Punta Arenas—his gold empire on the northern part of the island remained under constant threat of collapse. Food supplies arrived late or never, wage payments were eternally delayed, leading to endemic mutinies and desertions, and rival adventurers kept pouring in from Chile to try their luck. With local authorities confined beyond the Cordillera at Ushuaia, Popper took the law into his own hands, issuing his own money for wages and payments, and postal stamps (indicating "Auricosta" as their place of postage) for communications. To fend off competitors he deployed his private militia, increased for the occasion by straw dummies strapped onto horses to give the impression of overwhelming force. Leaving his brother Máximo in charge of his mining posts, Popper spent most of his final years in Buenos Aires, lobbying national government to sack unsympathetic officials in the Far South and to grant official status to his militia as a territorial police force. An astonishingly gifted writer, in his newspaper chronicles on Tierra del Fuego Popper ably wielded a cannonade of styles and registers in defense of his cause, from the adventure tale to the gallant anecdote, the landscape vignette to the ethnographic description, the burlesque dialogue to the political intrigue. The late imperial hero, the *bourgeois conquérant*, needs to be fluent in more than one idiom—Winchesters and violence on the remote frontier; entertainment, causeries, and small talk in the salons and boudoirs of the capital. Popper was one of the mirror images of Roca, a farcical double of the "conqueror of the desert": both relied on the same symbolic capital, Roca to convert it into political power, Popper into money.

Popper's short-lived Fuegian gold empire, in fact, presents us with a peculiar version of state capture and primitive accumulation, where everything from money and communications to military occupation and policing appears in "as if" mode. Popper's photographic album makes explicit the farcical nature of state expansion because, on the frontier, he had to play all the leading roles himself: military commander, collecting naturalist, travelling dandy, and so on. To cover up the precarious, insubstantial character of each and every one of these subject positions, he had to "overact" them. Thus, in fact, Popper involuntarily brought to the fore of the image the element of farce that was always present in the expansion of colonial power. Colonial power, as the partial presence of history and the (Western) subject, in Popper's Fuegian adventure became itself the absent model, the distant reality that his travelling circus of uniforms, tents, and Winchesters sought to conjure through its imitation. Internal colonialism on the Latin American late nineteenth-century frontier, we might say, was doubly specular: it repeated a model that was already a repetition (a copy), a re-presentation of the European signifier in a space this same representation posited as one of irreducible difference.

It is interesting to note, moreover, that the protagonist of this farce of capture was himself a marginal one: Popper, as a Romanian-born Jew whose parents had fled anti-Semitism in Poland, was in many ways a nomadic, stateless body, a "bare life" that could cast itself as a subject of power only in the no-man's-land of South America's ultimate frontier—the "uttermost part of the earth," in the words of another pioneer-settler.[10] As we have seen, the "substantial insubstantiality" of Popper's liminal power depended on the exposure of the bare life of the indigenous other, a life over which even Popper could take power. It is the founding scene of this simultaneous empowerment and absolute subjection, then, which we see represented in the elementary geometry of bodies on the second of Popper's "combat pictures" (fig. 49). The dead man's horizontal body virtually sustains Popper's vertical, upright body, the two composing a pyramidal figure that is further emphasized by the triangle of Popper's legs and the parallel horizontals of bow and rifle. An iconic image of the simultaneous imposition of sovereignty and sacrality, it is an image of violence turned into, indeed generating, visual order.

The annexation of the frontier as a private enterprise repeated as well as anticipated the violent expansion of the state in the mode of a murderous farce. Popper's pictures of his "conquest" of Tierra del Fuego imitate Pozzo's of the annexation of Patagonia from the previous decade, with the only (but decisive) difference that the image's violent origin, which Pozzo's album had deferred beyond the horizon of the frame, is now at the center of the composition. The "offering" of the murdered Selk'nam, and that of his belongings as a decoratively arranged collection of trophies, is the object of a symbolic exchange between capital and the state. If the latter had brought the desert under the rule of law, only to divide it, as real estate, among the private financiers of military expansion, Popper's private invasion claimed to act as a law-making force, even though its appropriation of the land could only take place in the lawless space of the frontier. If this mode of imperial expansion had its condition of possibility in an "extraterritorial" lawlessness, all the more did it therefore have to cast its initial act of violence as one in defense of the law, in the name of a sovereignty that preexisted its own invocation. Indeed, the production and display of this visual narrative on the foundation/defense of the law was at least as important for the success of Popper's enterprise as that of gold samples (the second of the combat pictures, in fact, appeared again on the cover page of the English-language edition of Popper's travelogue, superimposed on a landscape view from a mountaintop). For, only in exhibiting a violence at the origin of the law did the conqueror become the legitimate owner of the land, on the one hand, because this violence guaranteed, vis-à-vis Popper's official and private patrons, the actual exercise of territorial dominion, on the other, because only the demonstrative capacity and readiness to use violence could hold in check the threat of mass desertion that was constantly hanging over his mining empire. It is highly possible, given the careful and detailed staging of the images, including the use of uniforms and the poses of military drill adopted by Popper and his travel companions, that this was a scene already on the expedition's script before any real encounter with native Fuegians had taken place. To take possession of the land had always implied a chase for its inhabitants, a chase for a visual trophy.

## The Optical Unconscious

I want to turn now to the haunting images of the siege of Canudos produced by Flávio de Barros on the verge and in the immediate aftermath of the final assault and destruction of the millennialist settlement in the Bahian backlands. As

Robert Levine has shown, the attack on Canudos was the ultimate consequence of a larger, conflictive process of state intervention into the rural interior, which clashed with the established power of local landlords even as it reinforced traditional patterns of plied labor and herd vote. For the landless population, the state capture of social relations previously regulated in terms of "pastoral power" implied formerly unknown degrees of external intervention into cultural and religious practices, independent economic activities, and interpersonal relations.[11]

Whereas Popper's pictures have been largely forgotten in Argentina, some of Barros's photographs have become iconic images of national tragedy in Brazil, due to their inclusion in the first edition of Euclides da Cunha's *Os sertões*, perhaps the key work of the Brazilian literary canon. Yet the original purpose of these images, like that of Popper's, was to promote the cause of the victors—here essentially the second military column under General Carlos Eugênio de Andrade Guimarães (brother of the commander in chief Artur Oscar), who appears to have personally appointed Barros as "fotógrafo expedicionário" and to have closely monitored his work, choosing themes and motifs that included mock attacks and posed scenes of man-to-man combat. Arriving at the scene just days before the final attack on October 1, 1897, Barros dedicated himself primarily to the documentation of life on the front: large group shots of the different regiments comprise by far the largest number of prints, followed by leisure scenes (barbecues, soldiers inside their huts or having a smoke). In short, the album transmits an image of war as a collective adventure, in which advanced technology and efficient strategy but also comradeship and esprit de corps finally grant victory in a hostile environment (the first nine images of Barros's album are made up of panoramic shots of Canudos and the barren and dry *sertão* landscape).

According to Alan Trachtenberg, the new kind of mechanized long-range warfare that photographers first encountered in the U.S. Civil War challenged them in two fundamental ways: if their chemical and mechanic equipment was hardly designed for recording real-time fighting, the way in which war was now being waged also defied attempts to represent it according to the chivalric conventions of painterly Romanticism. Staged scenes of everyday life on the front therefore came closest to what former studio photographers had in their aesthetic arsenal to respond to this double challenge.[12] Although flexible negative film had been introduced in 1888 by Eastman Kodak, Barros was still using dry plates (glass plates covered with a silver nitrate emulsion). While these considerably reduced exposure time compared to traditional collodion plates, thus allowing capture of moving scenes, they made it difficult to process the photographs on site, due to the extreme variations of temperature in the *sertão*. Barros thus only developed and selected his prints on his return to Salvador. From there he directly traveled on to Rio de Janeiro, arriving in the capital by the end of October, at the same time as General Oscar and his high command. A private screening of lantern-slide versions of his pictures for journalists of the newspaper *O País* was arranged on October 29, which suggests that the selection of images must have been made by then; whether or not this was done in consultation with the military commanders is unclear. It can be assumed, though, that individual pictures of battalions and officers were sold by Barros to those portrayed in them.[13]

Yet whatever the ultimate function and use of Barros's images, it is clear that his recruitment at a fairly late stage of the conflict, when criticism about mismanagement of supplies and about excessive and systematic brutality was starting to spread through the press, was intended from the outset as a piece of active counterpropaganda that invoked the indexical power of the photographic image to forge an official memory under which critical voices could be effectively buried. One clearly staged image, for instance, captioned "Medical Staff and Injured Bandit" (*Corpo sanitário e uma jagunça ferida*, fig. 52) suggests that, far from massacring their "bandit" (*jagunço*) enemies of Canudos, the army was actually providing medical treatment to those it had "rescued" from the bastion of fanaticism.

As in the second of Popper's combat pictures, the scene is simultaneously one of empowerment and subjection, suggested by the image's geometrical arrangement of horizontal and vertical bodies. But unlike in Popper's image, there

FIGURE 52. Flávio de Barros, "Medical Staff and Injured Bandit (*jagunça*)." Albumin print (1897). Instituto Moreira Salles, Rio de Janeiro.

is an excess of vertical bodies here, exploding the frame on both ends. A second and third row of spectators breaks through the first row of medics and officers, disavowing their static posture and stern-faced expression. Note the darker shade of the faces in the back rows, and the way in which their attempts to wrestle their way into the image, stepping on their toes, hands on their front men's shoulders, distorts the visual order of the front row and turns it into a palisade. If the multitude of bodies disavows the picture's legend, which seeks to present it as an image of "care," exposing instead the trophy character of the young woman who is offered up to the viewer's gaze as a freakish specimen of barbarism, the disorder that invades the second plane of the image also undercuts its claims of orderliness and control. The staged scene of medical officers and their patient, which just as Popper's pictures takes the immobilized body of the other as its principal requisite, is here invaded by the indexical: there is too much to see (and too many urging to be seen) for the central scene to retain its exclusive command over our gaze. This sense of an explosion of the scene, spilling out beyond the limits of a frame no longer capable of containing it, is further heightened by the appearance of a second *sertaneja* (backlands woman) in the lower right-hand corner. This enigmatic face not only opens the frame towards the front, pointing us to its blind field—are there further bandits awaiting treatment? have they already been operated on?—it also engages in a dialogue with the faces and bodies in the back of the scene, which likewise intrude into its self-enclosed visual order. Hence the scene of civilization—the medical intervention on a "barbarous" body in need of assistance, which is in fact a synecdoche of the entire military operation—is exposed as beleaguered and besieged from multiple sides, rather than as a situation under control. The staging of the real, we could say, has to surrender under the pressure of the indexical that overruns its borders on each side, an excess that the photographic apparatus cannot help but record.

In part, we could try to understand this effect of subversion, indeed explosion, of staged reality by referring to Barthes's notion of the *punctum* as the "unrevealed" of the photograph. The *punctum* is that which eludes the intention of the photographer (or even the observation of the photographer, since it only comes to exist in the engagement between image and spectator), the insistence of the supplementary that refuses to let the image close in on itself, opening up a blind field.[14] Yet in these pictures it is not so much a minuscule detail or element that punctures our gaze. Rather, it is as though the represented were constantly inverting the stakes, turning upside down the voyeuristic logic of the gaze imposed on them, and exposing photography's (its authors' and viewers') complicity with violence. I will argue that this inverted return of meaning is the result of an overwriting of Barros's photographs by *Os sertões* and its process of reception. Even before, however, it had already been in the eye of the beholder as a disavowed, repressed presence. Nothing in Euclides's text, in other words, had not previously been in Barros's pictures, but it had been actively unseen, cast as the invisible.

I shall borrow Benjamin's controversial notion of the "optical unconscious" in order to grasp this historical dynamic by which the other's ghost, the indexicality that refuses to go away, becomes a phantasmatic truth-speaker. For Benjamin, the optical unconscious is that aspect of material reality that is repressed by the physiology of human vision but which can be disinterred by the technically enhanced speed of photographic illumination. The optical unconscious is thus at once technical and historical; it is an unconscious without a subject, proper to the material world: the way in which things desire to break out of the artificial places assigned to them under the commodity's regime, exploding the false naturalness of the marketplace's way of seeing.[15] But if photography in industrial Europe, for Benjamin, is therefore the true chronicler of modernity as "messianic time" (a time in which redemption has become a real historical possibility), on the margins of the West the camera turned into the forensic tool of an archaeology of sheer destruction. Hence, if there is a peripheral or colonial optical unconscious, it is one that exposes a different kind of potentiality, or "fullness of time"—a potentiality of radical destruction, of unmaking—civilization's own space of death. This other unconscious, which photography becomes burdened with as part of the technical apparatus of imperial expansion, begs linguistic supplementation; like the mass grave discovered by forensic archaeology, it at once defies and cries out for language. We could thus usefully connect it to the final reflections in Benjamin's essay on authenticity and the caption. For, if Benjamin urges for the inscription to become the principal component of the image, he is precisely not, as Susan Sontag maintains, making a moral demand on the photograph to "do what no photograph can ever do—speak," the caption thus becoming the photograph's "missing voice […] expected to speak for truth."[16] Rather, if photographic shock can produce a rupture in the "associative mechanism" of bourgeois historical thinking, in exactly the way in which it disrupts a self-delusive way of seeing, this shock only becomes a transformative force to the extent to which it inspires a new language. Rather than to occupy and fill in the image's place of lack, this new language uses it to inscribe a radical interruption in the discourse of history.

It is in this sense that I want to explore the collapse and reconstruction of historical meaning in the palimpsest of images and captions composed of Barros's photographs and their reedition as visual quotations in *Os sertões*. As I have argued, this double session is necessary since our own gaze is inexorably framed by the way Euclides's text has taken hold of these pictures, or rather of the space in which they can be seen. Conversely, by reintroducing Barros's photographs into a discussion of *Os sertões*, we can reassess Euclides's writing as an attempt to contain photography's visual excess, and thus to reconstitute meaning from the catastrophic immediacy of Barros's images. It is important to bear in mind that Barros's photographs had neither been publicly exhibited nor reprinted during the conflict itself, thus only becoming known to a large audience on the inclusion of three of them in *Os sertões*, one of the best-selling books in Brazilian literary history at the time. Even more importantly, as Berthold Zilly has shown, Euclides's text also recaptioned many of the photographs it did *not* reproduce visually, some of them repeatedly and at different instances of the narrative (thus the case of the various views of Canudos—*golpes de vista*, or "blows of vision," as Euclides calls them—that revisit the panoramic opening shots of Barros's album, only to undermine their certainty of appropriating the space of the other).[17] Here the caption eliminates its photographic referent altogether, abolishing the unequivocal presence of the visual image. The text culminates in an admission of the indescribable that turns on the trope of a visual deception, associating the inadequacy and impropriety of historical writing with the collapse of modernity's visual regime of perspective: "We shall spare ourselves the task of describing the last moments. We *could* not describe them. [...] We are like one who has ascended a very high mountain. On the summit, new and wide perspectives unfold before him, but along with them comes dizziness."[18]

Indeed, it is possible to read Euclides's monumental work almost entirely from the point of view of the two critiques sketched out in this passage: on the one hand, a critique of historical narrative's mimetic illusion, on the other, a critique of the indexical truth claims of those modern technologies of seeing (photography, cartography, geodesy, etc.) which *Os sertões* must nevertheless constantly refer to in order to interrupt and question the linearity of history's plot. Hence the almost cinematographic structure of the text, its continuous scansion and critique of the diegesis by iconic "takes," which are themselves the result of a captioning and overwriting of the visual image that eliminates its claim to immediacy. If, on incorporating Barros's photographs into his work Euclides was undoubtedly calling on their indexical value in order to strengthen his own claims to historical veracity, his text is simultaneously a denunciation of the insufficiency of photographic realism. This critique, I suggest, is at work most strikingly where Euclides's text takes the place of an image that is left out, entirely overwritten by the mnemonic script, as in the case, notably, of Barros's only picture of an enemy fighter, "Captured Bandit" (*Jagunço preso*) (fig. 53).

Barros was asked to take this picture by General Artur Oscar, the head of

FIGURE 53. Flávio de Barros, "Captured Bandit." Albumin print (1897). Instituto Moreira Salles, Rio de Janeiro.

command, who had offered a reward for bringing living prisoners into his presence to be questioned and photographed in order to document their orderly
treatment.[19] "*Preso*" (captured), then, simultaneously refers to a certain legal
status and to a state of visual exposure that warrants it. Paradoxically, it is precisely the *jagunço*'s absolute exposure to the photographic apparatus that allows
the composition of a visual space of legality. Barros's "bandit" is no less a visual
trophy than Popper's Selk'nam, yet he needs to be presented to the camera in a
state that is located simultaneously before and after Popper's moment of capture. Both pictures show a body in a state of total submission, exposed to a sovereign power that the photographic image both depicts and embodies. Both the
Selk'nam's and the *jagunço*'s are bodies before the law, but whereas the corpse of
the former figures in "Killed in the Field of Honor" as an indexical trace of an
extralegal violence in which the law has its origin and foundation, in "Captured
Bandit" the camera itself has become the eye of the law. It verifies the legality and

justness of military action against the Bahian peasantry by organizing the frame as a space of legality in which the camera itself takes the position of judge. Like Popper, Barros uses military uniforms and poses as devices for the composition of visual order, which simultaneously emphasizes and contains the excessive physical presence of the other. But although his state of unlimited exposure to a sovereign gaze reveals his true status as bare life, the *jagunço* in Barros's photograph nonetheless still represents a legal subject. He is exposed to the judgment of the viewer, to whom his military custodians have duly turned him over. Furthermore, and most important of all, he is (still) alive, and has to be, of course, in order for the scene to represent an image of the law: an image of the law's defense and not of its epic foundation, as in "Killed in the Field of Honor." Therefore Barros's caption must refer to the penal code—a "captured bandit" is someone who has been captured as a bandit, on the grounds of his criminal acts—rather than to that of war, which is how the law refers to its own suspension and origin.

But it is precisely this violence of origin, which Euclides inscribes once again into Barros's photograph, at the very moment, moreover, when narrative continuity in *Os sertões* is interrupted for a "cry of protest" in view of the sheer monstrosity of what the narrator has just referred. In Euclides's version of the scene, the moment of the *jagunço's* presentation and interrogation in the military camp is merely a brief instant of passage from the battlefield to the *caatinga*, the wilderness, where, "outside the law," the torture, execution, and dismemberment summarily described in the following chapter will take place. This recaptioning of the visual record explodes the frame by returning to the fore the violence that the photograph had expunged through visual composition. Euclides's restaging of the scene crosses out the photograph's mise-en-scène (the *studium*, in Barthes's terms); at the same time, however, it confirms the involuntary veracity of its formal composition, which reveals the *jagunço* as a tragic hero even in the moment of defeat, infinitely superior to his tormentors in the service of the state.

### Death Is Not the End

Roland Barthes, towards the end of *La chambre claire*, comments on Alexander Gardner's iconic portrait of Lewis Payne, a Confederate political prisoner awaiting execution, suggesting that it is "punctuated" not by a minor detail that "infects" and overturns the entire composition, but by the intensification of a disruptive temporality.[20] This "other *punctum*" is located neither in the photograph nor in the caption but in the gap that opens up in the simultaneous reading of discontinuity—of the "before" of the photographic session and the "after" that is already inscribed in it. In this violent caesura of time, the image is at once produced as a document and as a monument. *Os sertões* writes out this immediately monumental nature of history: it shows that what is "other" in "Captured Bandit" is not the *jagunço* but the scene in which he is caught. Yet in its fractured, monumental narrative of catastrophe, *Os sertões* offers, paradoxically, a way of containing the catastrophic excess to which it refers: by narrating the collapse of representation, *Os sertões* simultaneously permits representation to recommence. This is also the spatiotemporal exteriority, according to Euclides, that constitutes Canudos as the event that is fundamental, yet impossible to assimilate, in the constitution of the state: "It was a parenthesis, a hiatus. It was a vacuum. It did not exist. [...] History would not go as far as that."[21]

But then, liberal history, the history of the state, never returns to its original scene, which it must narrate as having always already occurred, if narrative is to take place. Photography is a way of seeing that is proper to this disjunctive temporality, which it casts as the time of things themselves. Things and bodies do indeed look battered in nineteenth-century photographs, as if they had just come out of a coma or recovered from a natural catastrophe. But this, I have argued, does not so much point to some existential transience as to these photographs' historical condition as images of primitive accumulation. Photography was an active agent of this process, not least because it attributed its effect to the objects themselves of which it took hold. Hence, it naturalized and objectified the *historical forms* primitive accumulation and state capture wrested from things and bodies (the commodity form, subjectivity, citizenship, race, gender, and so forth).

In this chapter, I have turned to photographs in search of a foundational scene of state capture in which the violence implied or erased in geographical representations of marginal spaces would come to the fore of the image. I have argued that, as a visual narrative, the expansion of the liberal state and the capitalist form of production work by means of the capture of subaltern bodies and "natural" spaces, in a temporality that moves towards a constantly deferred scene in which the capture of space and the violent submission of a body cast as bare life come to coincide. Territorial photography was instrumental in promoting new forms of visually inhabiting marginal spaces, offered up as prospective property or set aside for the geographers' and hygienists' engineerings of a new social order.[22] Meanwhile, the compilation of ethnic and social types, as in Christiano Júnior's *cartes de visite*, laid out the "terrain of the other" against which a visual economy of the bourgeois body and its social spaces could establish itself.[23] The photographs of state violence on the confines of national territory rendered explicit the violent condition of possibility of these visual languages of landscape and social typification. This, I have argued, is why explicit images of violence are the exception rather than the rule in the late nineteenth century—not because of an act of piety on behalf of travelling photographers nor because their equipment lacked the sophistication to record live action, but because violence is the external margin, the horizon from which the photographic field receives its internal coherence, and not its object. It is what the camera relegates to the space outside the frame, the blind field, thus simultaneously positing it as the frontier toward which an accumulative visual economy must move.

It is because violence was the external condition of possibility of photography's visual economy, too, that the few attempts to ban it on the sensitized surface of the photographic plate irredeemably faltered. Indeed, the farcical nature of the images of violence analyzed in this chapter seems to stem from the impossibility of representing within photographic space an event that defines its own spatiotemporal limit. Visual primitive accumulation is immediately farcical because its relation to its object is always already a mimicry, a staging of the real, which therefore always remains at least partially absent. Of course, Popper and Barros were fully conscious of the staged nature of their images, but they nevertheless offered them up as truthful depictions of the very real violence in which they themselves participated. My point is thus not about photographers' good or bad faith, but rather about the way in which the indexical, in these images of violence, is bound up not with the documental but with the monumental. The indexical, in these farcical images of the event of sovereignty, is not the inconspicuous detail the social historian can turn to for a supply of data, but the way in which the formal composition collapses under the weight of an exteriority it cannot assimilate except by overacting: the way in which the monumental caesura is indicated in the falling apart of the image's internal cohesion.

Of course, there were fundamental differences in form and function between the capitalist adventurer Popper's gift to the state (an album that "contained" Tierra del Fuego as an already conquered portion of national territory) and the expeditionary photographer Flávio de Barros's state-commissioned visual narrative of an orderly violence against the landless peasantry. Popper's and Barros's albums point to the difference, the paradoxical instant of deferral between primitive accumulation and state capture, in which the decision over the other's life and death is (or rather, has always already been) taken. David Viñas, in his classical study on the genocidal origins of the Argentine state, has defined this difference as the space of tension between the negation of the "barbarian" and the negativity of the "savage." By inserting "*jagunço*" where Viñas wrote "gaucho," we can use his phrase to clarify the distinction between Popper's and Barros's fields of vision: "The key word of the [*jagunço*] is 'but'; that of the Indian is 'no.' In fact, what is at stake is the space that opens up between the penal code and war: the [*jagunço*] is never conquered but pressed into military service; the Indian, by contrast, is condemned to genocide."[24] This is why the body of the *jagunço* must be policed—overseen, confined, surrounded—but, unlike the Indian's, his corpse cannot be exhibited as a token of spatial capture, since the margin on which he dwells is an internal contradiction, not an external space of negativity. His is a body that needs to be cared for, the Indian's a corpse that will remain unburied. More importantly, this discourse of care, of a pastoral responsibility attributed to the state and the governing elite, has generally prevailed in Brazilian territorial discourse of the nineteenth and twentieth centuries over the surgical metaphors of removing the deviant and radically other that have instead dominated Argentine territorial organicism. As I have argued above, this does not necessarily imply that state capture of marginal spaces in Brazil was a more benign process than in Argentina; in fact, the Canudos massacre seems to suggest a rather sinister similarity with the repression of indigenous and rural agencies in Patagonia. Rather, my point has been about how power is imagined, in each case, in relation to that of which it takes hold. The photographic record, rather than as its empirical evidence, has to be taken very much as a form of working this imaginary relation between power and its objects onto the material spaces and physical bodies it collects.

# Conclusion

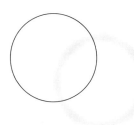

> We must therefore discard once and for all the view of the State as a completely united mechanism, founded on a homogeneous and hierarchical distribution of the centres of power moving from top to bottom of a uniform ladder or pyramid. According to this conception, the homogeneity and uniformity of the exercise of power is ensured by juridical regulation within the State: by a constitutional and administrative law that demarcates the fields of competence and activity of the various apparatuses. This is a radically false image, however.
>
> —Nicos Poulantzas, *State, Power, Socialism*

As I have attempted to show in this book, the state as visual form is found not *in* maps, museums, or photographs but in the way of seeing they called forth. This was a way of looking at social relations as beyond individual or collective intervention, as a natural or historical given, or rather, a "gift" from history and nature to the state. In the nineteenth century, as Marilena Chaui has argued in the case of Brazil, a vision of the nation emerged that saw national development as the work of transcendental agents transforming older colonial representations. First, nature and history gave the nation-form; the state, as the one receiving the gift, then transformed society in accordance with its providential destiny. The transformative action of the state was always already justified as the expression of nature's and history's mandate, returning the country to the Edenic state for which it was predestined. As a providential agent, the Brazilian state took power not just from but over nature, in a secular version of Portuguese messianic nationalism's narrative in which the resurgence of the Lusitanian Empire was to occur in the fullness of time. In this sense, late nineteenth-century notions of "redeeming" the backlands of the *sertão* through the state's modernizing intervention reinvented colonial visions of space as the domain of struggle between

Good and Evil. As "an effect of the image of Brazil-as-Nature […] the cosmic dispute between God and the Devil appears, from the very beginnings of colonization, not with regard to social divisions but as a division of and in Nature itself."[1]

Similarly, the violent conquest of the southern frontier in Argentina, which contemporary accounts celebrated as the apotheosis of four hundred years of colonization and thus as the beginning of a new, "postcolonial" temporality, posited nature as the origin of state power. Patagonian nature, as exposed to the gaze in maps, photographs, and museum exhibits, visualized state power as imposed on an inert, empty land, replacing the historical process of state formation with a founding myth from which the people were absent altogether. Indeed, where the national past was made to appear at all in the spectacles of state power, history itself took on the form of nature. History was turned into an external frame of society given by sovereign acts of foundation rather than made by the people-nation. The heroizing of founding fathers presented history as a gift bestowed on the nation by external agents, an exteriority that was nonetheless only produced through its performative enactment in the relation between spectators and objects. A different (but similarly manufactured) exteriority was imposed on native populations, who were removed from a plane of spatial coexistence into one of temporal anteriority. As "prehistoric" peoples (because, indeed, their place was before the state's mythical foundation of history), they could be exposed to the gaze of the museum visitor as spiritual ancestors, thus at the same time making them invisible as living contemporaries.

As Chaui points out, this sacralization of the state as the political expression of a natural or historical destiny is by no means contradictory to the continued existence of networks of favor and privilege that regulate local power. On the contrary, the state's abstract remoteness both opens the space in which these parallel networks can operate and makes it possible to cast the power of the local *coronel* or chieftain as similarly given or predestined. As the specular effect of performances of exhibiting and spectatorship—as a visual form—the state cannot but be inconsistent with the real practices of exercising power, at the same time as it contributes to their existence and reproduction. Thus the state as visual form is constantly under pressure from social practices that threaten to undermine its claim to stability and endurance. The truth-claims of the state's visual forms are always open to challenges on the grounds of insubstantiality, of giving a hollow or false image. As we have seen in the disputes between museum scientists and collectors such as Burmeister, Moreno, or Netto, or in the writings of geographers such as Fausto da Souza or Olascoaga urging viewers to "open their eyes" and look reality in the face, many of the images and forms of display we have analyzed were in fact created in reaction to such challenges. From the beginning, these were contested images, haunted by the very controversies they sought to expunge from their visual space. A constant refocusing of the real had to take place in order to maintain its apparent immutability and exteriority vis-à-vis social practices. Yet even those who challenged established representations and proposed to replace them by more truthful images only reaffirmed the mimetic pact that identified "the real" as something fully given and accessible to the gaze. What was left unchallenged, and has remained unchallenged even in the counterimages put forth in the twentieth century by the national-popular Left, is the visual form itself and the way in which it removed the nation-state from history into myth.

Having identified some of its enduring features, however, we need also to sum up the ways in which late nineteenth-century visual culture differed from the one that was to succeed it. If the period between approximately 1870 and 1900 witnessed the first attempts at a specular hegemonic articulation of national society, we are still a far cry from the national populist forms of interpellation identified most notoriously with the figures of Getúlio Vargas and Juan Domingo Perón. To therefore claim these figures as the beginning of modern politics in Brazil and Argentina, however, would be a mistake. Such a view risks misunderstanding the consolidation of the state form at the end of the nineteenth century as prepolitical, and thus naturalizing its production of national space and time. For, as I have just argued, this "naturalness" of the nation-state was what the visual forms construed in this period were all about. These forms certainly did not interpellate "the people" in ways even remotely comparable to the mass-communicational forms of Peronism or the Estado Novo, which were so crucially reliant on new audiovisual mass media such as the radio and the cinema. This should not be taken as a failure or shortcoming, however, as it was precisely not yet a "popular" subject they projected as their beholder. To discard the hegemonic character of these visual forms would be to confuse hegemony with populism. In fact, the notion of the state as a *natural* form, a living organism, was very much about the exclusion of the people as a political subject, though not as a subject of spectatorship.

Indeed, we might say that the optic of the state in the late nineteenth century exposed to the gaze the empty place of the people. This was a place reserved for some vague point in the future when there would be a subject to occupy it, a people entitled to take its place where nature and history had already indicated it. In this sense, the symbolic production of the state form at the close of the nineteenth century differs not only from twentieth-century national populism in Argentina and Brazil but also from postcolonial nation-state formations in Asia and Africa, so eloquently analyzed by Dipresh Chakrabarty, Partha Chatterjee, and Achille Mbembe, among others.[2] For there is not, as Chatterjee argues for the case of India, an inner or "spiritual domain" of national culture here that is hedged in and preserved in its distinctiveness against the simultaneous imposition of the external forms of the modern Western state. Instead, this inner domain is figured as one yet to come into being, although it is already encrypted in the forms of the outer domain of nature. This emphasis on nature and the emptying-out of the space of the people, I would argue, represent the particular and distinctive postcoloniality of the Latin American nation-state, the way in which it inherits and transforms older colonial representations and power relations. At the same time, "nature" provides the image that makes "the national" available for incorporation into global capitalist exchange. On behalf of, and as an expression of nature (and not the people-nation), the state turned into the titular subject of what Tulio Halperín Donghi calls a "new colonial compact" with imperial capital, fully consummated during the period under study here.[3]

As Chaui notes, however, a major change inside the picture would take place over the first decades of the twentieth century: "before, the emphasis had been on Nature, and now something else had appeared. In fact, not only was it necessary to continue celebrating Nature, but also to make a new character appear on the political stage: the Brazilian people."[4] As people-nation, however, the people now had to perform not merely as silent spectators but as actors in the very space of the image, which therefore had to become a "moving image." As an internal transformation in the statist way of seeing, the appearance of the people required the cinematic apparatus and its technologies of affect, in other words, a new kind of hegemonic interpellation that could no longer be achieved through the visual forms of the late nineteenth century. It is interesting to note that this crisis of a visual form that had relied on a static perspectival relation between exhibiting and spectatorship was also perceived by dissident members of the very social sectors whose dominance it had expressed. I have already discussed Euclides da Cunha's critique not merely of the "false images" of the landscape and history but of vision itself as a means of access to truth. Although paradoxically composed of iconic visual tableaus, Euclides's writing constantly warns against the delusive character of vision, the way in which the gaze misreads what lies beyond the appearance of the landscape and its inhabitants. A similar literary discourse of scopophobia appeared in Argentina around the same time in the writings of the first generation of cultural nationalists assembled around the journal *Ideas*. Perhaps its most thorough formulation was Manuel Gálvez's scathing attack on the Argentine Centenary Exhibition of 1910, in many ways the culmination and apogee of late nineteenth-century visual culture: "Superficiality! Here's the most deeply rooted condition among present-day Argentines! [...] She is the mirror, in which the Argentine people contemplate their external qualities, qualities that denounce an absolute emptiness of spirit. Here one lives in perpetual mise-en-scène, decoration triumphs while ethical and spiritual values are being mocked. [...] National life has become poisoned by exhibitionism. We only admire the exterior, that which glows and dazzles."[5]

In this critique of exhibitionism, which decries the inseparable link between the spectacle and commodity fetishism, a resistance not only against the exhibition as a visual form turned vulgar and hollow but against visual forms as such emerges that already anticipates conservative dismissals of cinema and of popular mass media in general. To the hollowness of visual forms, this conservative critique of the image will oppose the figure of an image fractured from within: the ruin. In the petrified, ruined nature and history of the old colonial northwest, Gálvez encounters the spiritual refuge of true Argentineness, just as Euclides had found in the natural forms of the *sertão*, tortured and splintered by the cataclysmic violence of drought, a cipher for Brazil that he opposed to conventional images of natural abundance. To the mobilization of national being in the affect-images of modern mass communication, this dissident, conservative nationalism counterposed its retreat into inorganic nature, into the mineral layers and cracks of the soil, just as it made history recoil into the petrified materiality of the ruin. As preserved in ruins, the spirit of nationality could be removed from change, becoming more identical to itself the more its external surface was being eroded by time, at the same time as it denounced in its slow disappearance the delusive nature of progress as an estrangement from the national essence, moving towards mere external appearance.

Conservative nationalism's anxiety to immobilize nature and history in geological forms was the cultural expression of its resistance to the full constitution of a national-popular hegemony. As an expression of resistance, however, it also bespeaks the extent to which nature and history, as visual forms of the exteriority of the real to social practices, still informed the national-popular movement-image. If "a new character," the people-nation, had made its appearance on "the political stage," in Chauí's words, this stage was still framed by nature and history as they had come down from the visual conventions of the nineteenth century. Ary Barroso, in the samba "Aquarela do Brasil" (1939), may have sung the praise of "sweet-talking mulattos" and "clever *morenas* of indiscreet glances," but these still made their appearance on the stage of "the good, tasty land" opened up "behind the curtain of the past" as well as, most importantly, within the frame of an imaginary picture. Even if exchanging the heavy texture of oil for the lighter, breezier substance of a watercolor (*aquarela*), the implicit notion of time and space as given by and to the gaze refers back to a previous visual form in which the people had still been mere spectators. The frame of the nation as image, in other words, still contains the movement unleashed by the samba anthem.

On one level, this persistence of nature as a visual form and as an emblem of nationality speaks to the continuity of the neocolonial inscription of Argentina and Brazil within global capitalist exchange, of which it had been an expression since the very beginnings of the nation-state. "Nature" continued to emblematize the distinctiveness of the national because, as a commodity, it represented the nation on the world market, despite successive attempts at national industrialization, import substitution, and the like. Ironically, today this specular performance of nature that both reproduces and disavows its commodity form has taken its last refuge in international tourism's visual consumption of landscape. The Web sites of national and regional tourist boards have now become the visual archive of the conventions of nineteenth-century landscape, cartography, and museology, offering to the gaze of the consumer the remainders of the state's visual sublime.

It is this crisis of the image—the crisis of vision as a purveyor of truth—and those of nature, history, and the state as visual forms this crisis entails, which has provided the critical distance that allowed me to return to the nineteenth-century image world without getting caught up in its aporias and tautologies. The crisis of the image that marks our own present also allows us today to recognize and challenge the ways in which nature, the state, and the image had previously been invested in one another, producing powerful effects of reality. It is what allows us to reclaim social memory and practice from nature and history facing us as an external, transcendental given. It has enabled new practices of struggle in the form of self-consciously performative appropriations of the nation-state's visual archives: the politicized restagings of natural pastoral by the Brazilian landless movement, for instance, or the resurgence of indigenous identities and memory practices in Argentina, which propose alternative space-times to the unifying totalizations of the state. Wherever possible, we should celebrate and support these new performances with our own critical efforts, without losing sight of the critical figure a dissident cultural nationalism had forged at a previous moment of crisis of the image. For the figure of the ruin might still have something to tell us today. It might remind us that the image of nature and of history as an external frame of our (national) existence has entered crisis only because the viability of national societies, and even of nature itself, has been placed under appeal by the forces of capitalism. To recognize the empowering aspects of this crisis, the extent to which it allows us to free ourselves from the optic of the state and invent new performances beyond its politics of identity, must not mean to lose sight of the real danger to which it exposes us, the question mark it puts behind our very existence.

# NOTES

I have opted to translate Spanish and Portuguese sources into English. Unless otherwise indicated, all these translations are mine.

## Introduction

*Epigraph.* "Criança! Jamais verás país nenhum como este. / Olha que céu, que mar, que floresta!"

1. For a useful history of state formation in Argentina and Brazil, see Emília Viotti da Costa, *Da monarquia à República: Momentos decisivos* (São Paulo: UNESP, 1998); Oscar Oszlak, *La formación del estado argentino* (Buenos Aires: Editorial de Belgrano, 1986); and Fernando Uricoechea, *The Patrimonial Foundations of the Brazilian Bureaucratic State* (Berkeley, CA: University of California Press, 1980).

2. Timothy Mitchell, "The Limits of the State: Beyond Statist Approaches and Their Critics," *American Political Science Review* 85, no. 1 (1991): 91, 94.

3. Erwin Panofsky, *Perspective as a Symbolic Form*, trans. Christopher S. Wood (New York: Zone Books, 1991), 68.

4. Pedro Karp Vasquez, "Juan Gutiérrez: The Penultimate Photographer of the Empire, First Photographer of the Republic," in *Juan Gutiérrez: Imagens do Rio 1892–1896*, ed. George Ermakoff (Rio de Janeiro: Capivara, 2001), 247–48.

5. José Murilo de Carvalho, *A formação das almas: O imaginário da República no Brasil* (São Paulo: Companhia das Letras, 1990), 55–73.

6. Walter Benjamin, *Ursprung des deutschen Trauerspiels*, in *Gesammelte Schriften* [hereafter *GS*] I, 1, ed. Rolf Tiedemann and Hermann Schwepenhäuser (Frankfurt am Main: Suhrkamp, 1991), 271–72, 358.

7. Susan Buck-Morss, *The Dialectics of Seeing: Walter Benjamin and the Arcades Project* (Cambridge, MA: MIT Press, 1989), 67, 82–83.

8. Hayden White, *Metahistory: The Historical Imagination in Nineteenth-Century Europe* (Baltimore, MD: Johns Hopkins University Press, 1973). On Latin America, the key reference on history as allegory in the nineteenth century is Doris Sommer's *Foundational Fictions: The National Romances of Latin America* (Berkeley, CA: University of California Press, 1991).

9. On baroque visual forms as means to mobilize public affections in an emergent mass society, see José Antonio Maravall, *Culture of the Baroque: Analysis of a Historical Structure* (Minneapolis, MN: University of Minnesota Press, 1986), especially pp. 251–63.

10. Clifford Geertz, *Negara: The Theatre State in Nineteenth-Century Bali* (Princeton, NJ: Princeton University Press, 1980), 121.

11. José Murilo de Carvalho, *Teatro das sombras: A política imperial* (Rio de Janeiro: UFRJ / Relume Dumará, 1996); Lilia Moritz Schwarcz, *As barbas do Imperador: D. Pedro II, um monarca nos trópicos* (São Paulo: Companhia das Letras, 1998).

12. Michel Foucault, *Surveiller et punir: Naissance de la prison* (Paris: Gallimard, 1975), 152–55.

13. Miguel Juárez Celman, Congreso Nacional, Cámara de Senadores, Diario de Sesiones: 18 de octubre de 1887. Quoted in Lilia Ana Bertoni, *Patriotas, cosmopolitas y nacionalistas: La construcción de la nacionalidad argentina a fines del siglo XIX* (Buenos Aires: Fondo de Cultura Económica, 2001), 103.

14. Estanislao S. Zeballos, "El Museo Nacional de Rio Janeiro," *Anales de la Sociedad Cienífica Argentina* 3 (1877): 275.

## Part 1: Museums

*Epigraph*. "Quem entra pela primeira vez n'uma exposição digna d'este nome, o primeiro impeto que tem é sahir d'ella" (Junio, "Pelas exposições").

1. Walter Benjamin, "Eduard Fuchs, der Sammler und Historiker," *GS* II, 2:465–505; id., "Ich packe meine Bibliothek aus: eine Rede über das Sammeln," *GS* IV, 1:388–96; id., "Konvolut H: Der Sammler," *Das Passagen-Werk* (Frankfurt am Main: Suhrkamp, 1983), 269–80.

2. Susan Stewart, *On Longing: Narratives of the Miniature, the Gigantic, the Souvenir, the Collection* (Durham, NC: Duke University Press, 1993), 156; also Jean Baudrillard, *The System of Objects* (London: Verso, 1996), 97.

3. Boris Groys, *Logik der Sammlung: Am Ende des musealen Zeitalters* (München: Hanser, 1997).

4. Didier Maleuvre, *Museum Memories: History, Theory, Art* (Stanford, CA: Stanford University Press, 1999), 38.

5. Paula Findlen, "The Museum: Its Classical Etymology and Renaissance Genealogy," in *Museum Studies: An Anthology of Contexts*, ed. Bettina Messias Carbonell, 23–50 (Malden, MA: Blackwell, 2004).

6. Carol Duncan and Alan Wallach, "The Universal Survey Museum," in Carbonell, *Museum Studies*, 59.

7. Erwin Panofsky, "Einleitung," in *Studien zur Ikonologie der Renaissance* (Köln: DuMont, 1997 [1939]), 30–61.

8. Baudrillard, *System of Objects*, 87.

9. Klaus Theweleit, *Male Fantasies I: Women, Floods, Bodies, History*, trans. Steve Conway (Cambridge: Polity Press, 1987), 205. Theweleit goes on to speculate "that it is above all the aliveness of the real that threatens these men. The more intensely life (emotions) impinges on them, the more aggressively they attack it, rendering it 'harmless' in extreme cases" (217).

10. Jonathan Crary, *Techniques of the Observer: On Vision and Modernity in the Nineteenth Century* (Cambridge, MA: MIT Press, 1990), 3.

11. Donald Preziosi, "Brain of the Earth's Body: Museums and the Framing of Modernity," in Carbonell, *Museum Studies*, 80.

12. Ibid., 79–80.

13. Johannes Fabian, *Time and the Other: How Anthropology Makes Its Object* (New York: Columbia University Press, 1983).

14. The exception is Susan Sheets-Pyenson's *Cathedrals of Science: The Development of Colonial Natural History Museums during the Late Nineteenth Century* (Kingston, Montréal: McGill-Queen's University Press, 1988), which provides a useful comparison between natural history museums in Latin America, Africa, and Oceania. A comparative history of museums in Latin America is still lacking; for a useful overview on the construction of an archaeological heritage, see Rebecca Earle, "Monumentos y museos: La nacionalización del pasado precolombino en la Hispanoamérica decimonónica," in *Galerías del progreso: Museos, exposiciones y cultura visual en América Latina*, ed. Beatriz González-Stephan and Jens Andermann (Rosario: Beatriz Viterbo, 2006), 27–63. On museums of natural history, see Maria M. Lopes, "Sociedades científicas y museos en América Latina," *Saber y Tiempo* 2, no. 7 (1999): 51–72; Maria M. Lopes and Irina Podgorny, "The Shaping of Latin American Museums," *Osiris* 15 (2000): 108–18.

15. Tony Bennett, *The Birth of the Museum: History, Theory, Politics* (London: Routledge, 1995), 47, 63.

## Chapter 1: Empires of Nature

1. Zeballos, "El Museo Nacional de Rio Janeiro," 269, 275. The Danish paleontologist Peter Wilhelm Lund, while in the service of the Museu Nacional of Rio de Janeiro, was one of the first to discover prehistoric human skulls at the site of Lagoa Santa between 1835 and 1844.

2. Timothy Mitchell, "The World as Exhibition," *Comparative Studies in Society and History* 31 (1989): 219. See also Krszysztof Pomian, *Collectors and Curiosities* (Oxford: Polity Press, 1990).

3. Michel Foucault, *The Order of Things: An Archaeology of the Human Sciences* (London: Routledge, 2002).

4. Bernardino Rivadavia, Circular del 7 de Agosto de 1812; quoted in Antonio Lascano González, *El Museo de Ciencias Naturales de Buenos Aires* (Buenos Aires, Ediciones Culturales Argentinas, 1980), 31. Apparently the only donation received was a collection of books and *naturalia* from Bartolomé Muñoz, confirmed in a government decree of 1814, which conferred them to the care of the city librarian.

5. Bernardino Rivadavia, *Decreto del 31 de diciembre de 1823*, Archivo del Museo Argentino de Ciencias Naturales "Bernardino Rivadavia," Buenos Aires.

6. D. João VI, *Decreto de Fundação do Museu Real*, quoted in Manuel Duarte Moreira de Azevedo, *O Rio de Janeiro: Sua história, monumentos, homens notáveis, usos e curiosidades* (Rio de Janeiro: Garnier, 1877), 220–21.

7. Vicente Stein Campos, *Elementos de museologia: História dos museus. Brasil* (Rio de Janeiro: Secretaria de Cultura, 1971), 13–14.

8. Maria Margaret Lopes, *O Brasil descobre a pesquisa científica: As ciências naturais e os museus* (São Paulo: Ed. Hucitec, 1998), 42–48.

9. Bruno Latour, *Science in Action: How to Follow Scientists and Engineers through Society* (Cambridge, MA: Harvard University Press, 1987), 236–43.

10. See Alvaro Fernández Bravo, "Catálogo, colección y colonialismo interno: Una lectura de la *Descripción de la Patagonia* de Thomas Falkner (1774)," *Revista de Crítica Literaria Latinoamericana* 30, no. 60 (2004): 229–49.

11. Dorinda Outram, "New Spaces in Natural History," in *Cultures of Natural History*, ed. Nicholas Jardine, James A. Secord, and Emma C. Spary (Cambridge: Cambridge University Press, 1996), 263.

12. F. de Castelnau, *Expédition dans les parties centrales de l'Amérique du Sud* (1843–47), quoted in Bruno Lobo et al., "O Museu Nacional de História Natural," *Archivos do Museu Nacional* 22 (Rio de Janeiro: Museu Nacional, 1923), 19–20.

13. Louis Agassiz, *A Journey in Brazil: By Professor and Mrs. Louis Agassiz* (Boston: Ticknor and Fields, 1868), 491.

14. Ladislau Netto, *Investigações históricas e científicas sobre o Museu Imperial e Nacional, acompanhadas de uma breve notícia das suas colecções e publicadas por ordem do Ministério de Agricultura* (Rio de Janeiro: Instituto Philomatico, 1870), 131.

15. Quoted in Luiz de Castro Faria, "As exposições de antropologia e arqueologia do Museu Nacional," *Publicações avulsas do Museu Nacional* 4 (1949): 4.

16. Lopes, *O Brasil descobre a pesquisa científica,* 51; Gil Baião Neto and Maria Rachel Fróis da Fonseca, "Museu Real," http://www.museunacional.ufr.br (accessed November 15, 2004).

17. Azevedo, *O Rio de Janeiro*, 223.

18. The origin of the museum's Egyptian collections is curious: Fiengo had previously sold these to the Rivadavia government in Argentina, only to find on his arrival at Buenos Aires that the new regime of Juan Manuel de Rosas had revoked the purchase. After unsuccessful negotiations, Fiengo left Buenos Aires with his merchandise, only to catch yellow fever on stopping over at Rio de Janeiro. It is not clear whether at least one mummy that appears in an inventory of the Museo Público of Buenos Aires of 1856 (another one from 1864 even mentions three mummies) was left behind. After Fiengo's death, his collections were seized by the Brazilian customs authorities and remitted, on Emperor Pedro I's request, to the National Museum.

19. Manuel Ricardo Trelles, *Memoria presentada a la Asociación de Amigos de la Historia Natural del Plata: Sobre el estado del Museo y demás relativo a la institución por el Secretario de la misma* (Buenos Aires: Imprenta "El Orden," 1856). Reprinted in Lascano González, *El Museo de Ciencias Naturales de Buenos Aires*, 72.

20. Trelles, *Memoria presentada a la Asociación,* 78.

21. Quoted in José M. Gallardo, *El Museo de Ciencias Naturales en la manzana de las luces* (Buenos Aires: Museo Argentino de Ciencias Naturales, 1976), 5.

22. Azevedo, *O Rio de Janeiro*, 234.

23. João Baptista de Lacerda, *Fastos do Museu Nacional: Recordações históricas e scientíficas fundadas em documentos authenticos e informações verídicas* (Rio de Janeiro: Imprensa Nacional, 1906), 44–45.

24. Germán Burmeister, "Sumario sobre la fundación y los progresos del Museo Público de Buenos Aires," *Anales del Museo Público de Buenos Aires*, 1 (1864–69), first fascicle (1864): 4.

25. Ibid., 10.

26. Ibid., 9.

27. Ibid., 7.

28. Germán Burmeister, "Al Señor Gefe de la Comision del Censo de los Bienes Nacionales, Dr. B. Zorrilla," Buenos Aires, 28 de Marzo de 1889, Archivo del Museo Argentino de Ciencias Naturales "Bernardino Rivadavia," legajo 1274.

29. Germán Burmeister, "Al Señor Ministro de Instrucción Pública, Dr. D. Filemon Posse," Buenos Aires, 10 de Marzo de 1888, Archivo del Museo Argentino de Ciencias Naturales "Bernardino Rivadavia," legajo 1089.

30. Germán Burmeister, "Al Señor Ministro de Instrucción Pública," Buenos Aires, 12 de Marzo de 1889, Archivo del Museo Argentino de Ciencias Naturales "Bernardino Rivadavia," legajo 1270.

31. Henry A. Ward, "Los museos argentinos," *Revista del Museo de La Plata* 1, no. 1 (1891): 145–46.

32. Dorinda Outram, *Georges Cuvier: Vocation, Science and Authority in Post-Revolutionary France* (Manchester: Manchester University Press, 1984), 176.

33. Lee Rust Brown, "The Emerson Museum," *Representations* 40 (1992): 70.

34. Netto, *Investigações históricas*, 149.

35. See, for instance, Burmeister's *Description physique de la République Argentine* (Paris: Savy; Buenos Aires: Coni, 1876–78), prepared for the Philadelphia exhibition of 1876. Copies of the museum's *Anales* were also on display at the universal exhibitions of Paris (1878) and Bremen (1884), where Burmeister also exhibited his *Los caballos fósiles de la pampa argentina* and *Erläuterungen zur Fauna Argentiniens*. (Archivo del Museo Argentino de Ciencias Naturales "Bernardino Rivadavia," legajos 503, 714).

36. Ladislau Netto, *Relatório do Museu Nacional: Apresentado ao Illustrissimo Exm. Sr. Conselheiro Tomás Jorge Coelho de Almeida pelo Dr. Ladislau Netto, Diretor Geral do Museu* (Rio de Janeiro: Imprensa Nacional, 1877), 5.

37. Lacerda, *Fastos*, 78.

38. Louis Couty, "O ensino superior no Brasil," *Gazeta Médica da Bahia* (1884): 225. Quoted in Lopes, *O Brasil*, 157.

39. Netto, *Investigações históricas,* 253, 255.

40. Lacerda, *Fastos*, 100–101.

41. I will limit my discussion here to the museums of Belém and São Paulo, as the other two regional museums founded in late nineteenth-century Brazil do not completely correspond to this characterization. The Museu Botânico do Amazonas of Manaus, directed by João Barbosa Rodrigues between 1882 and 1890, the year of his appointment as director of Rio's Botanical Garden and of the definitive closure of the museum, owed its brief existence to the local rubber boom; the Museu Paranaense de Curitiba, founded in the context of a provincial industrial exhibition in 1875, was chiefly designed to coordinate the province's representation at international trade fairs. See Lopes, *O Brasil*, 207–21.

42. Emil August Goeldi, *Relatório sobre o estado do Museu Paraense, apresentado a S. Exc. o Sr. Dr. Governador do Estado do Pará* (Belém: Typographia do Diário Official, 1894), 375.

43. Hermann von Ihering, "Bibliographia: Os Museus da America do Sul," *Revista do Museu Paulista* 1 (1895): 233.

44. Hermann von Ihering, "Historia do Monumento do Ypiranga e do Museu Paulista," *Revista do Museu Paulista* 1 (1895): 20.

45. Emil August Goeldi, "Parte administrativa," *Boletim do Museu Paraense de Historia Natural e Ethnographia* 2, no. 1 (1902): 108.

46. Hermann von Ihering, *O Museu Paulista em 1899 e 1900* (São Paulo: Diario Oficial, 1901), 8.

47. Bennett, *Birth of the Museum*, 42–43.

48. Richard Lydekker, "The La Plata Museum," *Natural Science* 4, no. 24 (1894): 2.

49. Bennett, *Birth of the Museum*, 186.

50. Ward, "Los museos argentinos," 148.

51. Francisco P. Moreno, "Museo de La Plata: El último informe de su director," *El Sudamericano* 2, no. 31 (1889): 99–100.

52. Francisco P. Moreno, "El Museo de La Plata: Rápida ojeada sobre su fundación y desarrollo," *Revista del Museo de La Plata* 1, no. 1 (1890–91): 39.

53. Domingo F. Sarmiento, "El Museo de La Plata" [1885], *Obras* (Buenos Aires: Imprenta y Litografía Mariano Moreno, 1899), tome 22, vol. 2, 311.

54. Lydekker, "The La Plata Museum," 4.

55. See Francisco P. Moreno, *El estudio del hombre sud-americano* (Buenos Aires: La Nación, 1878), 15–27; and *Antropología y arqueología: Importancia del estudio de estas ciencias en la República Argentina* (Buenos Aires: Imprenta Pablo E. Coni, 1881).

56. Moreno, "El Museo de La Plata," 39.

57. Francisco P. Moreno, "Carta al Ministro de Gobierno Manuel B. Gonnet," La Plata, May 9, 1886, Copiador del Museo de La Plata.

58. Quoted in Irina Podgorny, *El argentino despertar de las faunas y de las gentes prehistóricas* (Buenos Aires: Eudeba, 2003), 69.

59. Stephen Greenblatt, "Resonance and Wonder," in Karp and Lavine, *Exhibiting Cultures*, 42–56.

60. Moreno, "El Museo de La Plata," 33–34.

61. Elsewhere I have discussed Moreno's travel writings and their restaging in the material narrative of the museum. See "Evidencias y ensueños: El gabinete del Dr. Moreno," *Filología* 31, no. 1/2 (1998): 57–66; also "Moreno: La patria petrificada," in *Mapas de poder: Una arqueología literaria del espacio argentino* (Rosario: Beatriz Viterbo, 2000), 120–28.

62. Moreno, "El Museo de La Plata," 32.

63. Mary Louise Pratt, *Imperial Eyes: Travel Writing and Transculturation* (London: Routledge, 1993), 148.

64. On Moreno's scientific theories, see Mónica Quijada, "Ancestros, ciudadanos, piezas de museo: Francisco P. Moreno y la articulación del indígena en la construcción nacional argentina (siglo XIX)," *Estudios interdisciplinarios de América Latina y el Caribe* 9, no. 2 (1998). Accessed online at: http://www.tau.ac.il/eial/IX__2/quijada.html.

65. Domingo Faustino Sarmiento, "Mundos prehistóricos: Viaje aéreo a través del museo prehistórico de Moreno" [1878], in *Obras completas*, tome 22, vol. 2, pp. 135–45 (Buenos Aires: Imprenta y Litografía Mariano Moreno, 1899), 143.

66. Moreno, *Antropología y arqueología*, 26, 29.

67. On the museum's indigenous captives, see Irina Podgorny and Gustavo Politis, "¿Qué sucedió en la historia? Los esqueletos araucanos del Museo de La Plata y la Conquista del Desierto," *Arqueología contemporánea* 3 (1990–92): 73–79; Quijada, "Ancestros."

68. Moreno, "El Museo de La Plata," 346.

Chapter 2: Spectacles of Sacrifice

*Epigraph*. "Mas quem diria! Esses anthropofagos é que ficaram com medo de serem devorados pela curiosidade pública!"

1. Ladislau Netto quoted in Abelardo Duarte, *Ladislau Netto (1838–1894)* (Maceió: Imprensa Oficial, 1950), 167–69.

2. Giorgio Agamben, *Homo Sacer: Sovereign Power and Bare Life*, trans. Daniel Heller-Roazen (Stanford, CA: Stanford University Press, 1998), 111.

3. John Manuel Monteiro, "As 'raças' indígenas no pensamento brasileiro do Império," in *Raça, ciência e sociedade*, ed. Marcos Chor Maio and Ricardo Ventura Santos (Rio de Janeiro: Fiocruz, 1996), 15–22.

4. George W. Stocking Jr., "Bones, Bodies, Behavior," in *Bones, Bodies, Behavior: Essays on Biological Anthropology*, ed. George W. Stocking Jr. (Madison, WI: University of Wisconsin Press, 1988), 8.

5. Johannes Fabian, "Culture, Time, and the Object of Anthropology," in *Time and the Work of Anthropology: Critical Essays 1971–1991* (Chur, Switzerland: Harwood, 1991), 197; italics in original.

6. Lilia Moritz Schwarcz, *O espetáculo das raças: Cientistas, instituições e questão racial no Brasil, 1870–1930* (São Paulo: Companhia das Letras, 1993), 18, 61–65.

7. Manuela Carneiro da Cunha, "Política indigenista no século XIX," in *História dos índios no Brasil*, ed. M. Carneiro da Cunha (São Paulo: Companhia das Letras, 1998), 133–54.

8. David Brookshaw, *Paradise Betrayed: Brazilian Literature of the Indian* (Amsterdam: CEDLA, 1988), 8.

9. José Vieira Couto de Magalhães, *O selvagem* (Rio de Janeiro: Typographia Nacional, 1876), xxii.

10. Couto de Magalhães, *O selvagem*, 99.

11. Sílvio Romero, "Couto de Magalhães e a influencia dos selvagens no Folk-lore brazileiro," *Ethnographia brazileira*, 59. See also José Veríssimo's comments on *O selvagem*, in *Estudos Brazileiros (1877–1895)* (Belém: Tavares Cardoso & Cia., 1895), 57.

12. João Baptista de Lacerda and José Rodrigues Peixoto, "Contribuições para o estudo anthropologico das raças indigenas do Brazil, pelos doutores Lacerda Filho e Rodrigues Peixoto," *Archivos do Museu Nacional* 1 (1876): 71–72.

13. Hermann von Ihering, "A anthropologia do Estado de São Paulo," *Revista do Museu Paulista* 7 (1908): 202–57. Quoted after Luiz de Castro Faria, *Antropologia: Espetáculo e excelência* (Rio de Janeiro: Ed. UFRJ / Fabian, 1993), 64.

14. Faria, *Antropologia*: 65.

15. Lacerda, *Fastos*: 58.

16. *Guia da Exposição Anthropológica Brasileira realisada pelo Museu Nacional do Rio de Janeiro o 29 de julho de 1882* (Rio de Janeiro: Leuzinger, 1882); *Catálogo dos objectos expostos na Exposição Anthropológica do Rio de Janeiro* (Rio de Janeiro: Typographia Nacional, 1882).

17. J. Serra, "Meios de Catequese," *Revista da Exposição Antropológica Brasileira*, ed. Mello Morães Filho (Rio de Janeiro, 1882), 51.

18. Ladislau Netto, *Museu Nacional: Instrucções sobre a preparação e remessa das colecções que lhe forem destinadas* (Rio de Janeiro: Imprensa Nacional, 1890).

19. See Ladislau Netto, *Conférence faite au Muséum National en présence de LL. MM. Impériales, par le Dr. Ladislau Netto, Directeur Général du Muséum National de Rio de Janeiro* (Rio de Janeiro:

Machado & Cia., 1885) 9; "Investigações sobre a archeologia brazileira," *Archivos do Museu Nacional* 6 (1885), ii.

20. Ladislau Netto, letter from February 1882, quoted in Duarte, *Ladislau Netto*, 164–65.

21. Ladislau Netto, *Le Muséum National de Rio de Janeiro et son influence sur les sciences naturelles du Brésil* (Paris: Charles Delagrave, 1889), 58.

22. Netto, *Conférence*, 11–12.

23. Ibid., 7.

24. Ibid., 9.

25. Ibid., 26.

26. Ladislau Netto, opening speech to the Anthropological Exhibition, quoted in Duarte, *Ladislau Netto*, 168–69.

27. Elizabeth Edwards, *Raw Histories: Photographs, Anthropology, and the Museum* (Oxford: Berg, 2001), 31–32.

28. Jeff Rosen, "Naming and Framing Nature in *Photographie Zoologique*," *Word and Image* 13, 4 (1997): 381.

29. David Jenkins, "Object Lessons and Ethnographic Displays: Museum Exhibitions and the Making of American Anthropology," *Comparative Studies in Society and History* 36 (1994): 244.

30. Susan Sontag, *On Photography* (Harmondsworth: Penguin, 1979), 4.

31. Angelo Agostini, quoted after Schwarcz, *O espetáculo das raças*, 76–77.

## Chapter 3: Antiques and Archives

*Epigraph.* "Si carecemos de próceres, los inventaremos; como han hecho otros y como los pueblos son más sugestionables que los individuos, los pueblos acabarán por convencerse de que tienen próceres. Una vez convencidos de su existencia, lo estarán también de sus hazañas; los poetas escribirán himnos en su elogio y en el de la heroica nación que los ha producido, y los escultores fijarán sus fisonomías en el mármol y en el bronce."

1. José Honório Rodrigues, "Introdução," in *Catálogo da Exposição de História do Brasil* (Brasília: Editora da Universidade de Brasília, 1981 [1881]), ix.

2. Alvaro Fernández Bravo, "Material Memories: Tradition and Amnesia in Two Argentine Museums," in *Images of Power: Iconography, Culture and the State in Latin America*, ed. Jens Andermann and William Rowe (Oxford, New York: Berghahn, 2005), 78–95.

3. Andreas Huyssen, *Twilight Memories: Making Time in a Culture of Amnesia* (London: Routledge, 1997), 7.

4. Junio, "Pelas exposições," *Revista Illustrada*, 17 December 1881, 7. All further quotes are from the same issue and page.

5. Philippe Hamon, *Expositions: Littérature et architecture au XIXième siècle* (Paris: José Corti, 1989), 142.

6. Benjamin Franklin Ramiz Galvão, ed., *Catálogo da Exposição de História do Brazil, realizada pela Bibliotheca Nacional do Rio de Janeiro a 2 de Dezembro de 1881* (Rio de Janeiro: G. Leuzinger & Filhos, 1881), index.

7. Quoted after Maria Inez Turazzi, "Imagens da nação: A *Exposição de História do Brasil* de 1881 e a construção do patrimônio iconográfico," in González-Stephan and Andermann, *Galerías del progreso*, 130.

8. Ramiz Galvão, *Catálogo*, xi.

9. Turazzi, "Imagens da nação," 146.

10. Ernesto Quesada, *Las reliquias de San Martín: Estudio de las colecciones del Museo Histórico Nacional* (Buenos Aires: Imprenta de la Revista Nacional, 1900), 10–11.

11. Mário Barata, "Origens dos museus históricos e de arte no Brasil," *Revista do Instituto Histórico e Geográfico Brasileiro* 147, 350 (1986): 22–30.

12. *Colección Lamas: Catálogo de los objetos que se encuentran en la Exhibición de las Señoras Damas de la Caridad. En el Salón Alto del Teatro de la Ópera. 6 de Octubre de 1878* (Buenos Aires: Imp. de Juan A. Alsina, 1878).

13. "Borrador de Andrés Lamas, donde hace consideraciones para que se lleve a cabo la Exposición Continental de 1879" [actually 1882, J.A.], Buenos Aires, Archivo General de la Nación, Archivo Andrés Lamas, legajo 61.

14. *La Libertad*, 15 March 1882. See Andrés Lamas, "Carta al Dr. Carlos D' Amico, Ministro de Gobierno de la Provincia de Buenos Aires," Buenos Aires, Archivo General de la Nación, Archivo Andrés Lamas, legajo 61; "Exposición histórica: Acuerdo extraordinario de la Comisión," *La Libertad*, 15 March 1882.

15. José Luis Romero, "Prólogo," in *Pensamiento conservador* (Caracas: Biblioteca Ayacucho, 1978), x.

16. Oscar Terán, *Vida intelectual en el Buenos Aires fin-de-siglo (1880–1910): Derivas de la 'cultura científica'* (Buenos Aires: Fondo de Cultura Económica, 2000), 57.

17. Federico Tobar, "Estudios: *La Revolución Argentina*, por del dr. Vicente López," *Revista Nacional* 8 (1889): 289–96.

18. Domingo Faustino Sarmiento, *Condición del extranjero en América* [1887], in *Obras completas* (Buenos Aires: Luz del Día, 1944), tome 36: 206–7.

19. Lucio V. López, "Discurso en la colación de grados en la Facultad de Derecho," 24 March 1890. Quoted in Bertoni, *Patriotas*, 165.

20. Bertoni, *Patriotas*, 22.

21. Miguel Cané, *Prosa ligera* (Buenos Aires: La Cultura Argentina, 1919 [1903]), 123. A similar nostalgia for the uncontested hierarchies of a harmonious past was widespread among Brazilian writers of the turn of the century, even those who, before 1888, had campaigned for the abolition of slavery. See, for instance, Joaquim Nabuco, *Um estadista do Império: Nabuco de Araújo, sua vida, suas opiniões, sua época* (Rio de Janeiro: H. Garnier, 1898–1900).

22. Dora López, "Historia y museo: ¿Encuentro o desencuentro? Los primeros cincuenta años del Museo Histórico Nacional," in *Primeras Jornadas 'Nuestros museos': 500 años de historia a través de su patrimonio* (Buenos Aires: Ministerio de Cultura y Educación, 1992), 67–79; also Miguel Cané, *Programa de Historia Contemporánea* (Buenos Aires: Imprenta y Librerías de Mayo, 1878).

23. Response of Domingo F. Sarmiento, in "La Pirámide de Mayo: La cuestión de si debe ó no ser demolida," *Revista Nacional (Historia Americana - Literatura - Jurisprudencia)*, Año 4, tomo 13, no. 57 (1891): 13–14. All further quotes from the survey belong to the same reference.

24. "La Pirámide de Mayo," 15–16.

25. Ibid., 18.

26. Ibid., 47.

27. Jacques Derrida, *Archive Fever: A Freudian Impression*, trans. Eric Prenowitz (Chicago, IL: University of Chicago Press, 1995), 17.

28. "La Pirámide de Mayo," 62.

29. Ibid., 31.

30. Ibid., 57; italics in original.

31. In 1894, Carranza reported having suggested the rechristening of the towns of Tres Arroyos, Tordillo, Vecino, Pila, and Pilar, as, respectively, Rodríguez Peña, Rondeau, Vicente López, General Viamonte, and Escalada, "for reasons of patriotism and national spirit." "Informe al Ministro del Interior," *El Museo Histórico* 2 (1894): 302.

32. Adolfo P. Carranza, "Informes sobre el Museo Histórico Nacional al Ministro del Interior," *El Museo Histórico* 1–4 (1892–97); Ernesto Quesada, "Las colecciones del Museo Histórico Nacional," *Nosotros* 9, no. 19:77 (1915): 5–6.

33. Carranza quoted in Stella Maris García, "La revista *El Museo Histórico*: Una aproximación," *Primeras Jornadas 'Nuestros museos': 500 años de historia a través de su patrimonio* (Buenos Aires: Ministerio de Cultura y Educación, 1992), 37.

34. *El Monitor* 186 (1890): 540–41.

35. "El Museo Histórico Nacional," *La Prensa*, 31 August 1890.

36. Quesada, "Las colecciones," 8–10.

37. Ibid., 25.

38. Ibid., 4.

39. Ernesto Quesada, *El Museo Histórico Nacional: Su importancia patriótica, con motivo de la inauguración del nuevo local en el Parque Lezama* (Buenos Aires: G. Kraft, 1897), 20.

40. Quesada, *El Museo Histórico*, 5.

41. Museo Histórico Nacional, *Catálogo* (Buenos Aires: Imprenta Europea, 1891).

42. Quesada, *El Museo Histórico*, 24.

43. "Una visita al Museo Histórico," *El Coleccionista Argentino: Revista de Bellas Artes, Bibliografía, Historia, Numismática, Prensa Periódica* 1, no. 2 (1892): 1.

44. Miguel Cané, "De cepa criolla," in *Prosa ligera*, 129–31.

45. Quesada, "Las colecciones," 12.

46. Quesada, *Las reliquias*, 3.

47. Maleuvre, *Museum Memories*, 135.

48. Eduardo Wilde, *La lluvia y otros relatos* (Buenos Aires: Centro Editor de América Latina, 1992), 27.

49. Baudrillard, *The System of Objects*, 90.

50. *La Prensa*, September 1931, quoted in López, "Historia y museo," 74.

## Part 2: Maps

1. Cassini's *Carte Générale* comprised 180 sheets of 10 x 10 meters on a scale of 1:86,400, which were presented to the National Assembly in the very year of the Revolution (yet, for military reasons, only made public in 1815). See George Kish, *La carte, image des civilisations* (Paris: Seuil, 1980), 56–57.

2. Derek Gregory, *Geographical Imaginations* (Oxford: Blackwell, 1994), 70–205.

3. Carlos María Moyano, "Patagonia Austral: Exploración de los ríos Gallego, Coile, Santa Cruz y Canales del Pacífico," *Boletín del Instituto Geográfico Argentino* 8, no. 12 (1888): 320–21 (the italics are Moyano's own).

4. Moyano, "Patagonia Austral," *Boletín del Instituto Geográfico Argentino* 7, no. 12: 325–26; 9, no. 2:25.

5. Ibid., 9, no. 2:27.

6. Ramón Serrano M., "Geografía patagónica: Discusión sobre los Andes australes," reproduced in *Boletín del Instituto Geográfico Argentino* 9, no. 8 (1888): 195–97.

7. Carlos M. Moyano, "Respuesta al Sr. Serrano, Carta al Sr. Presidente de la Comisión Especial del Mapa y Atlas de la República Argentina, Dr. Estanislao S. Zeballos," *Boletín del Instituto Geográfico Argentino* 9, no. 8 (1888): 198.

8. Pratt, *Imperial Eyes*, 188.

9. See Pierre Nora, "Between Memory and History," in *Realms of Memory: Rethinking the French Past*, vol. 1, *Conflicts and Divisions*, trans. Arthur Goldhammer (New York: Columbia University Press, 1992), 1–20.

10. Schwarcz, *O espetáculo das raças*, 110.

11. Augusto Fausto de Souza, "Estudo sobre a divisão territorial do Brasil," *Revista do Instituto Historico e Geographico Brasileiro* 43, no. 2 (1880): 49.

12. Souza, "Estudo sobre a divisão territorial," 29–30, italics in the original.

13. Michel Roncayolo, "Le paysage du savant," in *Les lieux de mémoire*, ed. Pierre Nora (Paris: Gallimard-Quarto, 1997), vol. 1, 1006.

14. Michel Foucault, "Le panoptisme," in *Surveiller et punir: Naissance de la prision* (Paris: Gallimard, 1975), 228–64.

15. Souza, "Estudo sobre a divisão territorial," 76.

16. Carlos Corra Luna, "La obra del Instituto Geográfico Argentino," *Boletín del Instituto Geográfico Argentino* 17 (1896): 239.

17. On state power as the return of nature into society, see Pierre Clastres's groundbreaking work *La société contre l'état: Recherches d' anthropologie politique* (Paris: Minuit, 1974); see also Giorgio Agamben's analogy between "state of nature" and "state of exception," in Agamben, *Homo sacer*, 37–38.

18. Karl Marx, *Das Kapital: Kritik der politischen Ökonomie* (Berlin: Dietz, 1983 [*Marx Engels Werke*, vol. 23]), 779.

19. On railways as catalysts of the expansion of the state and of capital in Argentina and Brazil, see Oszlak, *La formación del estado argentino*, 139, 151–53; Francisco Foot Hardman, *Trem fantasma: A modernidade na selva* (São Paulo: Companhia das Letras, 1988).

20. David Harvey, *The Limits to Capital* (London: Verso, 1999), 373–412.

21. Nísia Trindade Lima, *Um sertão chamado Brasil: Intelectuais e representação geográfica no Brasil* (Rio de Janeiro: UPERJ / Editora Revan, 1999), 57–61.

22. Pereira quoted in Lima, *Um sertão chamado Brasil*, 84.

23. Nancy Leys Stepan, *Picturing Tropical Nature* (London: Reaktion Books, 2001), 133.

24. Alvaro Fernández Bravo, *Literatura y frontera: Procesos de territorialización en las culturas argentina y chilena del siglo XIX* (Buenos Aires: Sudamericana, 1999), 159ff.; also Susana López, *Representaciones de la Patagonia: Colonos, científicos y políticos* (La Plata: Eds. Al Margen, 2003).

25. Gabriela Nouzeilles, "Patagonia as Borderland: Nature, Culture, and the Image of the State," *Journal of Latin American Cultural Studies* 8, no. 1 (1999): 36.

1. Angel Rama, *The Lettered City* (Durham, NC: Duke University Press, 1996). On the symbolic exchanges between mysticism and modernism in the conception and construction of Brasília, see Caroline S. Tauxe, "Mystics, Modernists, and Constructions of Brasília," *Ecumene* 3, no. 1 (1996): 43–61.

2. For a discussion of the concepts of "origin" vs. "beginning," see Edward Said, *Beginnings: Intention and Method* (New York: Basic Books, 1975).

3. Luiz Cruls, "Relatório do Dr. L. Cruls" [1894], in Cruls, *Planalto Central do Brasil* (Rio de Janeiro: José Olympo, 1957), 65. All further quotes to the Planalto Commission's report refer to this edition.

4. Cruls, *Planalto Central do Brasil*, 66–67.

5. Ibid., 58.

6. Commissão Exploradora do Planalto Central do Brazil, *Relatório apresentado a S. Ex. o Sr. Ministro da Industria, Viação e Obras Publicas. Publicado por L. Cruls, Chefe da Commissão* (Rio de Janeiro: H. Lombaerts / C. Impressores do Observatorio, 1894). A further volume was published in 1896.

7. Commissão Exploradora do Planalto Central do Brazil, *Atlas dos Itinerários, Perfis longitudinais e da zona demarcada. Publicado por L. Cruls, Chefe da Commissão* (Rio de Janeiro: H. Lombaerts / C. Impressores do Observatorio, 1894).

8. Among the most interesting readings of Brasília are David G. Epstein, *Brasília, Plan and Reality: A Study of Planned and Spontaneous Urban Development* (Berkeley, CA: University of California Press, 1973); Valerie Fraser, "The Origins of Brasília," in *Building the New World: Studies in the Modern Architecture of Latin America, 1930–1960* (London: Verso, 2000), 215–40; James Holston, *The Modernist City: An Anthropological Critique of Brasília* (Chicago, IL: University of Chicago Press, 1989); and Aldo Paviani, ed., *Brasília, ideologia e realidade: Espaço urbano em questão* (São Paulo: Projeto, 1985).

9. Timothy Mitchell, *Colonising Egypt* (Cambridge, New York: Cambridge University Press, 1989), 60.

10. Cruls, *Planalto Central do Brasil*, 59.

11. Ibid., 59–60.

12. Ibid., 60.

13. Djalma Poli Coelho, "Mudança da capital, problema geopolítico" [1946], quoted in Ernesto Silva, *História de Brasília: Um sonho, uma esperança, uma realidade* (Brasília: Coordenadora Editora de Brasília, 1970), 56–57. Italics in original.

14. Demétrio Magnoli, *O corpo da pátria: Imaginação geográfica e política externa no Brasil (1808–1812)* (São Paulo: UNESP / Moderna, 1997), 131.

15. Luiz Cruls, "Amazônia," in *Federação*, 4 May 1901, quoted in Cruls, *Planalto Central do Brasil*, 24.

16. Cruls, *Planalto Central do Brasil*, 50.

17. Gilles Deleuze and Félix Guattari, *A Thousand Plateaus: Capitalism and Schizophrenia II* (London: Athlone, 1988), 362–63.

18. Cruls, *Planalto Central do Brasil*, 50.

19. Ibid., 54.

20. Stepan, *Picturing Tropical Nature*, 133.

21. On the colonial and imperial history of Goiás, see Antônio Americano do Brasil, *Súmulo da história de Goiás* (Goiânia: Departamento Estadual de Cultura, 1961).

22. Marilena Chaui, *Brasil: Mito fundador e sociedade autoritária* (São Paulo: Fundação Perseu Abramo, 2000), 63.

23. Cruls, *Planalto Central do Brasil*, 247.

24. Ibid., 129.

25. Ibid., 87.

26. Paul Carter, *The Road to Botany Bay: An Essay in Spatial History* (London: Faber & Faber, 1987), 112.

27. Foucault, *Surveiller et punir*, 175–83.

28. Michel De Certeau, *The Practice of Everyday Life* (Berkeley, CA: University of California Press, 1984), 91–130.

29. Victor Turner, *The Ritual Process: Structure and Anti-Structure* (New York: Aldine, 1969).

30. James R. Ryan, *Picturing Empire: Photography and the Visualization of the British Empire* (London: Reaktion Books, 1997), 50–51.

31. Cruls, *Planalto Central do Brasil*, 69.

32. Ibid., 91–92; italics in original.

33. Lúcio Costa quoted in William Holford, "Brasília: A New Capital City for Brazil," *Architectural Review* 122 (1957): 399.

34. Chaui, *Brasil*, 45.

35. Denis Cosgrove, *Social Formation and Symbolic Landscape* (Madison, WI: University of Wisconsin Press, 1998), 61.

36. Lima, *Um sertão chamado Brasil*, 65.

37. Chaui, *Brasil*, 33.

## Chapter 5: An Essay in Segmentarity

*Epigraph.* "Il faut à ce sol ascétique un homme au cœur dur, indomptable et sans attente: rien à recevoir et tout à donner, combien à imposer s'il est besoin, à faire partager de force. Et nul site en ce parfait espace. Ce n' est qu' un vaste champ au déploiement d' une vigueur."

1. On the military history of the "Conquest of the Desert," see Juan Carlos Walther, *La conquista del desierto: Síntesis histórica de los principales sucesos occuridos y operaciones realizadas en La Pampa y Patagonia, contra los indios (años 1527–1885)* (Buenos Aires: Eudeba, 1970); Néstor Tomás Auza, "La ocupación del espacio vacío: De la frontera interior a la frontera exterior, 1876–1910," in *La Argentina del ochenta al centenario*, ed. Gustavo Ferrari and Ezequiel Gallo, 62–89 (Buenos Aires: Sudamericana, 1980); Nora Siegrist de Gentile and María Haydée Martín, *Geopolítica, ciencia y técnica a través de la campaña del desierto* (Buenos Aires: Eudeba, 1981); Comisión Nacional de Homenaje al Centenario de la Conquista del Desierto, ed., *Congreso Nacional de Historia sobre la Conquista del Desierto celebrado en la ciudad de Gral. Roca del 6 al 10 de noviembre de 1979* (Buenos Aires: Academia Nacional de la Historia, 1980). Perhaps needless to say, these texts, as well as others cited or referred to in this chapter, continue to celebrate the genocidal racism of turn-of-the-century military discourse, more or less explicitly allegorizing the ethnic cleansing of 1880 as a precedent for the annihilation of revolutionary, trade union, and democratic activism in the "Dirty War" of 1976–83, a line of interpretation which cynically anticipates David Viñas's critique of the authoritarian state

in *Indios, ejército y frontera* (Buenos Aires: Siglo Veintiuno, 1983). Yet precisely because they explicitly bring these continuities to the fore, these right-wing texts have at least the merit of spelling out what "progressive" histories of state formation prefer to keep silent (or, if mentioned at all, treat as an unpleasant but more or less unavoidable side effect of state formation), namely, the genocidal condition of liberal modernity and the state in Argentina.

2. María Aurora Sánchez, *Julio Argentino Roca* (Buenos Aires: Círculo Militar, 1969), 372.

3. Estanislao S. Zeballos, *La conquista de 15000 leguas* (Buenos Aires: La Prensa, 1878), 318–19.

4. The idea of the desert's "incrustation" in the institutions created in order to subdue it provides one of the main argumentative threads in Martínez Estrada's œuvre between *Radiografía de la pampa* (1933) and *Muerte y transfiguración de Martín Fierro* (1948). "The ills," he argues in a passage from the latter, "that *Martín Fierro* had localized in frontier individuals are already encrusted in the very same institutions created as bastions in order to combat them. Today the struggle is a social one against spectres that inhabit the bodies of those who tell us they are fighting for civilization." Ezequiel Martínez Estrada, *Muerte y transfiguración de Martín Fierro* (Buenos Aires: Centro Editor de América Latina, 1983), 738.

5. Angel Floro Costa, *La conquista del desierto—Una visita al taller del pintor Blanes: Su cuadro alegórico 'La revista sobre el Río Negro'—Reflexiones históricas, políticas y artísticas alrededor del gran cuadro* (Montevideo: Imprenta de "El Siglo," 1893). The edition has no page numbers.

6. Laura Malosetti Costa, *Los primeros modernos: Arte y sociedad en Buenos Aires a fines del siglo XIX* (Buenos Aires: FCE, 2001), 61–81.

7. Julio Vezub, *Indios y soldados: Las fotografías de Carlos Encina y Edgardo Moreno durante la 'Conquista del Desierto'* (Buenos Aires: El Elefante Blanco, 2002), 67–71.

8. Floro Costa, *La conquista del desierto*, n. p.

9. Ibid.

10. In medieval and baroque emblematics, dogs are connoted both with rage and melancholy as with inquisitiveness and physical endurance. A companion of princes and noblemen, the dog shares and emphasizes their troubled, saturnine nature as divinely appointed rulers thrown into a carnal and abandoned world. See Benjamin, *Ursprung des deutschen Trauerspiels*, 329–32.

11. Interestingly, on the version of Blanes's painting that features on the 100-peso note (introduced during the speculation-fueled era of President Menem), the traces of the desert—the dog and the Indians—have been removed, replaced by a saber and a parchment representing the law authorizing Roca's expedition to the Río Negro. On the banknote, which symbolized, more than anything, Argentina's aspiration to enter the First World, the desert is erased and replaced by emblems of the state's legal and military apparatuses.

12. Norman Bryson, *Vision and Painting: The Logic of the Gaze* (Basingstoke: Palgrave, 1983), 96.

13. Deleuze and Guattari, *A Thousand Plateaus*, 447, 444.

14. See Eduardo Racedo, *Memoria militar y descriptiva de la 3a División Expedicionaria* (Buenos Aires: Plus Ultra, 1965 [1879]), 236–38.

15. Hebe Clementi, *La frontera en América* (Buenos Aires: Leviatan, 1977), tome 4, 91–94; Colin M. Lewis, "La consolidación de la frontera argentina a fines de la década del 70," in Ferrari and Gallo, *La Argentina del ochenta al centenario*, 469–83; Oszlak, *La formación*, 106–8; Walther, *La conquista*, 576–78.

16. Oscar Ricardo Melli, "El coronel Manuel José Olascoaga y la geografía argentina," *Boletín de la Academia Nacional de la Historia* 53 (1980): 189–211.

17. Ramiro Martínez Sierra, *El mapa de las pampas* (Buenos Aires: Plus Ultra, 1975), 256–57.

18. Deleuze and Guattari, *A Thousand Plateaus*, 212.

19. See Colin M. Lewis, *British Railways in Argentina, 1857–1914* (London: Athlone, 1983), 63.

20. Manuel José Olascoaga, *Estudio topográfico de La Pampa y Río Negro* (Buenos Aires: Eudeba, 1974 [1880]), 159.

21. Ibid., 159–60.

22. Ibid., 166.

23. Ibid., 161.

24. See Paul Virilio, *Speed and Politics*, trans. Mark Polizotti (New York: Semiotext, 1986), 12–13.

25. Carl von Clausewitz, "Gegend und Boden," in *Vom Kriege*, 359–63 (München: Cormoran, 2000 [1832]).

26. Henri Lefebvre, *The Production of Space*, trans. Donald Nicholson-Smith (Oxford: Blackwell, 1991), 39.

27. W. J. T. Mitchell, "Imperial Landscape," in *Landscape and Power*, ed. W. J. T. Mitchell (Chicago, IL: University of Chicago Press, 1994), 17.

## Chapter 6: Disappearing Acts

1. Sontag, *On Photography*, 16.

2. Abel Alexander and Luis Priamo, "Recordando a Christiano," in José Christiano de Freitas Henriques Júnior (Christiano Júnior), *Un país en transición: Fotografías de Buenos Aires, Cuyo y el Noroeste (1867–1883)* (Buenos Aires: Eds. Fundación Antorchas, 2002), 22.

3. Héctor Alimonda and Juan Ferguson, "Imagens, 'deserto' e memória nacional: As fotografias da campanha do exército argentino contra os índios, 1879," in *De sertões, desertos e espaços incivilizados*, ed. A. Mendes de Almeida, B. Zilly, and E. N. de Lima (Rio de Janeiro: FAPERJ / Mauad, 2001), 201–3.

4. "Economic potency," Marx, *Kapital*, I, 779.

5. Homi K. Bhabha, *The Location of Culture* (London: Routledge, 1994), 89.

6. The genitals of indigenous men, José María Borrero asserts in his historical chronicle of Patagonia's and Tierra del Fuego's exploitation after 1879, *La Patagonia trágica*, were accepted by the new landowning class of (mostly European) sheep farmers as proof that the subject in question had effectively been murdered, a reward thus being paid out to his killer. In the initial period after the Campaña del Desierto, estate owners had accepted ears, but later changed their policy following several incidents where bounty hunters had merely mutilated their indigenous victims without killing them. See José María Borrero, *La Patagonia trágica* (Buenos Aires: Peña Lillo / Eds. Continente, 2003 [1928]).

7. Julius Popper, *The Popper Expedition: Tierra del Fuego. A Lecture Delivered at the Argentine Geographical Institute, 5 March 1887*, trans. J. E. O'Curry (Buenos Aires: L. Jacobsen & Co., 1887), 39.

8. Timothy Sweet, *Traces of War: Poetry, Photography, and the Crisis of the Union* (Baltimore: Johns Hopkins University Press, 1990), 130–32.

9. Arnaldo Canclini, *Julio Popper: Quijote del oro fueguino* (Buenos Aires: Emecé, 1993), 35.

10. E. Lucas Bridges, *Uttermost Part of the Earth* (London: Hodder & Stoughton, 1951).

11. Robert D. Levine, *Vale of Tears: Rewriting the Canudos Massacre in Northeastern Brazil, 1893–1897* (Berkeley, CA: University of California Press, 1992).

12. Alan Trachtenberg, *Reading American Photographs: Images as History, Mathew Brady to Walker Evans* (New York: Hill & Wang, 1989), 73–74.

13. Cícero Antônio F. de Almeida, "O álbum fotográfico de Flávio de Barros: Memória e representação da guerra de Canudos," *Historia, Ciências, Saúde: Manguinhos* 5 (1998): 284–87.

14. Barthes, *La chambre claire*, 48–49.

15. Benjamin, "Kurze Geschichte," 371–72.

16. Sontag, *On Photography*, 108–9.

17. Apart from "400 jagunços prisioneiros" (which he recaptioned "As prisioneiras," eliminating the male prisoners from the title even before their physical elimination by the federal army), Euclides included in *Os sertões* the pictures "Monte Santo (Base de operações)" and "Acampamento dentro de Canudos." See Berthold Zilly, "Flávio de Barros, o ilustre cronista anônimo da guerra de Canudos: As fotografias que Euclides da Cunha gostaria de ter tirado," *Historia, Ciências, Saúde: Manguinhos* 5 (1998): 316–20.

18. Euclides da Cunha, *Rebellion in the Backlands*, trans. Samuel Putnam (Chicago, IL: University of Chicago Press, 1944 [1902]), 475.

19. Almeida, "O album fotográfico," 311.

20. Barthes, *La chambre claire*, 150.

21. Cunha, *Rebellion*, 443–44.

22. Joel Snyder, "Territorial Photography," in Mitchell, *Landscape and Power*, 175–201.

23. Deborah Poole, *Vision, Race and Modernity: A Visual Economy of the Andean Image World* (Princeton, NJ: Princeton University Press, 1997), 132–33.

24. Viñas, *Indios, ejército y frontera*, 159–60.

## Conclusion

1. Chaui, *Brasil*, 66.

2. Dipresh Chakrabarty, *Provincializing Europe: Postcolonial Thought and Historical Difference* (Princeton, NJ: Princeton University Press, 2000); Partha Chatterjee, *The Nation and Its Fragments: Colonial and Postcolonial Histories* (Princeton, NJ: Princeton University Press, 1993); Achille Mbembe, "The Banality of Power and the Aesthetics of Vulgarity in the Postcolony," *Public Culture* 4, no. 2 (1992): 1–30.

3. Tulio Halperín Donghi, *The Contemporary History of Latin America*, trans. John Charles Chasteen (Durham, NC: Duke University Press, 1993), 158–207.

4. Chaui, *Brasil*, 37–38.

5. Manuel Gálvez, *El diario de Gabriel Quiroga* (Buenos Aires: Taurus, 2001 [1910]), 142. On scopophobia in the literary reactions to the Argentine and Brazilian Centenary Exhibitions of 1910 and 1922, see Alvaro Fernández Bravo, "Celebraciones centenarias: Nacionalismo y cosmopolitismo en las conmemoraciones de la Independencia (Buenos Aires, 1910–Rio de Janeiro, 1922)," in González-Stephan and Andermann, *Galerías del progreso*, 333–74.

# BIBLIOGRAPHY

## Primary Sources

Agassiz, Louis. *A Journey in Brazil: By Professor and Mrs. Louis Agassiz*. Boston: Ticknor and Fields, 1868.

Azevedo, Manuel Duarte Moreira de. *O Rio de Janeiro: Sua história, monumentos, homens notáveis, usos e curiosidades*. Rio de Janeiro: Garnier, 1877.

Barros, Alvaro. *La guerra contra los indios*. Buenos Aires: Imprenta y Librerías de Mayo, 1877.

Berg, Carlos. *Comunicaciones del Museo Nacional de Buenos Aires*. Buenos Aires: Alsina, 1898–1901.

Borrero, José María. *La Patagonia trágica*. Buenos Aires: Peña Lillo / Eds. Continente, 2003 [1928].

Bridges, E. Lucas. *Uttermost Part of the Earth*. London: Hodder & Stoughton, 1951.

Burmeister, Germán [Konrad Hermann]. "Al Señor Gefe de la Comission del Censo de los Bienes Nacionales, Dr. B. Zorrilla," Buenos Aires, 28 de Marzo de 1889. Archivo del Museo Argentino de Ciencias Naturales "Bernardino Rivadavia," legajo 1274.

———. "Al Señor Ministro de Instrucción Pública," Buenos Aires, 12 de Marzo de 1889. Archivo del Museo Argentino de Ciencias Naturales "Bernardino Rivadavia," legajo 1270.

———. "Al Señor Ministro de Instrucción Pública, Dr. D. Filemon Posse," Buenos Aires, 10 de Marzo de 1888. Archivo del Museo Argentino de Ciencias Naturales "Bernardino Rivadavia," legajo 1089.

———. *Description physique de la République Argentine*. Paris: Savy / Buenos Aires: Coni, 1876–78.

———. "Sumario sobre la fundación y los progresos del Museo Público de Buenos Aires." *Anales del Museo Público de Buenos Aires*, vol. 1 (1864–69), first fascicle: 1–64.

Cané, Miguel. *Programa de Historia Contemporánea*. Buenos Aires: Imprenta y Librerías de Mayo, 1878.

———. *Prosa ligera*. Buenos Aires: La Cultura Argentina, 1919 [1903].

Carranza, Adolfo Pedro. *Los grandes ciudadanos: Primera série*. Buenos Aires: Imprenta de M. A. Rosas, 1905.

————. *Homenajes patrióticos: Discursos*. Buenos Aires: Revista Nacional, 1900.

————. "Informes sobre la gestión." *El Museo Histórico* 1–4 (1892–97).

————. *Noticia sobre la vida y servicios del coronel Juan Isidro Quesada*. Buenos Aires: Imp. Europea de M. A. Rosas / Museo Histórico Nacional, 1903.

*Catálogo dos objectos expostos na Exposição Anthropológica do Rio de Janeiro*. Rio de Janeiro: Typographia Nacional, 1882.

*Colección Lamas: Catálogo de los objetos que se encuentran en la Exhibición de las Señoras Damas de la Caridad. En el Salón Alto del Teatro de la Ópera. 6 de Octubre de 1878*. Buenos Aires: Alsina, 1878.

Commissão Exploradora do Planalto Central do Brazil. *Atlas dos Itinerários, Perfis longitudinais e da zona demarcada. Publicado por L. Cruls, Chefe da Commissão*. Rio de Janeiro: H. Lombaerts / C. Impressores do Observatorio, 1894.

————. *Relatório apresentado a S. Ex. o Sr. Ministro da Industria, Viação e Obras Publicas. Publicado por L. Cruls, Chefe da Commissão*. Rio de Janeiro: H. Lombaerts / C. Impressores do Observatorio, 1894.

Corra Luna, Carlos. "La obra del Instituto Geográfico Argentino." *Boletín del Instituto Geográfico Argentino* 17 (1896): 239.

Cruls, Luiz. *Planalto Central do Brasil*. Rio de Janeiro: José Olympo, 1957.

Cunha, Euclides da. *Rebellion in the Backlands*. Translated by Samuel Putnam. Chicago, IL: University of Chicago Press, 1944 [1902].

"Exposición histórica: Acuerdo extraordinario de la Comisión." *La Libertad*, 15 March 1882, 1.

Floro Costa, Angel. *La conquista del desierto—Una visita al taller del pintor Blanes: Su cuadro alegórico 'La revista sobre el Río Negro'—Reflexiones históricas, políticas y artísticas alrededor del gran cuadro*. Montevideo: Imprenta de "El Siglo," 1893.

Gálvez, Manuel. *El diario de Gabriel Quiroga*. Buenos Aires: Taurus, 2001 [1910].

Goeldi, Emil August. "Parte administrativa." *Boletim do Museu Paraense de Historia Natural e Ethnographia* 2, 1 (1902): 108.

————. *Relatório sobre o estado do Museu Paraense, apresentado a S. Exc. o Sr. Dr. Governador do Estado do Pará*. Belém: Typographia do Diário Official, 1894.

*Guia da Exposição Anthropológica Brasileira realisada pelo Museu Nacional do Rio de Janeiro o 29 de julho de 1882*. Rio de Janeiro: Leuzinger, 1882.

Henriques Júnior, José Christiano de Freitas [Christiano Júnior]. *Un país en transición: Fotografías de Buenos Aires, Cuyo y el Noroeste (1867–1883)*. Buenos Aires: Ediciones Fundación Antorchas, 2002.

Ihering, Hermann von. "A anthropologia do Estado de São Paulo." *Revista do Museu Paulista* 7 (1908): 202–57

————. "Bibliographia. Os Museus da America do Sul." *Revista do Museu Paulista* 1 (1895): 233–45.

————. "Historia do Monumento do Ypiranga e do Museu Paulista." *Revista do Museu Paulista* 1 (1895): 9–31.

————. *O Museu Paulista em 1899 e 1900*. São Paulo: Diario Oficial, 1901.

Junio. "Pelas exposições." *Revista Illustrada*, 17 December 1881, 7.

Lacerda, João Baptista de. *Fastos do Museu Nacional: Recordações históricas e scientíficas fundadas em documentos authenticos e informações verídicas*. Rio de Janeiro: Imprensa Nacional, 1906.

Lacerda, João Baptista de, and José Rodrigues Peixoto. "Contribuições para o estudo anthropologico das raças indigenas do Brazil, pelos doutores Lacerda Filho e Rodrigues Peixoto." *Archivos do Museu Nacional* 1 (1876): 47–83.

Lamas, Andrés. "Borrador de Andrés Lamas, donde hace consideraciones para que se lleve a cabo la Exposición Continental de 1879." Buenos Aires, Archivo General de la Nación, Archivo Andrés Lamas, legajo 61.

———. "Carta al Dr. Carlos D' Amico, Ministro de Gobierno de la Provincia de Buenos Aires." 1879. Buenos Aires, Archivo General de la Nación, Archivo Andrés Lamas, legajo 61.

Lydekker, Richard. "The La Plata Museum." *Natural Science* 4, no. 24 (1894): 1–21.

Magalhães, José Vieira Couto de. *O selvagem*. Rio de Janeiro: Typographia Nacional, 1876.

Moreno, Francisco Pascasio. *Antropología y arqueología: Importancia del estudio de estas ciencias en la República Argentina*. Buenos Aires: Imprenta Pablo E. Coni, 1881.

———. "Carta al Ministro de Gobierno Manuel B. Gonnet." La Plata, 9 May 1886. Copiador del Museo de La Plata.

———. *El estudio del hombre sud-americano*. Buenos Aires: La Nación, 1878.

———. "Museo de La Plata. El último informe de su director." *El Sudamericano* 2, no. 31 (1889): 99–100.

———. "El Museo de La Plata. Rápida ojeada sobre su fundación y desarrollo." *Revista del Museo de La Plata* 1, no. 1 (1890–91): 28–55.

Moyano, Carlos María. *Exploración de los ríos Gallegos, Coile y Santa Cruz*. Ushuaia: Zagier & Urruti, 2002 [1887].

———. "Patagonia Austral: Exploración de los ríos Gallego, Coile, Santa Cruz y Canales del Pacífico." *Boletín del Instituto Geográfico Argentino* vol. 8, no. 12 (1887)–vol. 9, no. 7 (1888).

———. "Respuesta al Sr. Serrano, Carta al Sr. Presidente de la Comisión Especial del Mapa y Atlas de la República Argentina, Dr. Estanislao S. Zeballos," *Boletín del Instituto Geográfico Argentino* 9, no. 8 (1888): 198.

*El Museo Histórico*. Vols. 1–4. Buenos Aires: Museo Histórico Nacional, 1892–97.

"El Museo Histórico Nacional." *La Prensa*, 31 August 1890, 1.

Museo Histórico Nacional. 1891. *Catálogo*. Buenos Aires: Impr. Europea, 1891.

———. *Catálogo*. Buenos Aires: Museo Histórico Nacional, 1892.

Nabuco, Joaquim. *Um estadista do Império. Nabuco de Araújo, sua vida, suas opiniões, sua época*. Rio de Janeiro: Garnier, 1898–1900.

Netto, Ladislau. *Conférence faite au Muséum National en présence de LL. MM. Impériales, par le Dr. Ladislau Netto, Directeur Général du Muséum National de Rio de Janeiro*. Rio de Janeiro: Machado & Cia., 1885.

———. *Investigações históricas e cientificas sobre o Museu Imperial e Nacional, acompanhadas de uma breve notícia das suas colecções e publicadas por ordem do Ministério de Agricultura*. Rio de Janeiro: Instituto Philomatico, 1870.

———. "Investigações sobre a archeologia brazileira." *Archivos do Museu Nacional* 6 (1885): 330–424.

———. *Museu Nacional: Instrucções sobre a preparação e remessa das colecções que lhe forem destinadas*. Rio de Janeiro: Imprensa Nacional, 1890.

———. *Le Muséum National de Rio de Janeiro et son influence sur les sciences naturelles du Brésil*. Paris: Charles Delagrave, 1889.

————. *Relatório do Museu Nacional. Apresentado ao Illustrissimo Exm. Sr. Conselheiro Tomás Jorge Coelho de Almeida pelo Dr. Ladislau Netto, Diretor Geral do Museu*. Rio de Janeiro: Imprensa Nacional, 1877.

Olascoaga, Manuel José. *Estudio topográfico de La Pampa y Río Negro*. Buenos Aires: Eudeba, 1974 [1880].

Payró, Roberto Jorge. *La Australia argentina*. Buenos Aires: Centro Editor de América Latina, 1982 [1898].

"La Pirámide de Mayo. La cuestión de si debe ó no ser demolida." *Revista Nacional (Historia Americana - Literatura - Jurisprudencia)*, year 4, tome 13, no. 57 (1891).

Popper, Julius. *Atlanta: Proyecto para la fundación de un pueblo marítimo en Tierra del Fuego, y otros escritos*. Buenos Aires: Eudeba / Ushuaia: Museo del Fin del Mundo, 2003.

————. *The Popper Expedition: Tierra del Fuego. A Lecture Delivered at the Argentine Geographical Institute, 5 March 1887*. Translated by J. E. O'Curry. Buenos Aires: L. Jacobsen & Co., 1887.

Quesada, Ernesto. "Las colecciones del Museo Histórico Nacional." *Nosotros* 9, 19: 74 (1915): 1–35.

————. *El Museo Histórico Nacional: Su importancia patriótica, con motivo de la inauguración del nuevo local en el Parque Lezama*. Buenos Aires: G. Kraft, 1897.

————. *Las reliquias de San Martín: Estudio de las colecciones del Museo Histórico Nacional*. Buenos Aires: Imprenta de la Revista Nacional, 1900.

Racedo, Eduardo. *Memoria militar y descriptiva de la 3a División Expedicionaria*. Buenos Aires: Plus Ultra, 1965 [1879].

Ramiz Galvão, Benjamin Franklin, ed. *Catálogo da Exposição de História do Brazil, realizada pela Bibliotheca Nacional do Rio de Janeiro a 2 de Dezembro de 1881*. Rio de Janeiro: G. Leuzinger & Filhos, 1881.

Rodrigues, Raimundo Nina. 1894. *As raças humanas e a responsibilidade penal no Brasil*. Bahia: Imprensa Popular.

Romero, Silvio. *Ethnographia brazileira: Estudos criticos sobre Couto de Magalhães, Barbosa Rodrigues, Theophilo Braga e Ladislão Netto*. Rio de Janeiro: Alves & Cia., 1888.

Sarmiento, Domingo Faustino. *Condición del extranjero en América* [1887]. In *Obras completas*, tome 36. Buenos Aires: Luz del Día.

————. "Mundos prehistóricos: Viaje aéreo a través del museo prehistórico de Moreno" [1878]. In *Obras completas*, tome 22, vol. 2, pp. 135–45. Buenos Aires: Imprenta y Litografía Mariano Moreno, 1899.

————. "El Museo de La Plata" [1885]. In *Obras completas*, tome 22, vol. 2, pp. 310–13. Buenos Aires: Imprenta y Litografía Mariano Moreno, 1899.

Serra, J. "Meios de Catequese." *Revista da Exposição Antropológica Brasileira*, ed. Mello Morães Filho. Rio de Janeiro, 1882.

Serrano Montaner, Ramón. "Geografia patagónica: Discusión sobre los Andes australes." *Boletín del Instituto Geográfico Argentino* 9, no. 8 (1888): 195–97.

Souza, Augusto Fausto de. "Estudo sobre a divisão territorial do Brasil." *Revista do Instituto Historico e Geographico Brasileiro* 43, no. 2 (1880): 27–113.

Tobar, Federico. "Estudios: *La Revolución Argentina*, por del dr. Vicente López." *Revista Nacional* 8 (1889): 289–96.

Trelles, Manuel Ricardo. *Memoria presentada a la Asociación de Amigos de la Historia Natural del Plata: Sobre el estado del Museo y demás relativo a la institución por el Secretario de la misma*. Buenos Aires: Imprenta "El Orden," 1856.

Veríssimo, José. *Estudos Brazileiros (1877–1895)*. Belém: Tavares Cardoso & Cia., 1895.

"Una visita al Museo Histórico." *El Coleccionista Argentino: Revista de Bellas Artes, Bibliografía, Historia, Numismática, Prensa Periódica* 1, no. 2 (1892): 1.

Ward, Henry A. "Los museos argentinos." *Revista del Museo de La Plata* 1, no. 1 (1891): 145–46.

Wilde, Eduardo. *La lluvia y otros relatos*. Buenos Aires: Centro Editor de América Latina, 1992.

Zeballos, Estanislao Severo. *La conquista de 15000 leguas*. Buenos Aires: La Prensa, 1878.

———. "El Museo Nacional de Rio Janeiro." *Anales de la Sociedad Cienífica Argentina* 3 (1877): 265–76.

## Critical Readings

Abreu, Regina. *A fabricação do imortal: Memória, História e estratégias de consacração no Brasil*. Rio de Janeiro: Rocco / Lapa Produções, 1996.

Agamben, Giorgio. *Homo Sacer: Sovereign Power and Bare Life*. Translated by Daniel Heller-Roazen. Stanford, CA: Stanford University Press, 1998.

Alexander, Abel, and Luis Priamo. "Recordando a Christiano." In *Un país en transición: Fotografías de Buenos Aires, Cuyo y el Noroeste: 1867–1883 / Christiano Junior*. Buenos Aires: Ediciones Fundación Antorchas, 2002.

Alimonda, Héctor, and Juan Ferguson. "Imagens, 'deserto' e memória nacional: As fotografias da campanha do exército argentino contra os índios, 1879." In *De sertões, desertos e espaços incivilizados*, edited by A. Mendes de Almeida, B. Zilly, and E. N. de Lima, 199–218. Rio de Janeiro: FAPERJ / Mauad, 2001.

Almeida, A. Mendes de, Berthold Zilly, and Eli N. de Lima, eds. *De sertões, desertos e espaços incivilizados*. Rio de Janeiro: FAPERJ / Mauad, 2001.

Almeida, Cícero Antônio F. de. "O álbum fotográfico de Flávio de Barros: Memória e representação da guerra de Canudos." *Historia, Ciências, Saúde: Manguinhos* 5 (1998): 309–15.

———. "O sertão pacificado, ou, o trabalho de Flávio de Barros no front." *Cadernos de fotografia brasileira* 1 (December 2002): 270–99.

Althusser, Louis. *Lenin and Philosophy and Other Essays*. Translated by Ben Brewster. London: New Left Books, 1971.

Andermann, Jens. "Crónica de un genocidio: Últimas instantáneas de la frontera." In *Historia crítica de la literatura argentina*, vol. 2, *La lucha de los lenguajes*, edited by Julio Schvartzman. Buenos Aires: Emecé, 2003.

———. "Entre la topografía y la iconografía: Mapas y nación, 1880." In *La ciencia en la Argentina entre siglos: Textos, contextos e instituciones*, edited by Marcelo Montserrat. Buenos Aires: Manantial, 2000.

———. "Evidencias y ensueños: El gabinete del Dr. Moreno." *Filología* 31, no. 1/2 (1998): 57–66.

———. *Mapas de poder: Una arqueología literaria del espacio argentino*. Rosario: Beatriz Viterbo, 2000.

———. "Reshaping the Creole Past: History Exhibitions in Nineteenth-Century Argentina." *Journal of the History of Collections* 13, no. 2 (2001): 145–62

———. "El sur profundo: Geografía, paisaje y conquista en la Campaña del Desierto." *Estudios: Revista de investigaciones literarias y culturales* 8, no. 16 (2000): 105–27.

Andermann, Jens, and William Rowe, eds. *Images of Power: Iconography, Culture and the State in Latin America*. London: Berghahn Books, 2005.

Anderson, Benedict. *Imagined Communities: Reflections on the Origin and Spread of Nationalism*. London: Verso, 1983.

Andrade, Joaquim Marçal Ferreira de. "A fotografia de guerra e o episódio de Canudos." *Cadernos de Fotografia Brasileira* 1 (December 2002): 238–69.

Ansaldi, Waldo, and José Luis Moreno, eds. *Estado y sociedad en el pensamiento nacional: Antología conceptual para el análisis comparado*. Buenos Aires: Cantaro, 1989.

Arantes, Antonio Augusto, ed. *Produzindo o passado: Estrategias de construção do patrimonio cultural*. São Paulo: Brasiliense, 1984.

Auza, Néstor Tomás. "Germán Burmeister y la Sociedad Paleontológica, 1866–1868." *Investigaciones y Ensayos* 46 (1996): 137–55.

———. "La ocupación del espacio vacío: De la frontera interior a la frontera exterior, 1876–1910." In Ferrari and Gallo, *La Argentina del ochenta al centenario*, 62–89.

Azevedo, Fernando de, ed. *As ciências no Brasil*. Rio de Janeiro: UFRJ, 1994.

Babini, José. *Historia de la ciencia en la Argentina*. Buenos Aires: Solar-Hachette, 1968.

Barata, Mário. "Origens dos museus históricos e de arte no Brasil." *Revista do Instituto Histórico e Geográfico Brasileiro* 147, no. 350 (1986): 22–30.

Barthes, Roland. *La chambre claire: Note sur la photographie*. Paris: Cahiers du Cinéma / Gallimard / Seuil, 1980.

Basalla, George. "The Spread of Western Science." *Science* 156 (May 1967): 611–22.

Baudrillard, Jean. *The System of Objects*. London: Verso, 1996.

Benjamin, Walter. *Gesammelte Schriften*. Edited by Rolf Tiedemann and Hermann Schweppenhäuser. Frankfurt am Main: Suhrkamp, 1991.

———. *Das Passagen-Werk*. Frankfurt am Main: Suhrkamp, 1983.

Bennett, Tony. *The Birth of the Museum: History, Theory, Politics*. London: Routledge, 1995.

Bernard, Tomás Diego. "Carranza y Udaondo: Dos precursores de la museografía argentina." *Historia* 12, no. 48 (1967): 96–103.

Bertoni, Lilia Ana. *Patriotas, cosmopolitas y nacionalistas: La construcción de la nacionalidad argentina a fines del siglo XIX*. Buenos Aires: Fondo de Cultura Económica, 2001.

Bhabha, Homi K. *The Location of Culture*. London: Routledge, 1994.

Bolton, Ralph, ed. *The Contest of Meaning: Critical Histories of Photography*. Cambridge, MA: MIT Press, 1989.

Botana, Natalio. *El orden conservador: La política argentina entre 1880 y 1916*. Buenos Aires: Hyspamérica, 1986.

Brasil, Antônio Americano do. *Súmulo da história de Goiás*. Goiânia: Departamento Estadual de Cultura, 1961.

Brookshaw, David. *Paradise Betrayed: Brazilian Literature of the Indian*. Amsterdam: CEDLA, 1988.

Brown, Lee Rust. "The Emerson Museum." *Representations* 40 (1992): 57–80.

Bryson, Norman. *Vision and Painting: The Logic of the Gaze*. Basingstoke: Palgrave, 1983.

Bucich Escobar, Ismael. *El Museo Histórico Nacional en su cincuentenario (1889–1939)*. Buenos Aires: Museo Histórico Nacional, 1939.

Buck-Morss, Susan. *The Dialectics of Seeing: Walter Benjamin and the Arcades Project*. Cambridge, MA: MIT Press, 1991.

Canclini, Arnaldo. *Julio Popper: Quijote del oro fueguino*. Buenos Aires: Emecé, 1993.

Carbonell, Bettina Messias, ed. *Museum Studies: An Anthology of Contexts*. Malden, MA: Blackwell, 2004.

Carter, Paul. *The Road to Botany Bay: An Essay in Spatial History*. London: Faber & Faber, 1987.

Carvalho, José Murilo de. *A construção da ordem: A elite política imperial*. Rio de Janeiro: Campus, 1980.

———. *A formação das almas: O imaginário da República no Brasil*. São Paulo: Companhia das Letras, 1990

———. *Pontos e bordados: Escritos de historia e política*. Belo Horizonte: Ed. UFMG, 1999.

———. *Teatro das sombras: A política imperial*. Rio de Janeiro: UFRJ / Relume Dumará, 1996.

Castro Faria, Luiz de. *Antropologia: Espetáculo e excelência*. Rio de Janeiro: UFRJ / Tempo Brasileiro, 1993.

———. "As exposições de antropologia e arqueologia do Museu Nacional." *Publicações avulsas do Museu Nacional* 4 (1949).

Chakrabarty, Dipresh. *Provincializing Europe: Postcolonial Thought and Historical Difference*. Princeton, NJ: Princeton University Press, 2000.

Chatterjee, Partha. *The Nation and Its Fragments: Colonial and Postcolonial Histories*. Princeton, NJ: Princeton University Press, 1993.

Chaui, Marilena. *Brasil: Mito fundador e sociedade autoritária*. São Paulo: Fundação Perseu Abramo, 2000.

Clastres, Pierre. *La société contre l'état: Recherches d'anthropologie politique*. Paris: Minuit, 1974.

Clausewitz, Carl von. *Vom Kriege*. München: Cormoran, 2000 [1832].

Clementi, Hebe. *La frontera en América*. Buenos Aires: Leviatan, 1977.

Comisión Nacional de Homenaje al Centenario de la Conquista del Desierto. *Congreso Nacional de Historia sobre la Conquista del Desierto celebrado en la ciudad de Gral: Roca del 6 al 10 de noviembre de 1979*. Buenos Aires: Academia Nacional de la Historia, 1980.

Cooke, Lynne, and Peter Wollen, eds. *Visual Display: Culture Beyond Appearances*. Seattle, WA: Bay Press, 1995.

Coombes, Annie E. "Museums and the Formation of National and Cultural Identities." *Oxford Art Journal* 11, no. 2 (1988): 57–68.

Corrêa, Mariza. *As ilusões da liberdade: A escola Nina Rodrigues e a antropologia no Brasil*. São Paulo: USP / FFLCH, 1983.

Cortés Rocca, Paola. "Entre el arte y la ciencia: La práctica fotográfica en el fin de siglo." *Filología* 24, no. 1/2 (1996): 21–23.

Cortesão, Jaime. *História do Brasil nos velhos mapas*. Rio de Janeiro: Instituto Rio Branco, 1965.

Cosgrove, Denis. *Social Formation and Symbolic Landscape*. Madison, WI: University of Wisconsin Press, 1998.

Cosgrove, Denis, and Stephen Daniels, eds. *The Iconography of Landscape: Essays on the Symbolic Representation, Design, and Use of Past Environments*. Cambridge: Cambridge University Press, 1988.

Costa, Emília Viotti da. *Da monarquia à República: Momentos decisivos*. São Paulo: UNESP, 1998.

Crary, Jonathan. *Techniques of the Observer: On Vision and Modernity in the Nineteenth Century*. Cambridge, MA: MIT Press, 1990.

Cresto, Juan José, ed. *Museo Histórico Nacional*. Buenos Aires: Manrique Zago, 1997.

Cunha, Manuela Carneiro da, ed. *História dos índios no Brasil*. São Paulo: Companhia das Letras, 1998.

De Certeau, Michel. *The Practice of Everyday Life*. Translated by Steven Rendall. Berkeley, CA: University of California Press, 1984.

Deleuze, Gilles. *L'image-mouvement: Cinéma I*. Paris: Minuit, 1983.

Deleuze, Gilles, and Félix Guattari. *A Thousand Plateaus: Capitalism and Schizophrenia II*. Translated by Brian Massumi. London: Athlone, 1988.

Derrida, Jacques. *Archive Fever: A Freudian Impression*. Translated by Eric Prenowitz. Chicago, IL: University of Chicago Press, 1995.

Duarte, Abelardo. *Ladislau Netto (1838–1894)*. Maceió: Imprensa Oficial, 1950.

Dujovne, Marta, and Ana María Telesca. "Museos, salones y panoramas: La formación de espacios de representación en el Buenos Aires del siglo XIX." In *Arte y espacio*, edited by Oscar Olea, 423–42. México: UNAM, 1987.

Duncan, Carol, and Alan Wallach. "The Universal Survey Museum." In Carbonell, *Museum Studies*, 59.

Earle, Rebecca. "Monumentos y museos: La nacionalización del pasado precolombino en la Hispanoamérica decimonónica." In González-Stephan and Andermann, *Galerías del progreso*, 27–63.

Edwards, Elizabeth. *Raw Histories: Photographs, Anthropology, and the Museum*. Oxford: Berg, 2001.

Elias, Maria José. *Museu Paulista: Memória e história*. São Paulo: FFLCH / USP, 1996.

Epstein, David G. *Brasília, Plan and Reality: A Study of Planned and Spontaneous Urban Development*. Berkeley, CA: University of California Press, 1973.

Ermakoff, George, ed. *Juan Gutiérrez: Imagens do Rio 1892–1896*. Rio de Janeiro: Capivara, 2001.

Estevão, Carlos. "Resumo histórico do Museu Paraense Emilio Goeldi." *Revista do Serviço do Patrimonio Histórico e Artístico Nacional* 2 (1938): 7–15.

Fabian, Johannes. *Time and the Other: How Anthropology Makes Its Object*. New York: Columbia University Press, 1983.

———. *Time and the Work of Anthropology: Critical Essays 1971–1991*. Chur, Switzerland: Harwood, 1991.

Fernández Bravo, Alvaro. "Catálogo, colección y colonialismo interno: Una lectura de la *Descripción de la Patagonia* de Thomas Falkner (1774)." *Revista de Crítica Literaria Latinoamericana* 30, no. 60 (2004): 229–49.

———. "Celebraciones centenarias: Nacionalismo y cosmopolitismo en las conmemoraciones de la Independencia (Buenos Aires, 1910–Rio de Janeiro, 1922)." In González-Stephan and Andermann, *Galerías de progreso*, 333–74.

———. *Literatura y frontera: Procesos de territorialización en las culturas argentina y chilena del siglo XIX*. Buenos Aires: Sudamericana, 1999.

———. "Material Memories: Tradition and Amnesia in Two Argentine Museums." In Andermann and Rowe, *Images of Power*, 78–95.

Ferrari, Gustavo, and Ezequiel Gallo, eds. *La Argentina del ochenta al centenario*. Buenos Aires: Sudamericana, 1980.

Ferrez, Gilberto. *Photography in Brazil, 1840–1900*. Albuquerque, NM: University of New Mexico Press, 1990.

Findlen, Paula. "The Museum: Its Classical Etymology and Renaissance Genealogy." In Carbonell, *Museum Studies*, 23–50.

Foot Hardman, Francisco. *Trem fantasma: A modernidade na selva*. São Paulo: Companhia das Letras, 1988.

Foster, Hal, ed. *Vision and Visuality*. New York: New Press, 1988.

Foucault, Michel. *L'archéologie du savoir*. Paris: Gallimard, 1969.

———. *The Order of Things: An Archaeology of the Human Sciences*. London: Routledge, 2002.

———. *Power: Essential Works of Foucault, 1954–1984*. Vol. 3, edited by James D. Faubion. Harmondsworth: Penguin, 2002.

———. *Surveiller et punir: Naissance de la prison*. Paris: Gallimard, 1975.

Fraser, Valerie. *Building the New World: Studies in the Modern Architecture of Latin America, 1930–1960*. London: Verso, 2000.

Gallardo, José M. *El Museo de Ciencias Naturales en la manzana de las luces*. Buenos Aires: Museo Argentino de Ciencias Naturales, 1976.

Galvão, Walnice Nogueira. *No calor da hora: A Guerra de Canudos nos jornais (4a Expedição)*. São Paulo: Ática, 1994.

García, Stella Maris. "La revista *El Museo Histórico*: Una aproximación." *Primeras Jornadas 'Nuestros museos': 500 años de historia a través de su patrimonio*. Buenos Aires: Ministerio de Cultura y Educación, 1992.

García Castellanos, Teodoro. *Breve historia de la Academia Nacional de Ciencias de Córdoba*. Córdoba: Academia Nacional de Ciencias, 1987.

Geertz, Clifford. *Negara: The Theatre State in Nineteenth-Century Bali*. Princeton, NJ: Princeton University Press, 1980.

Gómez, Juan. *La fotografía en la Argentina: Su historia y evolución en el siglo XIX, 1840–1899*. Buenos Aires: Abadía, 1986.

González Garaño, Alejo B., and Antonio Apraiz, eds. *Museo Histórico Nacional*. Buenos Aires: Museo Histórico Nacional, 1941.

González-Stephan, Beatriz, and Jens Andermann, eds. *Galerías del progreso: Museos, exposiciones y cultura visual en América Latina*. Rosario: Beatriz Viterbo, 2006.

Graham, Richard, ed. *The Idea of Race in Latin America, 1870–1940*. Austin, TX: University of Texas Press, 1990.

Graham, Richard. *Patronage and Politics in 19th Century Brazil*. Stanford, CA: Stanford University Press, 1990.

Greenblatt, Stephen. "Resonance and Wonder." In Karp and Lavine, *Exhibiting Cultures*, 42–56.

Gregory, Derek. *Geographical Imaginations*. Oxford: Blackwell, 1994.

Groys, Boris. *Logik der Sammlung: Am Ende des musealen Zeitalters*. München: Hanser, 1997.

Halperín Donghi, Tulio. *The Contemporary History of Latin America*. Translated by John Charles Chasteen. Durham, NC: Duke University Press, 1993.

———. *Una nación para el desierto argentino*. Buenos Aires: Centro Editor de América Latina, 1992.

Hamon, Philippe. *Expositions: Littérature et architecture au XIXième siècle*. Paris: José Corti, 1989.

Harvey, David. *The Limits to Capital*. London: Verso, 1999.

———. *Spaces of Capital: Towards a Critical Geography*. Edinburgh: Edinburgh University Press, 2001.

Holford, William. "Brasília: A New Capital City for Brazil." *Architectural Review* 122 (1957): 397–405.

Holston, James. *The Modernist City: An Anthropological Critique of Brasília*. Chicago, IL: University of Chicago Press, 1989.

Hooper-Greenhill, Eilean. *Museums and the Shaping of Knowledge*. London: Routledge, 1992.

Huyssen, Andreas. *Twilight Memories: Making Time in a Culture of Amnesia*. London: Routledge, 1997.

Jardine, Nicholas, James A. Secord, and Emma C. Spary, eds. *Cultures of Natural History*. Cambridge: Cambridge University Press, 1996.

Jenkins, David. "Object Lessons and Ethnographic Displays: Museum Exhibitions and the Making of American Anthropology." *Comparative Studies in Society and History* 36 (1994): 242–70.

Kaplan, Flora S., ed. *Museums and the Making of Ourselves: The Role of Objects in National Identity*. London: Leicester University Press, 1996.

Karp, Ivan, and Stephen D. Lavine, eds. *Exhibiting Cultures: The Poetics and Politics of Museum Display*. Washington, DC: Smithsonian Institution, 1991.

Kish, George. *La carte, image des civilisations*. Paris: Seuil, 1980.

Koselleck, Reinhart. *Vergangene Zukunft: Zur Semantik geschichtlicher Zeiten*. Frankfurt am Main: Suhrkamp, 1992.

Kossoy, Boris. *Dicionário Histórico-Fotográfico Brasileiro*. Rio de Janeiro: Instituto Moreira Salles, 2002.

———. *Origens e expansão da fotografia no Brasil, século XIX*. Rio de Janeiro: MEC / Funarte, 1980.

Kossoy, Boris, and Maria Luisa Tucci Carneiro. *O olhar europeu: O negro na iconografia brasileiro do século XIX*. São Paulo: USP, 1994.

Lascano González, Antonio. *El Museo de Ciencias Naturales de Buenos Aires*. Buenos Aires: Ediciones Culturales Argentinas, 1980.

Latour, Bruno. *Science in Action: How to Follow Scientists and Engineers through Society*. Cambridge, MA: Harvard University Press, 1987.

Lefebvre, Henri. *The Production of Space*. Translated by Donald Nicholson-Smith. Oxford: Blackwell, 1991.

Leite, Dante Moreira. *O caráter nacional brasileiro: História de uma ideologia*. São Paulo: Livraria Pioneiro, 1976.

Lessa, Renato. *A invenção republicana: Campos Salles, as bases e a decadência da Primeira República Brasileira*. Rio de Janeiro: Topbooks, 1999.

Levin, David Michael, ed. *Modernity and the Hegemony of Vision*. Berkeley, CA: University of California Press, 1993.

Levine, Robert D. *Images of History: Nineteenth and Early Twentieth Century Latin American Photographs as Documents*. Durham, NC: Duke University Press, 1989.

———. *Vale of Tears: Rewriting the Canudos Massacre in Northeastern Brazil, 1893–1897*. Berkeley, CA: University of California Press, 1992.

Lewis, Colin M. *British Railways in Argentina, 1857–1914*. London: Athlone, 1983.

———. "La consolidación de la frontera argentina a fines de la década del 70." In Ferrari and Gallo, *La Argentina del ochenta al centenario*, 469–83.

Lima, Luiz Costa. *O controle do imaginário: Razão e imaginação no Occidente*. São Paulo: Brasiliense, 1984.

———. *Terra ignota: A construção de Os sertões*. Rio de Janeiro: Civilização Brasileira, 1997.

Lima, Nísia Trindade. *Um sertão chamado Brasil: Intelectuais e representação geográfica no Brasil*. Rio de Janeiro: UPERJ / Editora Revan, 1999.

Lobo, Bruno, et al. *O Museu Nacional de História Natural*. Rio de Janeiro: Museu Nacional, 1923.

Lopes, Maria Margaret. *O Brasil descobre a pesquisa científica: As ciências naturais e os museus*. São Paulo: Ed. Hucitec, 1998.

———. "Sociedades científicas y museos en América Latina." *Saber y Tiempo* 2, no. 7 (1999): 51–72.

———. "Viajando pelo mundo dos museus: Diferentes olhares no processo de institucionalização das ciências naturais nos museus brasileiros." *Imaginário* 3 (1996): 59–78.

Lopes, Maria Margaret, and Irina Podgorny. "The Shaping of Latin American Museums." *Osiris* 15 (2000): 108–18.

López, Dora. "Historia y museo: ¿Encuentro o desencuentro? Los primeros cincuenta años del Museo Histórico Nacional." In *Primeras Jornadas 'Nuestros museos': 500 años de historia a través de su patrimonio*, 67–79. Buenos Aires: Ministerio de Cultura y Educación, 1992.

López, Susana. *Representaciones de la Patagonia: Colonos, científicos y políticos*. La Plata: Ediciones Al Margen, 2003,

Magnoli, Demétrio. *O corpo da pátria: Imaginação geográfica e política externa no Brasil (1808–1812)*. São Paulo: UNESP / Moderna, 1997.

Maio, Marcos Chor, and Ricardo Ventura Santos, eds. *Raça, ciência e sociedade*. Rio de Janeiro: Fiocruz, 1996.

Makino, Myoko. "Cronologia do Museu Paulista." *Diário Oficial do Estado de São Paulo* 107, no. 220 (15 November 1997): 1–3.

Maleuvre, Didier. *Museum Memories: History, Theory, Art*. Stanford, CA: Stanford University Press, 1999.

Malosetti Costa, Laura. *Los primeros modernos: Arte y sociedad en Buenos Aires a fines del siglo XIX*. Buenos Aires: FCE, 2001.

Maravall, José Antonio. *Culture of the Baroque: Analysis of a Historical Structure*. Minneapolis, MN: University of Minnesota Press, 1986.

Martínez Estrada, Ezequiel. *Muerte y transfiguración de Martín Fierro*. Buenos Aires: Centro Editor de América Latina, 1983.

Martínez Sierra, Ramiro. *El mapa de las pampas*. Buenos Aires: Plus Ultra, 1975.

Marx, Karl. *Das Kapital: Kritik der politischen Ökonomie*. 3 vols. Berlin: Dietz, 1983.

Mauad, Ana Maria. "Imagem e auto-imagem do Segundo Reinado." In *História da vida privada no Brasil*, vol. 2, edited by Fernando A. Novais and Luiz F. de Alencastro, 181–231. São Paulo: Companhia das Letras, 1998.

Mbembe, Achille. "The Banality of Power and the Aesthetics of Vulgarity in the Postcolony." *Public Culture* 4, no. 2 (1992): 1–30.

Melli, Oscar Ricardo. "El coronel Manuel José Olascoaga y la geografía argentina." *Boletín de la Academia Nacional de la Historia* 53 (1980): 189–211.

Miceli, Sérgio. *Imagens negociadas: Retratos da élite brasileira (1920–40)*. São Paulo: Companhia das Letras, 1996.

Mitchell, Timothy. *Colonising Egypt*. Cambridge: Cambridge University Press, 1989.

———. "The Limits of the State: Beyond Statist Approaches and Their Critics." *American Political Science Review* 85, no. 1 (1991): 77–96.

———. "The World as Exhibition." *Comparative Studies in Society and History* 31 (1989): 217–36.

Mitchell, W. J. T. *Iconology: Image, Text, Ideology*. Chicago, IL: University of Chicago Press, 1986.

———, ed. *Landscape and Power*. Chicago, IL: University of Chicago Press, 1994.

———, ed. *The Language of Images*. Chicago, IL: University of Chicago Press, 1974.

———. *Picture Theory*. Chicago, IL: University of Chicago Press, 1994.

Monteiro, John Manuel. "As 'raças' indígenas no pensamento brasileiro do Império." In *Raça, ciência e sociedade*, edited by Marcos Chor Maio and Ricardo Ventura Santos, 15–22. Rio de Janeiro: Fiocruz, 1996.

Montserrat, Marcelo, ed. *La ciencia en la Argentina entre siglos: Textos, contextos e instituciones*. Buenos Aires: Manantial, 2000.

Navarro Floria, Pedro. *Historia de la Patagonia*. Buenos Aires: Ciudad Argentina, 1999.

Neto, Gil Baião, and Maria Rachel Fróis da Fonseca, "Museu Real." http://www .museunacional.ufrj.br. Accessed 15 November 2004.

Neto, Maria Cristina Nunes Ferreira. "A Commissão Exploradora do Planalto Central do Brasil: A civilização a caminho do sertão." *Estudos—Humanidades* 29 (2002): 239–61.

Nora, Pierre. "Between Memory and History." In *Realms of Memory: Rethinking the French Past*, vol. 1, *Conflicts and Divisions*, 1–20. Translated by Arthur Goldhammer. New York: Columbia University Press, 1992.

———, ed. *Les lieux de mémoire*. 3 vols. Paris: Gallimard-Quarto, 1997.

———. *Realms of Memory: Rethinking the French Past*. Translated by Arthur Goldhammer. New York: Columbia University Press, 1992.

Nouzeilles, Gabriela. "Patagonia as Borderland: Nature, Culture, and the Image of the State." *Journal of Latin American Cultural Studies* 8, no. 1 (1999): 35–48.

Osborne, Peter D. *Travelling Light: Photography, Travel, and Visual Culture*. Manchester: Manchester University Press, 2000.

Oszlak, Oscar. *La formación del estado argentino*. Buenos Aires: Editorial de Belgrano, 1986.

Outram, Dorinda. *Georges Cuvier: Vocation, Science and Authority in Post-Revolutionary France*. Manchester: Manchester University Press, 1984.

———. "New Spaces in Natural History." In Jardine, Secord, and Spary, *Cultures of Natural History*. Cambridge: Cambridge University Press, 1996.

Paiva, Orlando Marques de. *Museu Paulista da USP*. São Paulo: Banco Safra, 1984.

Panofsky, Erwin. *Perspective as a Symbolic Form*. Translated by Christopher S. Wood. New York: Zone Books, 1991.

———. *Studien zur Ikonologie der Renaissance*. Köln: DuMont, 1997.

Paviani, Aldo, ed. *Brasília, ideologia e realidade: Espaço urbano em questão*. São Paulo: Projeto, 1985.

Podgorny, Irina. *El argentino despertar de las faunas y de las gentes prehistóricas*. Buenos Aires: Eudeba, 2003.

———. "Uma exibição científica dos pampas (apontamentos para uma história da formação das coleções do Museo de La Plata)." *Idéias* 5, no. 1 (1998): 173–216.

———. "El museo soy yo: Alfred Marbais Du Graty en la Confederación Argentina." *Ciencia Hoy* 7, no. 38 (1997): 48–53.

Podgorny, Irina, and Gustavo Politis. "¿Qué sucedió en la historia? Los esqueletos araucanos del Museo de La Plata y la Conquista del Desierto." *Arqueología contemporánea* 3 (1990–92): 73–79.

Pomian, Krzysztof. *Collectors and Curiosities*. Oxford: Polity Press, 1990.

Poole, Deborah. *Vision, Race and Modernity: A Visual Economy of the Andean Image World*. Princeton, NJ: Princeton University Press, 1997.

Poulantzas, Nicos. *State, Power, Socialism*. London: Verso, 2000.

Pratt, Mary Louise. *Imperial Eyes: Travel Writing and Transculturation*. London: Routledge, 1993.

Preziosi, Donald. "Brain of the Earth's Body: Museums and the Framing of Modernity." In Carbonell, *Museum Studies*, 79–80.

*Primeras Jornadas 'Nuestros museos': 500 años de historia a través de su patrimonio*. Buenos Aires: Ministerio de Cultura y Educación, 1992.

Quijada, Mónica. "Ancestros, ciudadanos, piezas de museo: Francisco P. Moreno y la articulación del indígena en la construcción nacional argentina (siglo XIX)." *Estudios interdisciplinarios de América Latina y el Caribe* 9, no. 2 (1998). http://www.tau.ac.il/eial/ IX__2/quijada.html.

Rama, Angel. *The Lettered City*. Durham, NC: Duke University Press, 1996.

Richards, Thomas. *The Imperial Archive: Knowledge and the Fantasy of Empire*. London: Verso, 1993.

Rodrigues, José Honório, ed. *Catálogo da Exposição de História do Brasil*. Brasília: Editora da Universidade de Brasília, 1981.

Romero, José Luis, ed. *Pensamiento conservador*. Caracas: Biblioteca Ayacucho, 1978.

Roncayolo, Michel. "Le paysage du savant." In *Les lieux de mémoire*, vol. 1, edited by Pierre Nora. Paris: Gallimard-Quarto, 1997.

Rosen, Jeff. "Naming and Framing Nature in *Photographie Zoologique*." *Word and Image* 13, no. 4 (1997): 377–91.

Ryan, James R. *Picturing Empire: Photography and the Visualization of the British Empire*. London: Reaktion Books, 1997.

Said, Edward. *Beginnings: Intention and Method*. New York: Basic Books, 1975.

Salles, Ricardo. *Nostalgia imperial: A formação da identidade nacional no Brasil do Segundo Reinado*. Rio de Janeiro: Topbooks, 1996.

Sánchez, María Aurora. *Julio Argentino Roca*. Buenos Aires: Círculo Militar, 1969.

Schwarcz, Lilia Moritz. *As barbas do Imperador: D. Pedro II, um monarca nos trópicos*. São Paulo: Companhia das Letras, 1998.

———. *O espetáculo das raças: Cientistas, instituições e questão racial no Brasil, 1870–1930*. São Paulo: Companhia das Letras, 1993.

Sheets-Pyenson, Susan. *Cathedrals of Science: The Development of Colonial Natural History Museums during the Late Nineteenth Century*. Kingston, Montréal: McGill-Queen's University Press, 1988.

Siegrist de Gentile, Nora, and María Haydée Martín. *Geopolítica, ciencia y técnica a través de la campaña del desierto*. Buenos Aires: Eudeba, 1981.

Silva, Ernesto. *História de Brasília: Um sonho, uma esperança, uma realidade*. Brasília: Coordena-dora Editora de Brasília, 1970.

Snyder, Joel. "Territorial Photography." In Mitchell, *Landscape and Power*, 175–201.

Sommer, Doris. *Foundational Fictions: The National Romances of Latin America*. Berkeley, CA: University of California Press, 1991.

Sontag, Susan. *On Photography*. Harmondsworth: Penguin, 1979.

Souza Lima, Antônio Carlos de. *Os museus de história natural e a construção do indigenismo*. Rio de Janeiro: Museu Nacional / UFRJ, 1989.

Stein Campos, Vicente. *Elementos de museologia: História dos museus. Brasil*. Rio de Janeiro: Secretaria de Cultura, 1971.

Stepan, Nancy Leys. *Beginnings of Brazilian Science: Oswaldo Cruz, Medical Research and Policy, 1890–1920*. New York: Science History Publications, 1976.

———. *The Hour of Eugenics: Race, Gender, and Nation in Latin America*. Ithaca, NY: Cornell University Press, 1991.

———. *Picturing Tropical Nature*. London: Reaktion Books, 2001.

Stewart, Susan. *On Longing: Narratives of the Miniature, the Gigantic, the Souvenir, the Collection*. Durham, NC: Duke University Press, 1993.

Stocking, George W., Jr., ed. *Bones, Bodies, Behavior: Essays on Biological Anthropology*. Madison, WI: University of Wisconsin Press, 1988.

———, ed. *Objects and Others: Essays on Museums and Material Culture*. Madison, WI: Wisconsin University Press, 1985.

Sweet, Timothy. *Traces of War: Poetry, Photography, and the Crisis of the Union*. Baltimore, MD: Johns Hopkins University Press, 1990.

Taussig, Michael. *Shamanism, Colonialism, and the Wild Man: A Study in Terror and Healing*. Chicago, IL: University of Chicago Press, 1987.

Tauxe, Caroline S. "Mystics, Modernists, and Constructions of Brasília." *Ecumene* 3, no. 1 (1996): 43–61.

Terán, Oscar. *Vida intelectual en el Buenos Aires fin-de-siglo (1880–1910): Derivas de la "cultura científica."* Buenos Aires: Fondo de Cultura Económica, 2000.

Theweleit, Klaus. *Male Fantasies I: Women, Floods, Bodies, History*. Translated by Steve Conway. Cambridge: Polity Press, 1987.

Trachtenberg, Alan. *Reading American Photographs: Images as History, Mathew Brady to Walker Evans*. New York: Hill & Wang, 1989.

Treece, David. *Exiles, Allies, Rebels: Brazil´s Indianist Movement, Indigenous Politics, and the Imperial Nation-State*. Westport, CT: Greenwood, 2000.

Turazzi, Maria Inez. "Imagens da nação: A *Exposição de História do Brasil* de 1881 e a construção do patrimônio iconográfico." In González-Stephan and Andermann, *Galerías del progreso*, 130.

———. *Marc Ferrez*. Rio de Janeiro: Cosac & Naify, 2000.

———. *Poses e trejeitos: A fotografia e as exposições na era do espetáculo (1839–1889)*. Rio de Janeiro: Funarte / Rocco, 1995.

Turner, Victor. *The Ritual Process: Structure and Anti-Structure*. New York: Aldine, 1969.

Uricoechea, Fernando. *The Patrimonial Foundations of the Brazilian Bureaucratic State*. Berkeley: University of California Press, 1980.

Vasquez, Pedro. *A fotografia no Império*. Rio de Janeiro: Jorge Zahar, 2002.

Vasquez, Pedro Karp. "Juan Gutiérrez: The Penultimate Photographer of the Empire, First Photographer of the Republic." In *Juan Gutiérrez: Imagens do Rio 1892–1896*, edited by George Ermakoff. Rio de Janeiro: Capivara, 2001.

Vezub, Julio. *Indios y soldados: Las fotografías de Carlos Encina y Edgardo Moreno durante la 'Conquista del Desierto.'* Buenos Aires: El Elefante Blanco, 2002.

Viñas, David. *Indios, ejército y frontera*. Buenos Aires: Siglo Veintiuno, 1983.

Virilio, Paul. *La machine de vision*. Paris: Galilée, 1988.

———. *Speed and Politics*. Translated by Mark Polizotti. New York: Semiotext, 1986.

Walther, Juan Carlos. *La conquista del desierto: Síntesis histórica de los principales sucesos ocurridos y operaciones realizadas en La Pampa y Patagonia, contra los indios (años 1527–1885).* Buenos Aires: Eudeba, 1970.

Wehling, Arno. *Estado, história, memória: Varnhagen e a construção da identidade nacional.* Rio de Janeiro: Nova Fronteira, 1999.

White, Hayden. *Metahistory: The Historical Imagination in Nineteenth-Century Europe.* Baltimore, MD: Johns Hopkins University Press, 1973.

Zilly, Berthold. "Flávio de Barros, o ilustre cronista anônimo da guerra de Canudos: As fotografias que Euclides da Cunha gostaria de ter tirado." *Historia, Ciências, Saúde:Manguinhos* 5 (1998): 316–20.

# INDEX

*Note:* Page numbers in italic type indicate illustrations.

117–18; indigenous peoples living in, 55, 59, 73–74; and knowledge representation, 28–29, 37–39, 51–52, 107; Latin American, 19–21; local concerns and, 38–39; modern, 6; and modernity, 13, 18–19; organizational principles in, 24–25, 31, 32, 34–35, 40, 72–73, 88–90, 108–10; and otherness, 62; photography and, 77–79, 81; private sphere and, 14; and reification, 12; research versus public collections in, 43–44, 110; revolutionary origins of, 13; and science, 42–44; and sovereignty, 28, 33; and spectacle, 49; spectatorship in, 45, 52, 57; state and, 14, 16, 18, 33, 51–52; and subject, 14, 19; and violence, 52, 56–57, 81, 85, 114; and visual form, 18, 44–45. *See also* collecting; exhibitions; objects

naming, 28, 33, 181–83
Namuncurá, Manuel, 161
National Archive, Argentina, 87, 88
national being: death of predecessors and, 55; Museo de La Plata interior decoration and, 49; museums and, 24, 25; theorists of, 26
National Education Council, Argentina, 106
National Exhibition (Brazil, 1873), 93
National Exhibition of Industries, Brazil (1881), 59
National Library, Rio de Janeiro, Brazil, 59, 86, *91*, 91–92
National Museum of Washington, D.C., 25
nationalism, conservative, 98–100, 105–6, 112–18, 211, 223n21
nature: appropriation of, 121; in baroque period, 6; in Brazil, 129–30, 137, 139–40, 143–44; empire versus economy of, 44–45; engineering and, 142; frontier and, 127; history and, 6; marginal populations and, 126; museums for study of, 26–27; state and, 7–8, 121–22, 126, 158, 207–12. *See also* landscape
Naturhistorisches Hofmuseum, Austria, 25
Neanderthal, 53
Neto, Pereira, *December 8th, 1889*, 9
Netto, Ladislau Souza de Mello e, 23–24, 26, 30, 33–34, 37–40, 59, 71–77, 84, 93, 208
Niemeyer, Oscar, 136
noble savages, 66
*Noções de coreografia brasileira* (Macedo), 86
noncoevalness, 19, 74, 75, 84. *See also* coevalness
Nora, Pierre, 122
*Nouvelle Division de la Terre par les différentes Espéces ou Races d'Hommes qui l'habitent* (Bernier), 60
Nouzeilles, Gabriela, 131

objectivity, 29
objects: archives versus museums as place for, 88; display of, 78–79, 81; exemplary versus singular character of, 35, 43; overabundance of, 88–89; photography of, 78–79, 81; relational approach to, 37

*Ocupación militar del Río Negro* (Blanes), 163, *167*, 167–74, 228n11
Olascoaga, Manuel José, 169, 174, 208; *Estudio Topográfico de La Pampa y Río Negro*, 174; *Plano Topográfico de La Pampa y Río Negro*, 163, 174–75, *176*, *177*, *182*, 177–83
optic of the state: explanation of, 1; Gutiérrez's photograph as example of, 2–5; and invisibility, 6. *See also* state: as visual form
optical unconscious, 199
opticality, modernity and, 18
*Origin of German Tragic Drama, The* (Benjamin), 6
Orléans e Saxe-Coburg-Gota, Luís Filipe Fernando Gastão de (Conde d'Eu), 59
Oscar, Artur, 196, 197, 200
Osório, Manuel Luís, equestrian monument of, 2–5, *3*
Ostwald & Martínez, 174
O'Sullivan, Timothy, 191
otherness: Brazilian Anthropological Exhibition and, 59–60; collecting and, 117; museums and, 62; subject constituted through, 76
Outram, Dorinda, 29, 37

painting: indigenous types rendered through, 81–82; Western, perceptual tradition of, 171
*País, O* (newspaper), 197
Paleontological Society of Buenos Aires, 36
paleontology, 35–36, 40
Pampa Indians, 160
Panofsky, Erwin, 2, 16
panoptic power, 124, 163, 180
Partido Autonomista Nacional, 164
Pasteur, Louis, 39
Patagonia: anthropology and, 54; Argentine role of, 131–32, 208; imperialism and, 130–31; military campaigns in, 160–62; scientific significance of, 36, 53–54; and violence, 131. *See also* Desert Campaign
Payne, Lewis, 202
Payró, Roberto Jorge, 132
Paz, José María, 87, 111
Pedro I, Emperor of Brazil, 3, 31, 64
Pedro II, Emperor of Brazil, 58, 66, 89, 92
Pehuenches, 161
Peixoto, Floriano, 41
people, the state and the, 209–10
Pereira, Miguel, 130
Perón, Juan Domingo, 209
perspective, 2
Philadelphia Universal Exhibition (1876), 25
photography: and Canudos, 195–202; and Desert Campaign, 187; and ethnography, 77–78; formats and presentation of, 186; and history, 203; imperialism and, 185; indexicality of, 192, 197–201, 204; and museum display, 77–79, 81; in nineteenth-century Latin America, 186–87;